MODERN
BRITISH
HISTORY ★ A
Garland
Series

Edited by
PETER STANSKY and
LESLIE HUME

THE NATIONAL UNION
OF WOMEN'S SUFFRAGE SOCIETIES
1897–1914

Leslie Parker Hume

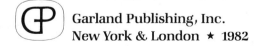

Garland Publishing, Inc.
New York & London ★ 1982

Library of Congress Cataloging in Publication Data

Hume, Leslie Parker.
  The National Union of Women's Suffrage Societies,
1897–1914.

  (Modern British history ; 3)
  Bibliography: p.
  Includes index.
  1. National Union of Women's Suffrage Societies—History.
2. Women—Suffrage—Great Britain—History.
  I. Title. II. Series.
JN979.H85 1982   324.6'23'06041   81-48371
ISBN 0-8240-5167-X

All volumes in this series are printed on acid-free,
250-year-life paper.
Printed in the United States of America

TABLE OF CONTENTS

Page

LIST OF TABLES

PREFACE

Although many historians have studied the women's suffrage movement in England during the late nineteenth and early twentieth centuries, the scholarship has focused exclusively on the militant aspect of the struggle for the vote and, in particular, on the activities of the Women's Social and Political Union (WSPU). Seemingly dazzled by all the excitement and sensationalism of stone throwing, arson, and forcible feeding, historians have lost sight of the less colorful, nonviolent, constitutional suffragists of the National Union of Women's Suffrage Societies (NUWSS). The few mentions of the NUWSS have, for the most part, repeated uncritically the militants' own judgments on the NUWSS and dismissed the NUWSS as an "old-fashioned and official gang" which did little to promote the cause of women's suffrage. In other words, historians have tended to treat the NUWSS as a static organization which, in 1914 as in 1897, differed very little from the suffrage organizations of the mid-Victorian period.

In fact, the NUWSS was important in its own right, and its history as related in this volume fills some of the gaps and omissions, and may dispel some of the misconceptions, which distort our present picture of the British women's suffrage movement. I hope that the history will provide a more complete understanding of the complexity of issues, personalities, and organizations that characterized the struggle for votes for women. The NUWSS, which by 1914 had over 50,000 adherents, was the single largest organization for the promotion of women's suffrage in Britain. Although in some ways the NUWSS was, in comparison with the WSPU, a less dramatic organization, much influenced by its Victorian heritage, it was, far more than its militant counterpart, responsible for laying the groundwork for the enactment of women's suffrage; the enfranchisement of women in 1918 was in large part the fruit of the prewar labors of the NUWSS.

Many persons have helped me in the research and writing of this book, and I should like to thank them here. In the early days of the project, Mildred Surrey and Rosemary Collier of the Fawcett Society, and Jean Ayton, Archivist of the Manchester Public Library, were of invaluable assistance in locating materials on the NUWSS. Andrew Rosen, Penny Kanner, and Margaret Barrow kindly shared their knowledge of archival sources and suffrage collections with me. On this side of the Atlantic, James Knox and David Rozkuszka of the Stanford University Libraries took great pains to help locate materials and proved endlessly patient in answering my queries.

I am indebted to Shirley Taylor for bringing her editorial skills to bear on the manuscript. I should also like to express my gratitude to Peter Stansky who, both as advisor and editor, was unfailingly enthusiastic about this study; his criticisms and encouragement aided me in every stage of the research and writing of the book. Finally, I should like to thank George Hume, who lived with the NUWSS for many years, and managed always to show interest in and support for this seemingly endless project.

L.P.H.

Stanford, California
8 June 1982

CHAPTER I

1897-1906: THE EARLY YEARS OF THE NUWSS

The formation of the National Union of Women's Suffrage Societies on October 14, 1897, and the first nine years of the NUWSS' activity were not so much the start of a new phase in the women's suffrage movement in England as they were the ending of the first long phase which began in the mid-1860's. Although there had been occasional voices crying in the wilderness for votes for women before the 1860's, nothing that could be termed a "movement for women's suffrage" existed before 1866.[1] The relative lateness of the date is not particularly surprising. Until the passage of the Reform Act in 1867, only one out of every five English men possessed the vote; therefore the stigma of being without a vote was more acceptable to women generally, since it was shared by the vast majority of English men. In the first half of the nineteenth century, other reforms were far more urgent to bring more immediate and concrete benefits to women, and the budding feminist movement tackled these reforms first. The two leading feminist groups of the 1860's, the Kensington Society and the Langham Place Circle, concentrated their energies on seeking the reform of property laws affecting married women and securing greater educational opportunities and expanding the spheres of employment for women.[2] These small groups of feminists seemed to believe that these practical reforms would lay the groundwork for the ultimate political enfranchisement of women and that in comparison with these much needed reforms, the vote was of secondary importance and largely of symbolic value.

One may speculate that the feminists refrained from embarking on a drive for the vote because they realized how controversial and explosive such a demand would be. Though many feminists were frank in their criticism of the status quo, they were quite aware of the heavy

---

[1]Constance Rover, Women's Suffrage and Party Politics in Great Britain, 1866-1914 (London, 1967), pp. 2-6.

[2]Helen Blackburn, Record of Women's Suffrage (London, 1902), p. 51; Ray Strachey, The Cause: A Short History of the Women's Movement in Great Britain (London, 1928), pp. 73-76, 89-104. The membership of the Kensington Society was only thirty-three in 1865; two years later it was sixty-seven. See Andrew Rosen, "Emily Davies and the Women's Movement, 1862-1867," unpub. MS.

hand of the Victorian social structure and their contemporaries' conviction that men and women were destined to have separate domains and duties.[3] It was as Tennyson defined it in The Princess (1847):

> Man for the field and woman for the hearth;
> Man for the sword, and for the needle she;
> Man with the head, and woman with the heart;
> Man to command, and woman to obey;
> All else confusion.   [pt. V, ll. 437-41]

Obviously, the political enfranchisement of women presaged the "confusion" of male and female roles, not only in its assumption that women had public duties and a political capacity, not just private duties and a domestic capacity, but also in its implied challenge of the notion of women as subordinates. The early feminists were quite aware of what the vote implied for relationships within the family, particularly for patriarchal authority; indeed, a re-ordering was what they were after, as they occasionally felt free to say. Lydia Becker, the most prominent figure in the early women's suffrage movement, expressed this idea frankly: "I think that the notion that the husband ought to have headship or authority over his wife, is the root of all social evils. . . . Husband and wife should be coordinate and co-equal, each owing to the other entire personal service and devotion, their obligations being strictly reciprocal and mutual. In a happy marriage there is no question of 'obedience' or which shall be 'paramount!'"[4]

It was a great leap, however, from verbally assaulting Victorian social dogma to beginning a political campaign that could topple one of the pillars of the Victorian social edifice. At any rate, whether the feminists were reluctant to commence this battle until they had tested their forces in less explosive ways, or simply had to do first things first, in 1866 they recognized that the time had come. They had achieved victories in the fields of child custody, married women's property, and employment; and in the House of Commons, where John Stuart Mill, the great Liberal champion of the rights of women, had recently won a seat, the question of franchise laws was being debated.[5] The auguries seemed favorable for the beginning of a movement for women's suffrage.

---

[3]For an excellent analysis of the Victorians' ideas about women, see Kate Millet, "The Debate Over Women: Ruskin vs. Mill," in Suffer and Be Still, ed. Martha Vicinus (Bloomington, 1973), pp. 121-39.

[4]As quoted in Blackburn, pp. 42-43.

[5]Josephine Kamm, Rapiers and Battleaxes (London, 1966), pp. 25-28, 89-105; Strachey, pp. 72-76, 89-99; A. P. W. Robson, "The Founding of the National Society for Women's Suffrage, 1866-1867," Canadian Journal of History, 8 (1973), no. 1:7.

From 1866 on, the supporters of women's suffrage conducted a continuous campaign for "votes for women" and established an organizational basis for their cause in London, Manchester, and other large cities in England and Scotland. Lydia Becker, who combined strong-mindedness and dedication with great energy and organizational ability, was the driving force behind the suffrage movement until her death in 1890; in 1872, at her instigation, a Central Committee was formed to work with members of the House of Commons to secure the enactment of women's suffrage.[6]

From 1867 to 1884 the women's suffrage issue generated a good deal of excitement and enthusiasm both inside and outside the House of Commons. Becker and her co-workers held public meetings, organized petitions, and established a suffrage journal to propagandize their cause. This was the "golden age" of reform, and whether the reforms were justified on liberal grounds—to protect individual rights and free the individual from artificial constraints—or in conservative terms—to knit the community together and promote social harmony—both Conservatives and Liberals seemed intent on giving legislative expression to their own particular vision of Victorian England. In such an atmosphere it was not difficult for the advocates of women's suffrage to gain a hearing for their cause. During the decade of the seventies the House of Commons debated the suffrage issue every year except 1874; in 1881 and 1883, resolutions in favor of women's suffrage were introduced in the House, and in 1884, William Woodall, a Liberal MP for Stoke-on-Trent, tried, without success, to secure the inclusion of women's suffrage in the second Reform Bill.[7]

The year 1884 was the high-water mark of the women's suffrage movement in the nineteenth century. With the enactment of the Reform Bill, Parliament seemed to lose interest in reform, and with it, women's suffrage, and the suffragists themselves, disappointed in their failure, lost most of their enthusiasm. The House of Commons became absorbed in the problems of the Empire and in the issue of Home Rule, and the whole question of women's suffrage, no longer curious or novel, ceased to attract attention or adherents.

In addition, the movement itself, especially after Becker's death in 1890, was weak and disorganized. The new women's auxiliaries of the parties—the Women's Council of the Primrose League, the Women's Liberal Federation, and the Women's Liberal Unionist Association— attracted much of the talent, energy, and ability which had once been

---

[6]Blackburn, pp. 119-21. The London National Society for Women's Suffrage did not join this committee until 1877.

[7]Rover, pp. 63, 218-19.

placed at the disposal of the suffrage societies.[8] The death of Becker, who for so long had led and sustained the movement, dealt a severe blow to the cause; her successor, Millicent Garrett Fawcett, was still not devoting all her energies to the movement and had not yet established the authority she was to have later. Political disagreements and personal hostilities had been endemic to the cause since its inception, and these continued to plague the suffrage movement and sap its strength. Besides lack of agreement over whether the several organizations should become active in other feminist causes, or whether they should remain neutral toward the political parties, there had always been clashes in temperament and personality.[9] After 1877 the movement had achieved a semblance of unity, but in 1888 serious political differences arose over the matter of permitting political groups, principally party organizations such as the Women's Liberal Federation, to affiliate with the suffrage societies. The minority group (including Becker and Fawcett), opposed to such a policy, broke off, keeping the old name, Central Committee of the National Society for Women's Suffrage. The majority took the new name, Central National Society for Women's Suffrage.[10]

For the next eight years the suffrage movement was directed by divided counsels, both based in London where they acted as a liaison committee between Parliament and the suffrage organizations outside London. In 1895, in anticipation of the upcoming General Election, the two branches, along with the most important Midlands group, the Manchester National Society for Women's Suffrage, agreed to coordinate their activities so as to make the most of their limited resources.[11] The temporary alliance worked well, and in January 1896 the three groups established a joint committee to take charge of promoting the suffrage cause in Parliament.[12] The Combined Sub-Committee, as this committee came to be called, soon included representatives of the Edinburgh

[8]Ibid., p.29. The Women's Council of the Primrose League was founded in 1885, the Women's Liberal Federation and the Women's Liberal Unionist Association in 1886.

[9]See Strachey, pp. 110-13, 269-77; Rover, pp. 53-55; Robson, pp. 1-22.

[10]Blackburn, pp. 175-77.

[11]Minutes of the executive committee of the Central National Society for Women's Suffrage, July 1, 1895, Fawcett Library, London.

[12]Millicent Fawcett, who was at that time a member of the executive of the Central Committee of the National Society for Women's Suffrage, suggested the establishment of a permanent joint committee. Minutes of the executive committee of the Central National Society for Women's Suffrage, December 15, 1895, Fawcett Library, London.

National Society for Women's Suffrage and the Bristol and West of
England Society for Women's Suffrage.[13] This committee adopted the
tactics Becker had used—meeting with parliamentary supporters of
women's suffrage, sending circulars to Members of Parliament asking them
to ballot for a day for a bill, and whipping up support whenever a
women's suffrage bill came before Parliament.[14] These same tactics were
also used by the NUWSS in its early years.

The next obvious step, once united action for pressure on
Parliament had been undertaken, was to coordinate activities elsewhere
in the country. To achieve this goal a conference of delegates from the
principal women's suffrage societies in the United Kingdom, representing
some twenty groups, was held in Birmingham on October 16, 1896.[15] The
conference decided that a geographical division was the most workable,
so that each suffrage society would have a definite area in which to
conduct its campaign, and it passed a resolution to that effect: "That
this Conference resolves that each society here represented undertake,
as far as is practicable, a definite area of Great Britain and Ireland,
with the object of extending the Women's Suffrage movement within that
area, each society being left free to work on its own lines."[16]

The Combined Committee and the Birmingham Conference proved
that the societies could work together. Much of the mistrust engendered
by the split of 1888 was dissipated, and the suffragists came to see
that their work would be easier and more productive if they united on a

---

[13]Central Committee of the National Society for Women's
Suffrage, Annual Report, 1897 (London, 1897), pp. 5-6.

[14]A Parliamentary Franchise (Extension to Women) Bill was
scheduled to be introduced by Faithfull F. Begg (Cons. Glasgow, St.
Rollox) on May 20, 1896, but the day was taken up by the Government.
Begg was more successful in 1897; his bill passed its second reading on
February 3 by a majority of 71, but it failed to reach the committee
stage. In 1896 and 1897 the efforts of the Combined Committee revolved
around these bills. Minutes of the Combined Sub-Committee, January 22,
1896-October 14, 1897, Fawcett Library, London.

[15]Delegates came from the Central National Society for Women's
Suffrage, the Central Committee of the National Society for Women's
Suffrage, the Women's Franchise League, the Parliamentary Committee, the
Bristol and West of England Society for Women's Suffrage, the Manchester
National Society for Women's Suffrage, the Edinburgh National Society
for Women's Suffrage, and suffrage organizations in Birkenhead,
Birmingham, Cambridge, Cheltenham, Leeds, Leicester, Liverpool, Luton,
Mansfield, Nottingham, Southport, Dublin, and the North of Ireland.
Woman's Signal, November 5, 1896.

[16]Ibid.

permanent basis; moreover, the formation of a united body of suffrage societies would do away with the appearance of dissension within the movement.[17] In October 1897 the societies which formed the Combined Committee agreed upon a scheme of federation, and reconstituted the Combined Committee as the executive committee of the National Union of Women's Suffrage Societies[18] At the invitation of the Combined Committee, twelve other suffrage societies agreed to join the new union; thus the newly formed National Union of Women's Suffrage Societies represented the seventeen largest, most important suffrage societies in Great Britain.[19]

Although the organizational structure of the new federation was highly decentralized and left the member societies with almost complete responsibility for promoting the suffrage cause within the geographical areas entrusted to them, the NUWSS did formulate certain rules which it expected the societies to adhere to: they were to be strictly neutral in regard to political parties (a victory for the Central Committee), and their sole object was to be the attainment of votes for women.[20] Nothing was said in 1897 about "law-abiding tactics" or "constitutional methods of agitation"; the new NUWSS simply assumed that these were the only methods which its constituent societies would use to agitate for the vote. It was not until 1908 that the NUWSS specifically stipulated that its member societies should use only "constitutional" means to propagandize for the cause.[21]

---

[17]Minutes of the Combined Sub-Committee, June 17, 1897, Fawcett Library, London.

[18]Central and Western Society for Women's Suffrage, Annual Report, 1898 (London, 1898), p. 10. The name of the Central National Society for Women's Suffrage was changed to Central and Western Society for Women's Suffrage. The Central Committee of the National Society for Women's Suffrage became the Central and East of England Society for Women's Suffrage. The Manchester National Society became the North of England Society for Women's Suffrage. This was done to indicate the areas in which the societies conducted their work.

[19]The twelve other societies were Birkenhead, Birmingham, Cambridge, Cheltenham, Halifax, Leeds, Leicester, Liverpool, Luton, Mansfield, Nottingham, and Southport. Englishwoman's Review, 29 (January 15, 1898): 24.

[20]Minutes of the executive committee of the National Union of Women's Suffrage Societies, February 10, 1898, Fawcett Library, London (hereafter cited as NUWSS, Ex. com. mins.).

[21]National Union of Women's Suffrage Societies, Annual Report, 1908 (London, 1909), p.1.

The newly formed federation was headed by an executive committee composed of representatives from the member societies, the numbers from each being determined by the size of the society and the geographic area that it covered.[22] The chief task of the executive, only vaguely defined, was "to place women's suffrage in this position, so that no government, of whatever party, shall be able to touch questions relating to representation without at the same time removing the electoral disabilities of women," or in a more simple formulation, "to obtain the Parliamentary Franchise for Women on the same terms as it is, or may be granted to men."[23] Its actual duties were limited to conferring with the Committee of Parliamentary Supporters of Women's Suffrage and assisting it in working for the suffrage cause within Parliament. In theory, the executive was also responsible for coordinating the societies' activities in the country, but it had virtually no power over the member societies and had very little say about how the societies conducted their local affairs. Thus it was less an executive body than a liaison committee between Parliament and the member societies. It had almost no funds at its disposal, and it relied on the staff of its member societies for clerical assistance.[24]

But if the committee in 1897 had few actual powers, its implied power was considerable, for its membership included some of the most distinguished women in England. The acknowledged leader of the NUWSS was Millicent Garrett Fawcett, who at the age of fifty was one of the most capable women of her generation. Born in 1847, the daughter of Newson Garrett, a Suffolk merchant and shipowner, she had been initiated into the women's movement at an early age as a result of the struggles of her sister Elizabeth to enter the British medical profession. But

---

[22]NUWSS, Ex. Com. Mins., February 10, 1898, Fawcett Library, London. The representatives were appointed by the local societies, which were free to change their representation as often as they liked; this changing in the membership was intentional.

[23]Central and Western Society for Women's Suffrage, Annual Report, 1898, p. 14; NUWSS, Ex. com. mins., February 10, 1898, Fawcett Library, London.

[24]The five largest societies were each asked to pay £5 into a common fund at the beginning of each parliamentary session. The smaller societies were asked to pay £1 or less. NUWSS, Ex. com. mins., January 20, 1898, Fawcett Library, London. The secretaries for the NUWSS were Marie Louise Baxter, Edith Palliser, and Esther Roper, who were the secretaries, respectively, for the Central and Western Society for Women's Suffrage, the Central and East of England Society for Women's Suffrage, and the North of England Society for Women's Suffrage. The NUWSS used the offices of the two Central Societies.

Newson Garrett was himself a staunch feminist and he and all his daughters, Louisa, Elizabeth, Alice, Millicent, and Agnes, were active in some aspect of the feminist movement.[25]

If the Garrett family circle nurtured Millicent Fawcett's interest in the women's movement, her marriage in 1867 to Henry Fawcett intensified her feminist inclinations. Fawcett, a Liberal MP for Brighton, was a close friend of John Stuart Mill and an ardent advocate of women's suffrage. Through Fawcett and her sister Louisa Garrett Smith, Millicent Fawcett gained an entry into London suffrage circles, and in 1867 she was present both at the first committee meeting of the London National Society for Women's Suffrage and at the debate on Mill's famous women's suffrage amendment to the Reform Bill.[26] Her interests during the 1870's and early 1880's went much beyond women's suffrage, however: she wrote several works on political economy, published two novels and several articles, helped found Newnham College, agitated for the Married Women's Property Act, and acted as secretary for her blind husband.[27]

It was not until after her husband died in 1884 that Millicent Fawcett began to devote herself wholeheartedly to political activity, particularly to the women's suffrage movement. Her political convictions were rooted in the liberal tradition and her sympathies lay with the Liberal Party, but Gladstone's opposition to women's suffrage and his conversion to Home Rule, which she regarded as both a base act of political expediency and a cowardly surrender to physical force, convinced her that the spirit of liberalism had left the party, and in 1887 she broke with the Liberals over the Home Rule issue. The

---

[25]Ray Strachey, Millicent Garrett Fawcett (London, 1931), p. 13; Robson, p. 2; Millicent Garrett Fawcett, What I Remember (London, 1924), p. 33; Theodore Stanton, ed., The Woman Question in Europe (New York, 1884), p. 1. Alice Garrett Cowell was one of the first women to participate in local government; she served as a member of the London School Board. Louisa Garrett Smith and Agnes Garrett were both active suffragists. Agnes was also one of the first women in England to become a professional house decorator. For the story of Elizabeth's struggle to become a doctor see Jo Manton, Elizabeth Garrett Anderson (New York, 1965).

[26]Fawcett, pp. 64-65; Strachey, Millicent Garrett Fawcett, pp. 42-43.

[27]Political Economy for Beginners was published in 1870; this was followed in 1872 by Essays and Lectures on Social and Political Subjects (written with Henry Fawcett) and in 1875 by her first novel, Jane Doncaster. Of her second novel, published under a pseudonym, all trace, even the title and date of publication, seems to have disappeared. Strachey, Millicent Garrett Fawcett, p. 55.

controversy over Home Rule had the positive effect of stimulating her interest in party politics; she joined the Women's Liberal Unionist Association and in the late 1880's and the 1890's was a prominent speaker against Home Rule. Her involvement in the association was a valuable preparation for her subsequent role in the suffrage movement, for it not only increased her knowledge of the political world and earned her a reputation for intelligence and integrity in Parliamentary circles but also gave her considerable organizational experience and trained her as a public speaker.[28]

Even while absorbed with the Home Rule issue, Fawcett found time to continue her association with the women's movement. She strongly supported W. T. Stead's attempts to put an end to the white slave traffic and was active in the National Vigilance Association.[29] More important, Fawcett continued to work for women's suffrage, as a member of the Central Committee of the National Society for Women's Suffrage. When Becker died in 1890 Fawcett had already established a reputation for devotion to women's suffrage combined with considerable political sagacity. There was no question who would succeed Becker as the leading proponent of women's suffrage in England.

Fawcett was in many ways a colorless and aloof figure, much in contrast to Emmeline and Christabel Pankhurst, her counterparts in the Women's Social and Political Union, but her rational, calm, understated exterior concealed a remarkable intellect, considerable organizational abilities, and great political acumen; moreover, she was completely dedicated to the women's suffrage movement. As head of the executive of the NUWSS, her dispassionate nature and practical outlook stood her in good stead: she never appeared discouraged, grew angry at her colleagues, or allowed the committee to lose its sense of purpose and direction.[30] In turn, her fellow suffragists felt great respect and

---

[28]Fawcett, What I Remember, pp. 112-15; Strachey, Millicent Garrett Fawcett, pp. 125-27.

[29]W. T. Stead, editor of the Pall Mall Gazette, was responsible for disclosing to the public the horrors of the White Slave Traffic. When he was imprisoned in 1885, Fawcett wrote to leading government officials, urging that Stead be made a first class misdemeanant. She wrote to Stead: "I honour and reverence you for what you have done for the weakest and most helpless among women." Her interest in the white slave traffic led her to join the National Vigilance Association, and to become a member of its executive committee. Fawcett Library Autograph Collection, vol. 11, M. G. Fawcett to W. T. Stead, November 9, 1885, Fawcett Library, London.

[30]Interview with Dame Margery Corbett-Ashby, a former member of the executive committee of the NUWSS, December 4, 1974, London.

"intense personal loyalty" for her.[31] The fact that she led the NUWSS
from 1897 to 1919 is an eloquent tribute both to her capabilities and to
the esteem in which she was held by her colleagues in the organization.

To a degree, Fawcett embodied the Victorian ideal of womanhood
in that she was, with everything else, a model wife and mother, and
therefore solid and respectable.[32] At a time when journalists such as
Eliza Lynn Linton were complaining about "modern mothers" and "ambitious
wives" and Victorian society was acutely conscious that its ideas about
women were being challenged, Fawcett's ladylike appearance and exemplary
behavior made her feminism seem less threatening than that generally of
the "shrieking sisterhood" of feminists.[33] She was never the impulsive,
emotional, hysterical female so often depicted as the stereotype by the
opponents of women's suffrage.[34] Indeed, her imperturbability and her
dispassionate nature tended to mute the importance and the urgency of
the women's cause. She was at times too cautious and too moderate in
pressing the suffragists' claims upon Parliament. Her idealism and
optimism, as in John Stuart Mill and Henry Fawcett, were rooted in the
soil of nineteenth-century liberalism. She sincerely believed in the
universality of reason and the inevitability of progress and thought
that Members of Parliament, being rational men, would accede to the
suffragists' demands because the enfranchisement of women was integral
to the whole notion of progress. An article which she published in 1886
summed up these ideas clearly, rather as the supporters of the Reform
Bills of 1832 and 1867 had expressed them:

> Women's suffrage . . . will come as a necessary corollary of the
> other changes which have been gradually and steadily modifying
> during this century the social history of our country. It will
> will be a political change, not of a very great or extensive
> character in itself, based upon social, educational, and

---

[31]Strachey, *Millicent Garrett Fawcett*, p. 266.

[32]The Fawcetts had one daughter, Philippa Garrett Fawcett. As
a student at Newnham College, she scored the highest marks in the
Mathematical Tripos of all those who took the exam; these marks placed
her "above the Senior Wrangler." *Ibid.*, pp. 142-44.

[33]Elizabeth Lynn Linton, *Modern Women and What Is Said of Them*
(New York, 1870), *passim*.

[34]One of the favorite arguments used by opponents of women's
suffrage was that women were impulsive and emotional and, therefore, by
nature, unsuited to having voting privileges. For an example of this
type of argument see *H. C. Deb. 4s.*, vol. 45, February 3, 1897, c. 1209.

economic changes which have already taken place. It will have the effect of adjusting the political machinery of the country to the altered social conditions of its inhabitants.[35]

Although Fawcett severed her ties with the Liberals, she never completely cast off the conviction that the Liberal Party was the political embodiment of liberalism, and that women's suffrage was part and parcel of the liberal ideology; this colored her attitude to the party and made her overly sympathetic to the excuses and blandishments of the Liberal politicians. Her conception of politics and the interconnection she made between women's suffrage, liberalism, and Liberalism, undermined her natural pragmatism and at times handicapped her ability to act as the effective leader of the suffrage movement.[36]

Fawcett's colleagues on the executive committee of the NUWSS were also exceptionally able women, though some were quite different from Fawcett in personality. Lady Frances Balfour, president of the Central and East of England Society, the daughter of the Duke of Argyll and sister-in-law of Arthur Balfour, was opinionated, quick-tempered, and often outspoken; her commitment to women's suffrage was personal and emotional. A staunch churchwoman and an ardent Liberal,[37] she reveled in political intrigue and continually prodded the indecisive Arthur Balfour to take a firm stand on the suffrage issue. She moved with great ease in political circles, and her connections were extremely useful to the NUWSS; undoubtedly had she been a man, she would have taken a seat alongside her numerous relatives in the House of Commons.[38]

---

[35]As quoted in Rover, p. 2.

[36]For an example of Fawcett's thoughts on the connection between Liberalism, liberalism, and women's suffrage, see the Correspondence of Millicent Garrett Fawcett with the London Society for Women's Suffrage, Fawcett Library, London, Millicent Garrett Fawcett to Miss Benecke, March 11, 1913.

[37]Like Fawcett, Lady Frances broke with the Liberal Party over the Home Rule issue but she returned to the party in 1904 at the time of the free trade controveresy. Affirming her commitment to the Liberal Party, Lady Frances wrote: "I should feel it as dishonourable to abandon my party name, as I should to become a Pagan or Papist, or a polyglot Anglo-Catholic, or call myself English instead of Scot." Lady Frances Balfour, Ne Obliviscaris: Dinna Forget (London, 1930), vol. 1, p. 189.

[38]The government acknowledged her considerable abilities when, in 1910, it appointed her to sit on the Commission to investigate the Matrimonial and Divorce Laws.

Many of the other members of the executive were equally distinguished, such as Helen Blackburn, long-time suffrage worker and editor of the Englishwoman's Review; Eleanor Rathbone, of the prominent Liverpool family, who was to become a Member of Parliament and a great champion of social reform; Priscilla Bright McLaren, sister of John and Jacob Bright, a crusader for women's rights and the matriarch of probably the most prominent suffrage family in England;[39] Louisa Stevenson, the first woman to be elected to a parochial board in Edinburgh; Eva Gore-Booth, who proselytized for women's suffrage in the cotton mills of Lancashire; and Eliza Wigham, a staunch supporter of Josephine Butler's crusade to repeal the Contagious Diseases Acts. Along with the rest of the total membership of twenty-six, these women shared certain characteristics of age and background.[40] They were middle-aged, mostly from the middle classes, and in religion were Evangelicals or Nonconformists; 20 percent of them were Quakers. They were all very much "insiders" in the world of Parliament, many of them being related to office holders (usually Members of Parliament), and were active in women's party organizations, such as the Women's Liberal Unionist Association; some had held ofice in their own right, often as Poor Law Guardians.[41] Not surprisingly, these suffragists were in no sense newcomers to the suffrage movement: many of them came from families which had supported women's suffrage, and approximately half of the committee had been actively working for women's suffrage for more than twenty years.

---

[39]Both Mrs. McLaren's stepson, Sir Charles McLaren, M.P. (Lib., Leicestershire, Bosworth), and her son, Walter McLaren, M.P. (Lib., Cheshire, Crewe), were leading parliamentry spokesmen for the suffrage cause. Her daughters-in-law, Lady Laura McLaren and Eva McLaren, were also prominent suffragists.

[40]In 1898 the members of the executive committee were: Mrs. Ashford, the Lady Frances Balfour, Mrs. Beddoe, Miss Helen Blackburn, Miss Bigg, Mrs. Broadley Reid, Mrs. Russell Cooke, Mrs. Enfield Dowson, Mrs. William Evans, Mrs. Fawcett, Mrs. Arthur Francis, Miss Eva Gore-Booth, Miss S. E. Hall, Mrs. Ashworth Hallett, the Hon. Mrs. Arthur Lyttelton, Miss Mair, Miss J. McLea, Miss Mellor, Mrs. Priscilla Bright McLaren, Mrs. Wynford Philipps, Miss Rathbone, Miss Roper, Miss Louisa Stevenson, Mrs. Taylor, Miss Tillotson, Miss Wigham. Secretaries: Marie Louise Baxter, Edith Palliser, Esther Roper. Central and Western Society for Women's Suffrage, Annual Report, 1898, p. 13.

[41]The profile of the NUWSS executive committee bears a striking resemblance to that of another feminist pressure group, the Ladies National Association for the Repeal of the Contagious Diseases Acts. See Judith R. Walkowitz, "We Are Not Beasts of the Field: Prostitution and the Campaign Against the Contagious Diseases Acts, 1869-1886" (Ph.D. diss., University of Rochester, 1974).

Although for most of the executive women's suffrage was the primary concern, a good many of the NUWSS leadership either had been or were currently involved in other causes connected to the feminist movement. They had agitated for moral reform, campaigned to open the medical profession and universities to women, encouraged women to participate in local government, and sought to improve the industrial position of women. They were a sort of feminist "cousinhood", linked not only by a common interest and involvement in the feminist movement but also in many cases by ties of long-time friendship or even blood relationship. Like their leader, Millicent Fawcett, the members of the NUWSS executive were eminently respectable and at least superficially conformed to the Victorian ideal of womanhood--sober, religious, decorous, good wives and model mothers.[42] In no sense, except in terms of sex, were they "outsiders." They belonged to the Victorian establishment, and, as able and energetic women, felt that their credentials of competence and intelligence should be acknowledged and utilized, regardless of sex. They believed that political privileges were the concomitants of duties and obligations and that the vote should be conferred on those who were so supremely qualified. Thus their feminism was circumscribed in a peculiarly Victorian manner by their acceptance of class distinctions and a political system which was built around these distinctions.[43] They were not attacking the political system but rather, as respectable representatives of the middle class, asking to be let in. Like their leader, they had a naïve confidence in the innate good sense of the Members of Parliament and were sure that it would not be long before Parliament bowed to reason and gave votes to women. Because they were so much "insiders" they gravely underestimated

---

[42]According to Geoffrey Best, respectability was "the sharpest of all lines of social division. . . . It signified at one and the same time intrinsic virtue and social value." For an excellent discussion of the value the Victorians placed on respectability, see Geoffrey Best, Mid-Victotrian Britain, 1851-75 (St. Albans, 1973), pp. 283-85.

[43]The relationship between feminism and class consciousness in late nineteenth- and early twentieth-century Britain is discussed in Robin Miller Jacoby, "Feminism and Class Consciousness in the British and American Women's Trade Union Leagues, 1890-1925," in Liberating Women's History, ed. Berenice A. Carroll (Urbana, 1976), pp. 137-60. See also R. S. Neale, "Working Class Women and Women's Suffrage," in Class and Ideology in the Nineteenth Century, ed. R. S. Neale (London, 1972), pp. 143-68.

the indestructability of the barrier of sex and minimized the fears and hostilities which their demand aroused.[44]

Despite the formation of the NUWSS, the suffrage issue remained in the parliamentary limbo to which the House of Commons had banished it in 1884. As Lady Frances Balfour noted, the period between 1897 and 1906 was very bleak for the suffragist cause: the suffrage issue "was always shoved onto a siding to let express trains go by, and even the slowest train was an express to those who wished the matter shelved."[45] The NUWSS had no new policies to offer the disheartened suffragists and employed the same tactics used by its predecessor, the National Society for Women's Suffrage. It continued Becker's policy of promoting a private member's suffrage bill, in hopes that the Government would eventually take up the question and adopt it as one of their own measures.[46] The NUWSS realized that it was extremely unlikely that a private member's bill would be passed into law, but it still felt that this was the only way in which the suffrage issue would be brought to the attention of the Government, the House of Commons, and the public. For a period of years, as in the days of Becker, the executive of the NUWSS continued to meet regularly with a Parliamentary Committee for Women's Suffrage to discuss the position of women's suffrage in the House of Commons.[47] At these meetings the parliamentary supporters of women's suffrage gave advice and instructions to the NUWSS representatives, and the NUWSS leadership listened to and followed these

---

[44]Brian Harrison, Separate Spheres: The Opposition to Women's Suffrage in Britain (London, 1978), gives an excellent analysis of these fears and hostilities. His contention that many of those who opposed women's suffrage did so because they feared the enfranchisement of women would break up the family is particularly interesting, as is his argument that many felt women were, because of temper and intellect, unworthy of the vote. Harrison, pp. 55-84.

[45]Balfour, vol. 2, p. 136.

[46]Becker adhered to the policy of supporting private members' bills except when an electoral reform bill was put before Parliament, in which case (as, for example, the Reform Bill of 1884) she favored the introduction of suffrage amendments to the bill. Blackburn, pp. 149-50. See also National Union of Women's Suffrage Societies, Annual Report, 1898 (London, 1898), p. 4.

[47]The composition of the committee varied from Parliament to Parliament depending upon who supported the suffrage cause. In Miss Becker's day women were not admitted to the meetings of the Committee, but were forced to wait outside the room. The executive of the NUWSS, however, attended the deliberations of the Committee. Blackburn, pp. 174-75.

suggestions.[48] Also in the Becker tradition, at the beginning of each session the NUWSS would send out a letter to all Members of Parliament friendly to the cause asking them to ballot for a day for a bill or for a resolution; when it appeared that a suffrage bill was to be brought before the House it would issue whips in support of the bill.[49] To supplement its activities within Parliament, the NUWSS sponsored meetings in support of women's suffrage and organized petitions to Parliament.[50] It kept the local societies informed of its dealings with the House of Commons and asked the societies to approach their local MP's about supporting suffrage—though not all of them did so.[51]

All these tactics were very much in the pattern of Victorian pressure groups generally, following in the tradition of the Anti-Corn Law League and the Liberation Society which relied on petitions, public meetings, and letters to MP's to advertise their causes and to influence Parliament.[52] The strategy was to create a parliamentary lobby and also an "enlightened public opinion which . . . was supposed to bear on government," to construct a network of local branches that would give evidence of a "national voice," and to apply electoral pressure to enlist the aid of particular MP's.[53]

During the early years of the NUWSS, and in particular from 1897 to 1903, the work of the member societies was actually far more interesting—and more important—than that of the central organization. While the NUWSS continued to function chiefly as a liaison between Parliament and the suffrage societies and as a committee which coordinated the activities of these societies, the affiliates, acting on

---

[48]For example, at the request of the Parliamentary Committee, the NUWSS agreed not to do any lobbying for a bill or resolution, as MP's disliked this. NUWSS, Ex. com. mins., February 20, 1899, Fawcett Library, London.

[49]See, for example, NUWSS, Ex. com. mins., March 3, 1898, and January 11, 1900, Fawcett Library, London.

[50]National Union of Women's Suffrage Societies, Annual Report, 1898, p.5; NUWSS, Ex. com. mins., October 21, 1900, Fawcett Library, London.

[51]NUWSS, Ex. com. mins., October 2, 1902, Fawcett Library, London.

[52]Brian Harrison, "State Intervention and Moral Reform in Nineteenth-century England,"in Pressure from Without in Early Victorian England, ed. Patricia Hollis (London, 1974), p. 292.

[53]Patricia Hollis, "Pressure from Without: An Introduction," in Pressure from Without, pp. 14-17.

their own initiative, were working to build a strong organizational foothold in the country and to make women's suffrage a truly popular cause.

In 1897 the Central and East of England Society for Women's Suffrage started a "local associate scheme" which was designed to expand the suffrage association to every parliamentary constituency within its territory.[54] A local secretary was appointed within each constituency and, working with a list of names of known sympathizers in the area, was supposed to seek their help in forming a local society. Gradually, working through church groups, political and debating societies, and other community organizations, the secretary could enlist a group of supporters for the suffrage cause and ultimately form a small suffrage society, with a local secretary to keep records and act as liaison with the Central Society.[55] Associate members, that is, women who sympathised with the cause but were not able to become subscribing members, were also welcomed, and together the associates and members in many places built up a strong local committee and gained a voice and a base for women's suffrage in the constituency. The object of the program was to make women's suffrage a political force strong enough to influence the legislative behavior of the local MP:

> The final aim should be, of course, to secure enough supporters of all parties in the constituency to constitute a political force and, though endless patience may be necessary, this work of building up a strong public opinion must in the end succeed, for, so soon as it is strong enough candidates and MPs will feel called upon to take such action as will immediately bring about legislation.[56]

By 1899, the Central and East of England Society had instituted the local associate scheme in eight constituencies and had succeeded in gaining 1,828 supporters and associates.[57] The Bristol, North of

---

[54] Central Committee of the National Society for Women's Suffrage, Annual Report, 1897, p. 5.

[55] National Union of Women's Suffrage Societies, Annual Report, 1898, pp. 6-7.

[56] Women's Suffrage Record, June 1903.

[57] Central and East of England Society for Women's Suffrage, Annual Report, 1899 (London, 1899), p. 7. In 1900 the Central and East of England Society and the Central and Western Society merged to form the Central Society for Women's Suffrage. By 1904, the Central Society had established local committees in eighteen constituencies. Central Society for Women's Suffrage, Annual Report, 1901 (London, 1901), pp. 6-7.

England, and Central and Western societies were so impressed by the success of the program that they also adopted the scheme. The establishment of local suffrage organizations to enlist public support for the women's cause and to put pressure on Members of Parliament was to become a principal goal of the National Union of Women's Suffrage Societies. Spurred on by the successful example of the Central and East of England Society, the NUWSS, in 1903, adopted the organizational scheme which had originated with its affiliate.

While the Central and East of England Society for Women's Suffrage was engaged in building up a network of local suffrage committees, the North of England Society, under the leadership of Eva Gore-Booth and Esther Roper, was attempting to shed its middle class image and bring working women into the suffrage movement. Both Gore-Booth and Roper were motivated by a genuine desire to improve the lot of the working woman, and they championed the enfranchisement of women as a necessary accompaniment to industrial and social reform.[58] They also realized that the addition of working women to the suffragist forces would be a way of making women's suffrage a "mass movement," both in terms of size and, more important, in terms of class basis, which would show Parliament that women's suffrage was not "a fad of the rich and well-to-do" and might also result in support from the labor movement.[59]

---

[58]Eva Gore-Booth, the daughter of an Irish landowner and sister of Countess Markiewicz, came to Manchester in 1897. There she joined forces with Esther Roper, a graduate of Victoria University, who had been working for the women's cause for two years. As active suffragists, Gore-Booth and Roper became members of the executive committee of the North of England Society and the National Union of Women's Suffrage Societies. In 1905 they left the North of England Society. The reasons for their departure are obscure, although it appears that many of the other members of the committee felt they were running the society into debt and were making the society exclusively a working class organization.

Christabel Pankhurst was friendly with both these women, and it was through them that she becme active in the North of England Society. In 1901, both Christabel and Emmeline Pankhurst subscribed to the North of England Society, and in 1903 Christabel was on the executive committee of the organization. She, too, resigned from the committee in 1905. Neither Gore-Booth nor Roper ever became involved with the WSPU, however, and though they left the North of England Society, they continued to cooperate closely with the NUWSS and favored constitutional methods rather than militancy.

[59]Bertha Mason, a member of the executive of the North of England Society, said the work of the society "caused many who had treated the question of women's suffrage as a fad of the rich and well-to-do" to take an interest in the movement. Manchester Guardian, October 5, 1909.

Unlike Fawcett, whose suffragist convictions were grounded in the liberal notion of natural rights, Gore—Booth and Roper looked at the vote as a matter of expediency: they were convinced that women needed the vote for their own protection.[60] Women were an important part of the work force in the textile industries of the North. In the cotton trade unions, for example, they outnumbered men by 96,820 to 69,999.[61] But though the women trade unionists paid dues to support the Labour Representation movement, they had no votes. Under the direction of Roper and Gore-Booth, the North of England Society set out to convince these women that the vote was necessary to rectify industrial grievances of working women. Assisted by Labour Churches, the Independent Labour Party (ILP), and the Women's Cooperative Guild, the North England Society sponsored meetings for working women and spoke to them about the suffrage cause.[62] Ultimately, a few suffrage committees were formed in North Lancashire industrial centers, such as Accrington, Bolton, and Salford, and working women began to press the question on trade unions.[63] The Northern Society's work with women textile workers inspired the Central Society to imitate its example; in 1903, the Central Society began to organize women working in the Staffordshire potteries.[64]

The North of England Society also tried to bring the political demands of the working woman to the attention of Parliament. In 1901 and 1902 it presented the House of Commons with petitions for the enfranchisement of women signed by some 66,835 women factory workers in

---

[60]Aileen S. Kraditor, The Ideas of the Woman Suffrage Movement, 1890–1920 (New York, 1965), notes that in 1890, the American suffragists began to base their arguments for the vote on expediency rather than natural rights. This shift in argument, she thinks, reflects both the entry of socially conscious women into the suffrage movement and a change in groups of men either in, or near power, to whom this appeal for suffrage could be directed. Her arguments seem to have some applicability to developments in the suffrage movement in the North of England. Gore—Booth and Roper did exemplify a new type of socially conscious, suffrage activist, and the Labour Party, a relative newcomer on the political scene, was fast becoming the target of the suffragists' propaganda. See Kraditor, pp. 45–74.

[61]North of England Society for Women's Suffrage, Annual Report, 1902 (Manchester, n.d.), pp. 6–7.

[62]North of England Society for Women's Suffrage, Annual Report, 1900 (Manchester, n.d.), pp. 8–9.

[63]North of England Society for Women's Suffrage, Annual Report, 1904 (Manchester, n.d.), pp. 6–7.

[64]Central Society for Women's Suffrage, Annual Report, 1903 (London, 1903), p. 5.

Yorkshire, Cheshire, and Lancashire.[65] At about the same time, the North of England Society, in conjunction with the Lancashire and Cheshire Women Textile and Other Workers' Representation Committee, took another bold step by deciding to sponsor a women's suffrage candidate at the next General Election; in July 1903 it presented this plan to the executive committee of the NUWSS which agreed to help raise funds for the candidacy.[66]

The North of England Society contended with two problems which the NUWSS was to face repeatedly—the problem of courting the working class, and the problem of convincing Parliament that women's suffrage was a matter of concern to this class—and its groundwork was extremely important both in giving the NUWSS an organizational foothold in the industrial centers of the North and in helping to show the House of Commons that the suffrage cause was not the exclusive property of the middle and upper classes. In its dealings with the trade unions, the North of England Society opened up the question of the relationship between the labor and suffrage movements, and hinted at the possibility of linking the two. Its promotion of the policy of running a woman's suffrage candidate stimulated the NUWSS to take a more aggressive interest in elections, and eventually, in 1907, to sponsor its own suffrage candidate.

The activity of the North of England Society demonstrates that although the NUWSS was primarily a middle class organization, led by representatives of the middle class, its members nonetheless recognized

---

[65]On March 18, 1901, a petition asking for enfranchisement signed by 29,359 female factory operatives from Lancashire was presented to Members of Parliament. This was followed on February 18, 1902, by a petition signed by 33,184 textile workers in Yorkshire and 4,292 textile workers in Cheshire. North of England Society for Women's Suffrage, Annual Report, 1901 (Manchester, n.d.), p. 4; Central Society for Women's Suffrage, Annual Report, 1902 (London, 1902), p. 4.

[66]The Lancashire and Cheshire Women Textile and Other Workers' Representation Committee was formed by Esther Roper, Eva Gore-Booth, and Sarah Reddish in 1903. This organization, in conjunction with the Lancashire and Cheshire Women's Suffrage Society (founded in 1905) and the Manchester and Salford Women's Trade and Labour Council, worked to improve the position of women in industry. In 1906 it sponsored a women's suffrage candidate to contest Wigan. The candidate, Thorley Smith, ran on a labour-suffrage platform, and polled 2,205 votes out of a poll of 5,778. So far as I have been able to determine, the one record of the committee's activities is the following: Lancashire and Cheshire Women's Suffrage Society, Lancashire and Cheshire Women's Textile and Other Workers' Representation Committee, Manchester and Salford Women's Trade and Labour Council, Annual Report, 1905-1906 (Manchester, n.d.). See also NUWSS, Ex. com. mins., July 9, and December 3, 1903, Fawcett Library, London.

the necessity of broadening its base of support and attracting working women into the suffrage movement. This aspect of the NUWSS is often overlooked, and credit is given to the Women's Social and Political Union for drawing women workers to the suffrage cause; the financial and organizational support which the North of England Society gave to the women textile workers is forgotten.[67] It is true that in this early period, the efforts of the Northern Society were only partly successful and had no real effect on the middle class orientation of the NUWSS. But those efforts influenced other branches of the NUWSS, so that eventually, as other branches began efforts among the working class, the central organization had to take notice.

During this early period, while the branch societies were launching the suffrage movement among women textile and pottery workers, the executive committee of the NUWSS rested. Though its main function was to act as a parliamentary lobby, it was unable to prod the House of Commons to action. Between 1897 and 1904 not one resolution or bill on the subject of women's suffrage was discussed in the House of Commons.[68] In great measure it was the attitude of the leadership and the structure of the NUWSS itself that was to blame. As "insiders" the executive committee respected the political establishment and had confidence in the good faith and good sense of MP's. They were more deferential toward and more reluctant to criticize the House of Commons than were the leaders of other pressure groups, such as the London Working Men's Association or even the Anti-Corn Law League, and this attitude, along with their firm belief that it was inevitable that the House of Commons would give votes to women, made them reluctant to lobby aggressively for their cause.[69] Letter writing, petitions, and most important, the innate "reasonableness" of the average MP would eventually bring about the enactment of women's suffrage, and as old feminists who had received their political schooling from Becker and her colleagues, they were quite used to the necessity of slow, patient work on behalf of all feminist reforms. Women had, after all, finally gained the local franchise, and had been admitted to the universities and the medical profession. The same sort of efforts would gain them the parliamentary vote.

---

[67]See, for example, Sheila Rowbotham, Hidden from History (New York, 1976), pp. 78-79.

[68]On March 16, 1904, Sir Charles McLaren introduced a motion "That the disabilities of women in respect to the Parliamentary Franchise, ought to be removed by legislation." The resolution passed by a majority of 182 to 68. H. C. Deb. 4s, vol. 131, March 16, 1904, cc. 1339-66.

[69]Alexander Wilson, "The Suffrage Movement," in Pressure from Without, pp. 80-104; David Martin, "Land Reform," ibid., pp. 131-58.

The NUWSS was also handicapped by the weakness of its organizational structure. Though the executive committee had purposely been set up not to be permanent, with members appointed by the local societies and with no fixed term of office for these local representatives, the resulting lack of continuity proved to be a weakness rather than a strength. The central organization had to compete with the strong sense of independence of the local societies. The local societies looked upon the NUWSS mainly as an administrtive convenience to facilitate dealings with Parliament, and they did not want the NUWSS to direct their affairs; and because the NUWSS was totally dependent upon the goodwill of its branches—for funds, offices, and clerical staff—it was in no position to enforce its ideas upon them or make any demands.[70]

The political climate both magnified and aggravated the suffragists' own failures in promoting the suffrage cause in Parliament. The fortunes of the women's suffrage movement tended to fluctuate with the fortunes of franchise reform: within the context of comprehensive reform, the women's suffrage cause prospered, but at other times the suffragists were hard put to gain a hearing.[71] Between 1897 and 1903, franchise reform was neglected for a host of other political issues, including protection, licensing, education and labor disputes, and, even more, the Boer War, which from 1899 to 1902 completely overshadowed all other concerns. Given the conservative inclinations of the NUWSS leadership, it was hardly a proper time for promoting the cause of women's suffrage, and Fawcett herself was preoccupied with war responsibilities, particularly as a member of a Government commission which went to South Africa in 1901 and 1902 to investigate conditions in the internment camps.[72]

---

[70]One can only guess what the financial position of the NUWSS was at this time, for in these early years the NUWSS did not issue a balance sheet. The annual report of 1907 noted that the NUWSS had almost no money in the 1897–1903 period: "Beyond small affiliation fees to pay printing expenses, the Union had no funds at its disposal, although on isolated occasions money was given for specific purposes." National Union of Women's Suffrage Societies, Annual Report, 1907 (Uxbridge, 1907), p. 5.

[71]As one historian has noted, pressure groups were generally more successful in securing the repeal, rather than the introduction of legislation: "Positive legislation, including parliamentary reform, is likely to have a pedigree of its own, independent of pressure from without." Women's suffrage did not have this "pedigree." See Hollis, p. 24.

[72]Fawcett later commented: "Two fires cannot burn together and the most ardent suffragist felt that while war lasted it was not a fitting time to press their own claims and objects." See Millicent Garrett Fawcett, Women's Suffrage: A Short History of a Great Movement (London, 1912), p. 59, and Fawcett, What I Remember, pp. 153–74.

In October 1903, however, with the war over and rumors of a General Election in the air, the NUWSS, at the prodding of W. T. Stead and Elizabeth Wolstenholme-Elmy, agreed to sponsor a National Convention in Defense of the Civic Rights of Women.[73] This was the beginning of a new, aggressive stage. On October 16 and 17, two hundred delegates, representing all the NUWSS societies as well as many other women's organizations such as the Women's Liberal Federation and the British Women's Temperance Association, gathered in London. The convention passed four resolutions which instructed the NUWSS to take steps to make women's suffrage an issue at the next General Election: the NUWSS was asked to request all Cabinet members and leaders of the opposition to receive deputations on women's suffrage, to write all parliamentary candidates a letter on the subject, to raise a fund of £2,000 per annum for three years to agitate and organize for women's suffrage, and, most important:

> The National Union of Women's Suffrage Societies should take immediate steps to form a committee, where none already exists, in every Borough, County, Riding, and, if possible, in every county division of Great Britain and Ireland, who would pledge themselves to press the question of Women's Suffrage, irrespective of party, upon every Member of Parliament and candidate prior to the next General Election; and that, so far as possible, such committees should try to influence the local party associations only to choose candidates who are in favour of Women's Suffrage.[74]

In December the NUWSS appointed a subcommittee to consider how to implement the instructions of the convention. The committee issued an appeal for funds to carry on "a vigorous Women's Suffrage campaign throughout the country in order to force the subject upon the attention of constituencies and the candidates at the next General Election."[75] In preparation for the election, it drafted a letter to all parliamentary candidates, asking them to pledge support for women's

---

[73]NUWSS, Ex. com. mins., September 17, 1903, Fawcett Library, London. Elizabeth Wolstenholme-Elmy was a long-time suffragist and former secretary of the Manchester National Society for Women's Suffrage. She and Stead had held a conference of suffrage groups in July 1903 to consider whether it would be better to work for adult suffrage (votes for all men and women) or to continue to concentrate exclusively on women's suffrage. The meeting decided to continue to work only for votes for women, and asked the NUWSS to call a convention to discuss women's suffrage. NUWSS, Ex. com. mins., July 9, 1903, Fawcett Library, London.

[74]Women's Suffrage Record, December 1903.

[75]Minutes of the subcommittee of the National Union of Women's Suffrage Societies, December 9, 1903, Fawcett Library, London.

suffrage.[76] It also began to work out a plan (modeled on the "local associate scheme" of the Central and East of England Society) for forming suffrage committees in each parliamentary constituency. The committees were to keep in close touch with party organizations and party agents in order to draw their attention to the suffrage issue, with the object of securing the selection of suffragists as parliamentary candidates. The NUWSS would give financial support to establish and to assist these committees.

As a result of the 1903 convention, the NUWSS emerged as something more than a consultative body or a liaison committee between Parliament and the member societies.[77] Whereas in the 1897-1903 period the affiliates were almost completely autonomous, and within their own geographical territories established and implemented their own programs, in the 1903-6 period, the NUWSS began to exert more control over its member societies. The prospect of a General Election gave the NUWSS an immediate goal and a practical reason for organizing the independent-minded affiliates into a cohesive national pressure group. Also, the General Election forced the NUWSS to shift its focus away from Parliament to the parliamentary constituencies and pay greater attention to the activities of the affiliated societies. Although the NUWSS did not successfully execute all the directives of the 1903 convention, it did establish 133 new suffrage committees and it raised an election fund of some £2,520.[78] The fund was especially important because it gave the NUWSS its own independent source of financing. Under the direction of the NUWSS, the member societies questioned all candidates on their attitude to women's suffrage and received 415 pledges of support for the cause.[79]

After a long period of inactivity on the suffrage issue, Parliament itself was beginning to take a new interest in the cause. Whereas from 1897 to 1903 the House of Commons did not once consider women's suffrage, in the 1904-6 period it debated the issue four times.[80] Although the NUWSS had helped promote these measures, it was

---

[76]Ibid., December 11, 1903.

[77]Common Cause, April 4, 1913 (hereafter cited as C.C.).

[78]NUWSS, Ex. com. mins., October 6, 1904, and June 1, 1905, Fawcett Library, London; Englishwoman's Review, 36 (January 16, 1905); 26, and 37 (January 15, 1906); 28.

[79]National Union of Women's Suffrage Societies, Annual Report, 1905-1906 (Uxbridge, 1907), p.5.

[80]Besides McLaren's resolution, already referred to, which passed the House on March 16, 1904 (see note 68 above), there were bills by Bamford Slack (Lib. Herts, Mid), Sir Charles Dilke (Lib., Gloucs.,

not the women's persuasive abilities but the change in the political climate that was responsible for this new interest in women's suffrage.[81] The impending General Election undoubtedly had a great deal to do with the change, since all the political parties, with an eye to the constituencies, were showing an interest in all sorts of issues, and Members of the House of Commons were eager to use parliamentary debates as a means of "testing the political wind" and gauging the response of the electors to a particular issue.

The Liberal victory in January 1906 gave the NUWSS hope that the House of Commons' renewed interest in women's suffrage would be translated into positive legislation. The NUWSS had always been irrationally optimistic about the Liberal Party. Compared with the Conservative Party, the Liberal Party was sympathetic to the suffrage cause: in the seventeen divisions which were held on women's suffrage between 1867 and 1904, the number of Liberals who supported women's suffrage outnumbered those who opposed it on ten occasions, whereas on the Conservative benches, the number of Conservatives who opposed women's suffrage outnumbered those who supported it on twelve occasions. Yet, on the average, only 26.7 percent of the total number of Liberal MP's voted for women's suffrage in these divisions; another 26.7 percent voted against it, and 46.6 percent did not vote at all.[82] The NUWSS, convinced that women's suffrage was a liberal cause, tended to ignore the figures and to exaggerate the Liberal Party's enthusiasm for the cause. The fact that Sir Henry Campbell-Bannerman, the new Prime Minister, was generally thought to be sympathetic to women's suffrage only increased the NUWSS optimism that great things would come from the

---

Forest of Dean), and Keir Hardie (Lab., Metthyr Tydvil). Slack introduced a women's suffrage bill for its second reading on May 12, 1905. Debate was adjourned, and on June 2 the bill was talked out. (H. C. Deb. 4s, vol. 146, May 12, 1905, cc. 217-36, and H. C. Deb. 4s, vol. 147, June 2, 1905, cc. 613-16.) On March 2, 1906, Dilke introduced an Adult Suffrage Bill, which was talked out. (H. C. Deb. 4s, vol. 152, March 2, 1906, cc. 1448-54.) On April 25, 1906, Hardie introduced a resolution on women's suffrage. The debate was interrupted by disturbances in the Ladies' Gallery, and the resolution was finally talked out. H. C. Deb. 4s, vol. 155, April 25, 1906, cc. 1570-87.

[81]For details on the lobbying see Minutes of the executive committee of the Central Society for Women's Suffrage, April 12, 1905, and Circulars of the London Society for Women's Suffrage, 1906, Circular from Edith Palliser and Frances Sterling, April 20, 1906, Fawcett Library, London.

[82]Brian Harrison, Separate Spheres, pp. 28-29, provided the information from which these figures were tabulated. On the average, only 16.1 percent of the total number of Conservative MP's voted for women's suffrage in these divisions, while 28.3 percent voted against it; 55.6 percent did not vote at all.

Liberals. Campbell-Bannerman's announcement that he would receive a deputation of suffragists seemed proof of his goodwill.[83] The NUWSS placed great hopes in the success of the deputation, which it interpreted as a sign that "the agitation has definitely entered the field of practical politics."[84] On May 19 a deputation of 350 persons, representing twenty-five women's organizations as well as parliamentary supporters of the cause, met with the Prime Minister; Emily Davies, founder of Girton College and a member of the executive of the Central Society for Women's Suffrage, spoke eloquently for the NUWSS.[85] But it quickly became clear that the suffragists had greatly overestimated Campbell-Bannerman's commitment to the cause.[86] The Prime Minister told

---

[83]On February 2, 1906, the executive committee of the Central Society for Women's Suffrage noted that a group of suffragist MP's were sponsoring a petition to request the Prime Minister to receive a deputation on women's suffrage. The disturbances in the Ladies' Gallery on April 25 complicated negotiations for the deputation and there were suggestions that the Women's Social and Political Union, the instigator of these disturbances, should be excluded; this step, however, was not taken. Minutes of the executive committee of the Central Society for Women's Suffrage, February 22 and May 1, 1906, Fawcett Library, London.

Sylvia Pankhurst maintains that the WSPU was responsible for prevailing upon Campbell-Bannerman to receive a deputation on women's suffrage. This seems unlikely. It is much more probable that the suffragist MP's were responsible for convincing Campbell-Bannerman to meet the deputation. E. Sylvia Pankhurst, The Suffragette Movement: An Intimate Account of Persons and Ideals (London, 1931), pp. 207-8.

[84]Women's Suffrage Record, July 1906.

[85]Among the MP's present were Philip Snowden (Lab., Blackburn), Geoffrey Howard (Lib. Cumb. N), Henry York Stanger (Lib., N. Kensington), Keir Hardie, and Sir Charles McLaren. The organizations represented included the NUWSS, the WSPU, the Women's Liberal Federation, the British Women's Temperance Association, the Women's Industrial Council, and the Women's Cooperative Guild. Account of the Deputation to Sir Henry Campbell-Bannerman, May 19, 1906, NUWSS pamphlet (n.p., n.d.).

[86]In fact, Campbell-Bannerman was never enthusiastic about women's suffrage. The following anecdote, which he told at a meeting of the Women's Liberal Federation in November 1903, gives a good picture of his attitude: "I was sitting one day, when the matter came up to be voted upon, by the side of Mr. John Bright, and he said 'What do you think about this?' I said, 'Well, I am in this position. I have voted for it, but I am not very much inclined to vote for it again,' and John Bright looked at me and said, 'Dear me, that's precisely my position; let's both do the same thing' And accordingly, we both walked out from the division. Ever since I have maintained that more or less neutral attitude." Women's Suffrage Record, December 1903.

them that it was not politically realistic to expect the Liberals to promote women's suffrage, and he blandly advised them to continue to work to convert the party, and the country, to women's suffrage: "I have only one thing to preach to you and that is the virtue of patience. . . . You canot shut your eyes to the fact that no party in the State, and no Government that has ever been formed or is now in existence, is united entirely on this question. . . . It would not do for me to make any definite statement or pledge on the subject in these circumstances."[87]

The Prime Minister's cool response at least had the positive effect of causing the NUWSS to take more active measures to stir up support for the suffrage cause. Although disillusioned by the Liberal leader's lack of interest, the NUWSS believed that if it could convert the opposition within the Liberal Party and, more particularly, within the Cabinet, the Liberal Government might introduce legislation to enfranchise women. Accordingly, in July 1906, the executive committee announced that it would organize special campaigns in the constituencies of prominent Liberal opponents of women's suffrage.[88] Poplar (Sydney Buxton, Postmaster General), Rossendale (Lewis Harcourt, First Commissioner of Works), Forfarshire (John Sinclair, Secretary for Scotland), and Fife (Herbert Asquith, Chancellor of the Exchequer) were its prime targets. In cooperation with local suffrage committees, the NUWSS held meetings, collected petitions, distributed literature, and organized deputations to win support for the cause in these constituencies.[89] In October 1906, it announced that it intended to sponsor its own parliamentary candidates to run against leading opponents of women's suffrage: "The National Union adopts the policy of running a Women's Suffrage candidate wherever a suitable opportunity occurs at a by election, and where none of the official candidates are preparing actively to support women's suffrage.[90]

The NUWSS actions had a largely symbolic value. Asquith's and Harcourt's hostility to the cause certainly did not evaporate under the

---

[87]Ibid. July 1906.

[88]The Times, July 5, 1906.

[89]National Union of Women's Suffrage Societies, Annual Report, 1905-1906, pp. 7-8.

[90]Women's Suffrage Record, November 1906; see also note 66 above. The Ladies' National Association, which some members of the NUWSS executive had supported, may have inspired both the North of England Society and the NUWSS to sponsor candidates at elections. The LNA, one of the most important feminist organizations of the nineteenth century, had used this tactic with some success. See Josephine E. Butler, Personal Reminiscences of a Great Crusade (London, 1911), pp. 26-33.

influence of the NUWSS. But increased activity in the constituencies and a more aggressive election policy were signs that the NUWSS was beginning to abandon its passive policy of patiently waiting for Parliament to act on the suffrage issue. The Convention of 1903 had put new life into the NUWSS; the efforts to form societies and to collect funds were indications that the NUWSS was beginning to promote its cause actively and that the central organization was at last emerging from its state of lethargy. Whereas before 1903 the NUWSS had almost exclusively concentrated on working within Parliament, leaving the member societies to organize activities in the constituencies, in the 1903-6 period the NUWSS gradually began to assume a directing role in organizing the constituencies. Instead of acting as a liaison committee for the member societies, it was beginning to formulate policies for these societies and to oversee and to manage their implementation.

The Liberals' return to power in 1906 intensified these tendencies within the NUWSS: it increased the organization's expectations that Parliament would enact some measure of women's suffrage and thereby infused the NUWSS with a new zeal for promoting its cause. The suffragists believed that they could persuade the Liberal Government to effect some measure of women's suffrage if they could show that there was real enthusiasm for the enfranchisement of women in the nation. There is no question that this belief was extremely naïve. It underestimated the antagonism aroused by women's suffrage, overestimated the Liberal's commitment to the cause, and tended to make women's suffrage into an abstract issue, totally divorced from the political context of party considertions and electoral reform. Yet, however deluded the NUWSS may have been in clinging to this conviction, it stimulated the NUWSS to press its case more actively in the parliamentary constituencies, and as a concomitant of this, to exert more direction over the activities of its member societies.

In 1906 the NUWSS was no longer merely an umbrella organization under which the member societies independently pursued their own activities but was an active central core which intended to determine policies for the affiliates. And with the change in the nature of the organization, new tactics were also being tried. The NUWSS was still an extremely weak organization and it had a long way to go before it aroused much public or parliamentary enthusiasm for the cause of women's suffrage, but a beginning had been made. The heritage of Becker and the nineteenth-century suffrage movement no longer shaped the features or the actions of the NUWSS in quite so authoritarian a fashion: the NUWSS had begun to emerge from the nineteenth into the twentieth century.

CHAPTER II

THE NUWSS AND THE WSPU

The next three years were a time of growth and organizational development for the NUWSS. In contrast to its early years, the organization now devoted its main energies to propagandizing for women's suffrage in the parliamentary constituencies, rather than lobbying for the cause within the House of Commons. The seeds of these developments were planted in the years between 1903 and 1906; yet, it was the example of the Women's Social and Political Union (WSPU) which, in the years between 1906 and 1909, both stimulated and conditioned the growth of the NUWSS and injected a new vitality into the constitutional suffrage movement. During this period the NUWSS defined its relations with the WSPU, and by 1909 a pattern of relationships was established within the suffrage movement which persisted until the outbreak of war in August 1914.

The WSPU had been founded in Manchester in October 1903, by Emmeline Pankhurst, the widow of Dr. Richard Pankhurst, a Radical politician and ardent suffragist, and Christabel Pankhurst, their eldest daughter. The new organization was designed to function politically as "a women's parallel to the I. L. P., though with primary emphasis on the vote."[1] From 1903 to 1905 the WSPU confined its activities to Lancashire. It was a small, parochial organization, closely tied to the ILP, and dependent on the ILP for audiences and financial support. The WSPU had not succeeded in attracting a large following, nor had it received national attention. Its methods of agitation were traditional: it had not yet adopted militant tactics as a means of publicizing its demand and enlisting support for the women's suffrage movement.[2]

In 1905 and 1906, the WSPU underwent a remarkable metamorphosis. The Pankhursts moved the organization from Manchester to London, shifted the focus of its energies from the working classes to the House of Commons, and began to sever its ties with the Labour Party; most important, they adopted militancy as a political tactic. There were two dimensions to the Pankhursts' decision to engage in militancy. Unquestionably there was a psychological motive for its adoption: militancy was an overt rejection of the Victorian ideal of

---

[1]Sylvia Pankhurst, The Suffragette Movement, p. 168.

[2]Andrew Rosen, Rise Up, Women! (London, 1974), p. 57.

womanhood, "of a moribund, a respectable, a smothering security."[3] It offered women the possibility of demonstrating strength and "challenging man's monopoly of traits which accorded him a dominant position in society"; it expressed "both indignation at man's indifference and woman's ability to protest as men would were they treated similarly."[4] It would be misleading, however, to imply that the only motives behind the decision to engage in militancy were psychological. The Pankhursts were more politically pragmatic than has often been suggested. Tactical considerations, as well as psychological motivations, led them to jettison conventional methods of agitation and to embark on a campaign of militancy, a campaign conceived against a background of stagnation and failure in the women's suffrage movement.[5] Petitions and polite conversations, the tactical hallmarks of nineteenth-century feminism, had failed to arouse much public or parliamentary enthusiasm for the women's cause; more strident techniques might meet with more success. According to Sylvia Pankhurst, the WSPU's object in resorting to militancy was: "To create an impression upon the public throughout the country, to set everyone talking about votes for women, to keep the subject in the press, to leave the Government no peace from it."[6]

Militancy was designed to create a mass movement for women's suffrage and thereby to force the House of Commons to enfranchise women. The militancy took a very mild form at the outset, not going beyond heckling Cabinet ministers, interrupting public meetings, and holding large processions and demonstrations.[7] These interruptions of

---

[3]George Dangerfield, The Strange Death of Liberal England (New York, 1961), p. 144.

[4]Ruth Freeman Claus, "Militancy in the English and American Woman Suffrage Movements" (Ph.D. diss., Yale University, 1975), pp. 34-47.

[5]F. W. Pethick-Lawrence, Fate Has Been Kind (London, 1943), p.68.

[6]Pankhurst, p. 223.

[7]The Pankhursts' association with the ILP influenced their decision to engage in militancy. Demonstrations, followed by imprisonments, followed by processions when the prisoners were released, had been very useful to the ILP in dramatizing its cause and gaining publicity. The Pankhursts were very aware of this and drew on the tactical experiences of the ILP. Rosen, pp. 19-23.
In the nineteenth century, pressure groups such as the National Reform League had held processions and mass meetings to popularize their demands. Unlike the ILP, however, they do not seem to have used imprisonments as a tactical weapon to create sympathy for their cause. Alexander Wilson, "The Suffrage Movement," in Pressure from Without, pp. 80-104.

meetings and disturbances in the Ladies' Gallery seem to have been of
only slight interest to the NUWSS and did not provoke any comment or
promote any action by the constitutionalists.[8] But the arrest and
imprisonment in October 1906 of eleven members of the WSPU could not be
ignored. The NUWSS, like much of the public and a large part of the
House of Commons, was shocked that the women should be sent to Holloway
as prisoners in the Second Division, as well as fined, and it thought
the punishment harsh and excessive in relation to the deeds.[9] Fawcett
publicly announced her support for the prisoners and urged her fellow
suffragists to stand by them:

> The real responsibility for these sensational methods lies
> with the politicians, misnamed statesmen, who will not attend
> to a demand for justice until it is accompanied by some form
> of violence. Every kind of insult and abuse is hurled at the
> women who have adopted these methods, especially by the
> "reptile" press. But, I hope the more old-fashioned
> suffragists will stand by them; and I take this opportunity of
> saying that in my opinion, far from having injured the
> movement, they have done more during the last twelve months to
> bring it within the region of practical politics than we have
> been able to accomplish in the same number of years.[10]

In a letter that Fawcett wrote to friends she added, "I feel that the
action of the prisoners has touched the imagination of the country in
a manner which quieter methods did not succeed in doing."[11]

---

[8]On October 13, 1905, Christabel Pankhurst and Annie Kenney,
representatives of the WSPU, interrupted Sir Edward Grey who was
speaking at a Liberal meeting in the Free Trade Hall, Manchester, and
asked him when the Liberals intended to give votes to women. As a
result of this action, the two women were sentenced to seven days in
prison. This incident marked the start of militancy by the WSPU.
Undoubtedly, it attracted new recruits into the suffrage movement.
But even though this and subsequent disturbances created by the WSPU
in 1905 and 1906 helped to enlist support for the suffrage movement,
they did not affect the policies of the NUWSS. Until October 1906,
the files of the NUWSS and the Central Society for Women's Suffrage
contain only a small amount of correspondence relating to the WSPU's
activities. After October 1906, this is not the case.

[9]One of the eleven arrested was Anne Cobden Sanderson, a
daughter of Richard Cobden and a friend of Fawcett's--an additional
reason for NUWSS reaction.

[10]The Times, October 27, 1906.

[11]As quoted in Emmeline Pethick-Lawrence, My Part in a Changing
World (London, 1938), p. 171.

The WSPU responded warmly to Fawcett's expressions of support. Emmeline Pethick-Lawrence, the treasurer, called Fawcett's action "a generous and noble gesture,"[12] and Elizabeth Robins, a member of the executive committee of the WSPU, thanked her effusively for her support:

> They are grateful to you--these women who are fighting the much- misunderstood battle in the open. Some of them know quite well they would stand a poor chance indeed, but for the past influence and present championship of yourself and others like you--if there are others. .... The generous attitude of one like yourself must be of invaluable help to those of us who cannot hope ever to be so well equipped, and yet have come to feel they must not hold back one voice through an ignoble fear of the bugbear charge of notoriety-hunting.[13]

Within the NUWSS, there was general indignation. Letters echoing Fawcett's sentiments poured into the NUWSS office.[14] The annual meeting of the Central Society for Women's Suffrage passed a resolution urging the constitutionalists to take note of the example set by the militants: "It recognizes the zeal shown by these women who have not hesitated to go to prison in support of their convictions and it calls upon this society and upon all women to show an equal zeal in furthering by every constitutional method the cause to which they are devoted."[15] On December 11, 1906, after the eleven arrested WSPU members had been released from Holloway, Fawcett and other members of

---

[12]Ibid.

[13]Archives, Manchester Public Library, M/50, Box 9, Elizabeth Robins to Millicent Garrett Fawcett, October 27, 1906. Eva Gore-Booth, on the other hand, asked Fawcett not to support the actions of the WSPU, as the militants' behavior was repugnant to working women: "There is no class in the community who has such good reason for objecting and does so strongly object to shrieking and throwing yourself on the floor and struggling and kicking as does the average working woman, whose dignity is very real to them. . . . It is not the fact of demonstrations or even violence that is offensive to them, it is being mixed up with and held accountable as a class for educated and upper class women who kick, shriek, bite, and spit." Archives, Manchester Public Library, M/50, Box 10, Eva Gore-Booth to Millicent Garrett Fawcett, October 25, 1906.

[14]See, for example, the Fawcett Library Autograph Collection, vol. 1, B2, Edith Kerwood to Frances Sterling, October 26, 1906, Fawcett Library, London (hereafter cited as FLAC).

[15]Minutes of the executive committee of the Central Society for Women's Suffrage, October 29, 1906, Fawcett Library, London.

the NUWSS executive gave a banquet in their honor as proof of their friendship and admiration.[16]

For all its demonstrations of sympathy and support, however, the NUWSS was faced with a real challenge by the actions of the WSPU and the willingness of its members to become martyrs for the sake of women's suffrage. The constitutional suffragists of the NUWSS and its affiliates had always maintained that moral force was a more effective, and a more honorable, weapon than physical force, and they feared that once the use of violence was countenanced, it would be impossible to put an end to it.[17] In the past, however, "moral force" had often been a synonym for inaction. The activities of the militants in a sense put the NUWSS and its constitutional methods on trial and forced the NUWSS into actions which would prove that they, too, could contribute to the progress of the suffrage movement, and that violence and martyrdom were not the only means of rousing the nation to take an interest in the cause. The almost frenetic activity of the NUWSS in the years 1906-9 was an attempt to emulate the dedication and determination of the militants and to vindicate the constitutional suffrage movement. During this period the example of the WSPU had a great influence on the policies of the NUWSS, and the NUWSS, following the lead of the WSPU, threw itself into processions, demonstrations, and extensive activity in elections.

The first sign that the NUWSS was preparing to take more active measures to promote women's suffrage came in January 1907, with the adoption of a new constitution.[18] This constitution--in preparation throughout the previous autumn--was designed to strengthen the organizational structure of the NUWSS. The executive committee was to be made more permanent than before, with members elected rather than appointed by the societies, for one-year terms. The new constitution

---

[16]The Times, December 12, 1906.

[17]Josephine Butler's success in obtaining the repeal of the Contagious Diseases Act was one source of inspiration to the NUWSS, and this example was often cited as proof of the efficacy of moral force. In 1907, for example, Frances Sterling, secretary of the NUWSS, wrote a long letter to Maud Arncliffe-Sennett, a member of the WSPU, in which she discussed the policies of the NUWSS and WSPU and expressed her admiration for Josephine Butler: "After that lesson it would take me a great deal of despair before I should adopt the new methods." British Museum, London, Arncliffe-Sennett Collection, vol. 1, Frances Sterling to Maud Arncliffe-Sennett, April 12, 1907.

[18]Representatives from the thirty-one societies in the NUWSS met in London on January 28, 1907 to hear the draft of the new constitution. National Union of Women's Suffrage Societies, Annual Report, 1907, p. 6.

also established a council composed of representatives from the local societies; this would meet four times a year to formulate policies.[19] The executive committee was responsible to the council of representatives, and any changes in policy would have to receive the approval of this body. The net effect of the new constitution was to facilitate communication and cooperation among the member societies, and to place the executive in a position to manage and supervise the activities of these societies. Other organizational innovations followed the adoption of the new constitution. The NUWSS moved into its own offices, obtained its own staff, and in the summer of 1906 began to contribute on a regular basis to Women's Franchise, a weekly newspaper.[20] The NUWSS was still decentralized, but it was now a "practical working organization" with independent resources and a strong executive.[21]

Shortly after the adoption of the new constitution the NUWSS started to work in earnest for the introduction of a women's suffrage bill in Parliament. The strategy of both the NUWSS and the WSPU at this time was to promote a private member's bill for women's suffrage.[22] Although both organizations recognized that it was unlikely that a private bill would pass through all its stages, they also realized that since no party was willing to support a women's suffrage measure, a private bill was the only parliamentary alternative available to

---

[19]The number of delegates that each society sent to the Council was determined by the size of the society. Societies numbering 20 to 50 members were allotted one delegate each; societies of 50 to 100 members were allotted two delegates. One additional delegate was allotted for every fifty members beyond 100.

[20]Minutes of the executive committee of the Central Society for Women's Suffrage, February 21, 1907; NUWSS, Ex. com. mins., 1907, passim; Fawcett Library, London.

[21]National Union of Women's Suffrage Societies, Annual Report, 1907, p. 6. The WSPU had also adopted a new constitution, in October 1906, which made many changes in organizational structure in an effort to make the Union more democratic. These changes, however, were never put into effect. See Rosen, pp. 72-73.

[22]Constance Rover is wrong when she implies that the NUWSS believed that a private member's bill could pass the House of Commons and that the NUWSS "preferred" this type of bill because it kept women's suffrage from becoming a party issue. Cf. Rover, Women's Suffrage and Party Politics in Great Britain, 1866-1914, pp. 68-69, and Ray Strachey, Millicent Garret Fawcett, p. 249.

them.[23] The private member's bill would have a "nuisance" value in that it would keep the women's suffrage issue in front of Parliament, the Government, and the public and publicize the cause. Also, private bills could be a way of persuading—and pressuring—the Government to introduce a women's suffrage measure. If a majority of Liberal MP's voted for the private bills, that evidence of support might force the Government to sponsor a bill of its own.

The main tasks for the moment were to get a member to introduce a bill, and after that to see that the bill successfuly passed its second reading. The way to achieve both these ends was to show Parliament that there was a demand for women's suffrage. Accordingly, the NUWSS summoned all supporters of the movement to join in a march from Hyde Park Corner to Exeter Hall. On February 9, led by Lady Frances Balfour, Fawcett, Jane, Lady Strachey, and Edith Pechey-Phipson, some 3,000 women representing forty organizations, all carrying banners and accompanied by bands, walked in the rain through the streets of London to advertise their cause.[24] This so-called "Mud March" was the largest public demonstration in support of women's suffrage that had ever been organized.[25]

Four days after the procession, the executive committee of the NUWSS met with the Parliamentary Committee for Women's Suffrage to discuss the introduction of a private member's bill.[26] On March 8, less than a month later, Willoughby H. Dickinson (Lib., St. Pancras, N.) introduced a Women's Enfranchisement Bill for its second reading.[27] The NUWSS had taken great pains to drum up support for the bill. All member societies had been asked to send letters and organize deputations to their local MP's and, where possible, to see that male electors in the constituencies approached their MP's about supporting

---

[23]The leaders of both the Labour and Conservative parties had refused the Pankhursts' request to sponsor a women's suffrage measure. Pankhurst, p. 204; Rosen, p. 94.

[24]The Times, February 11, 1907. Jane, Lady Strachey, mother of Lytton Strachey, was a long-time suffragist and president of the Women's Local Government Society. Edith Pechey-Phipson was one of the first women to enter the English medical profession. Both women were on the executive of the NUWSS.

[25]Ray Strachey, The Cause, p. 305. The processions of the WSPU had been on a much smaller scale.

[26]National Union of Women's Suffrage Societies, Annual Report, 1907, p. 8.

[27]H. C. Deb. 4s, vol. 170, March 8, 1907, c. 1102.

the bill.[28] All this activity, coming soon after the march, aroused great interest in the debate on Dickinson's bill, and an unusually large number of MP's turned up to hear the discussion. Significantly, Dickinson, in introducing the bill, pleaded with those present not to let militant methods alienate them from the suffrage movement.[29] The subsequent debate centered on whether the bill was wide enough in scope, and whether there was, in fact, any demand in the country for women's suffrage.[30] Unfortunately, no final judgment was given on the merits of the measure, as the Dickinson Bill, like its predecessors, was talked out.

The NUWSS had worked harder for the Dickinson Bill than for any other previous suffrage measure, and it had expected the House to give the matter serious consideration and at least to divide on the bill. Now the hard work had all come to nothing. The NUWSS was disappointed and angry at the insulting way in which the House of Commons had treated the bill, and it was now convinced that Members of Parliament were not seriously interested in women's suffrage and did not consider the issue to be of great consequence to the electorate. Instead of relying on Parliament, the NUWSS resolved to try and arouse interest in women's suffrage in the nation as a whole, specifically by working in by-elections. By-elections would give the suffragists an opportunity to appeal to the public and educate it about the women's cause; equally important, they would enable the NUWSS to force the issue on prospective Members of Parliament.

This strategy had already been adopted by the WSPU, which in August 1906 had announced that it would oppose all Liberal candidates,

---

[28]Correspondence of the London Society for Women's Suffrage, "Suggestions for work in support of the Women's Suffrage Bill," February 1907, Fawcett Library, London.

[29]H. C. Deb. 4s, vol. 170, March 8, 1907, c. 1102.

[30]Sir Henry Campbell-Bannerman was one of those who thought the bill was too limited. He, and others, maintained that the bill would not enfranchise many working women and that the 1,500,000 women who would be given votes would belong to the middle and upper classes. Philip Snowden (Lab., Blackburn) denied this, quoting statistics from a survey which the ILP had made in 1904. These statistics, based on reports from 50 districts, showed that 82.4 percent of the women voters on the municipal register belonged to the working class.
Though Campbell-Bannerman's fears were echoed by other Liberals, both in this debate and in subsequent debates on women's suffrage, in many cases the contention that the bill was "undemocratic" was not a matter of sincere conviction but rather a convenient excuse for not supporting the suffrage issue. The fact that many members of the Labour Party backed these supposedly "narrow" bills also casts doubt on the motives of these Liberal champions of working class women.

regardless of their views on women's suffrage, until the Government introduced a women's suffrage bill. As Emmeline Pankhurst freely admitted, the strategy was borrowed from Parnell and the Irish party:

> In 1885 . . . Dr. Pankhurst, stood as a Liberal candidate for Parliament in Rotherline. . . . Parnell was in command, and his settled policy was opposition to all Government candidates. So, in spite of the fact that Dr. Pankhurst was a staunch upholder of home rule, the Parnell forces were solidly opposed to him, and he was defeated. . . . my husband pointed out to me that Parnell's policy was absolutely right. With his small party he could never hope to win home rule from a hostile majority, but by constant obstruction he could in time wear out the Government, and force it to surrender. That was a valuable political lesson, one that years later I was destined to put into practice.[31]

The NUWSS policy differed from that of the WSPU in not being anti-Liberal; the NUWSS was ready to support "the best friend of women's suffrage," whatever his party, toward the goal of electing as many candidates as possible who would be on the suffragists' side:

> It [the NUWSS] believes that if a majority of members can be returned, publicly and definitely pledged to raise and support the question in the House, the Government then in office will see the absolute necessity of dealing with the matter. It, therefore, does not adopt the policy of opposing Liberal candidates merely because members of the present Government have so far declared themselves unable to bring in a Bill for the Enfranchisement of Women.[32]

Indeed, despite the poor performance of the Liberals, the NUWSS still thought there was a good chance that they would bring in a bill for women's suffrage. Undoubtedly this hope was partly determined by the pro-Liberal sympathies of the NUWSS executive, as well as by their belief that women's suffrage was in the best tradition of liberal reform.[33] In looking at the suffrage issue from a very abstract, moral perspective, they evidently failed to recognize, or at least they did not accept, the degree to which the Liberal Party was pragmatic and electorally minded in its attitude toward women's suffrage. Though

---

[31]Emmeline Pankhurst, My Own Story (London, 1914), p. 18.

[32]Women's Franchise, July 4, 1907.

[33]In 1907 ten of the twenty members of the NUWSS executive committee were in some way connected with the Liberal Party. Two members, Isabella Ford and Ethel Snowden, were linked with the Labour Party. Only one member, Lady Strachey, was affiliated with the Conservative Party.

there was no evidence to prove the point, many Liberals feared that if the vote were given only to women who fulfilled the qualifications that male voters had to meet, the reform would benefit the Conservatives more than it would the Liberals.[34]

Not all of the NUWSS policy was simply party loyalty, however. The Liberals had been in office for only a year, and the NUWSS felt that the Government should be given a reasonable amount of time to act on the question before they were condemned as opponents of women's suffrage. Though the WSPU disagreed, the NUWSS did not believe that it would help the women's cause to oppose Liberals at elections—not only because it would antagonize the ruling party, and, by the same token, help the Conservatives, but also because it would confuse the electorate.[35] If the voting records of the parties were any indication of future trends, the Liberals would be more likely than the Tories to support women's suffrage: in the seventeen divisions that were held on women's suffrage between 1867 and 1904, the Liberals had, on the average, contributed 59.7 percent of the votes for women's suffrage measures, and the Conservatives only 33.8 percent.[36] The NUWSS believed that the best way of encouraging the Government to bring in a suffrage bill was to strengthen the suffragist sentiment within the Liberal Party. It would be a mistake to associate the suffrage movement with anti-Liberal policies, and there was little point in a policy that indirectly assisted the Conservatives, who, during their long tenure in power, had done nothing for women and were not likely to

---

[34]In fact, the ILP survey of 1904 had shown that this was not the case. And, in the 1907 debate on the Dickinson Bill, Dickinson claimed that in his constituency, St. Pancras North, 60 percent of the women on the municipal register belonged to the working class. H. C. Deb. 4s, vol. 170, March 8, 1907, c. 1108. Neither of these surveys was solid evidence, of course, but the Liberals who argued that only wealthy women would be enfranchised offered no evidence at all.

[35]The By-Election Policies of the NUWSS and the WSPU Compared, NUWSS pamphlet (London, 1907).

[36]These figures have been computed on the basis of voting information provided in Brian Harrison, Separate Spheres, pp. 28-29. The Liberals, on the average, contributed 46.1 percent of the votes against women's suffrage, while the Conservatives contributed 51 percent. The votes of the Labour Party and the Irish Nationalist Party make up the remaining percentage.

change if returned to power.[37] And so far as the average elector was concerned, the sight of supporters of women's suffrage opposing the presumably suffragist Liberals would only be mystifying.

In part, the disagreement between the NUWSS and the WSPU on the matter of opposing or not opposing Liberals resulted from their differing ideas on the value of by-election campaigns. The educational value of these campaigns was extremely important to the NUWSS, and NUWSS members always stressed the opportunity to propagandize and enlist public support for the women's cause. The WSPU, on the other hand, was preoccupied with the political ramifications of by-elections: to them, by-elections were principally a means of putting pressure on the Government, through the loss of seats in the House of Commons, to introduce a measure for women's suffrage.

During 1907, the NUWSS participated in four by-elections: Hexham, Jarrow, Kirkdale,[38] and Wimbledon. At Hexham the NUWSS supported a Conservative, Colonel Bates; at Jarrow it supported a Labourite, Pete Curran; and at Kirkdale, finding none of the candidates satisfactory, it remained neutral and propagandized for the suffrage cause. Although only Curran was victorious, the NUWSS maintained that from an educational standpoint, these three by-election campaigns were great successes; as a result of the interest aroused, women's suffrage committees had been formed in all of these constituencies.[39] Encouraged by this response, the NUWSS, in October 1907, decided to take part in all future by-elections; it stressed that the educational value of these campaigns was as important, if not more important, than the return of a suffragist to Parliament:

> The main idea underlying this scheme of by-election policy is the education of constituencies in women's suffrage, and the utilization of these elections as an opportunity for organizing new women's suffrage societies, a by-election

---

[37]Arthur Balfour, the head of the Conservative Party, was a proponent of women's suffrage but not an ardent supporter. Both his sisters-in-law, Lady Frances Balfour and Lady Betty Balfour, complained of his lack of enthusiasm for the cause. FLAC, vol. 1, Bi, Lady Frances Balfour to Millicent Garrett Fawcett, September 22, 1898, Fawcett Library, London.

[38]National Union of Women's Suffrage Societies, Annual Report, 1907, p. 11.

[39]At Hexham a Liberal, R. D. Holt, defeated Colonel Bates. Three new women's suffrage committees were formed at Hexham, for example. NUWSS, Ex. com. mins., March 22, 1907, in Minutes of the executive committee of the Central Society for Women's Suffrage, Fawcett Library, London.

offering the best occasion for getting a hearing from voters and therefore the point to which the chief energy of the National Union could with most advantage be directed and on which its funds could be best expended.[40]

The NUWSS hoped that by exciting the country's interest in women's suffrage and creating a demand for the enfranchisement of women, it could force the Government to pay serious attention to the suffragists' cause.

The by-election at Wimbledon, in May 1907, was special in that the NUWSS for the first time sponsored a women's suffrage candidate— the Hon. Bertrand Russell, a member of the NUWSS executive committee and a well-known figure. Wimbledon was a Conservative stronghold, and its sitting Member, a prominent Tory, Sir Henry Chaplin, was an outspoken opponent of women's suffrage. The Liberals, believing the case to be hopeless, had decided to let Chaplin have the seat, but the NUWSS was unhappy with this decision because it felt that no confirmed opponent of women's suffrage should be returned to Parliament unopposed.[41] It therefore prevailed upon Russell, a Liberal and a Free Trader, to run on a women's suffrage platform.[42] In choosing him as

---

[40]Report of the Annual Council of the National Union of Women's Suffrage Societies, October 25, 1907, in Minutes of the executive committee of the Central Society for Women's Suffrage, Fawcett Library, London.

[41]W. S. B. McLaren outlined the reasons behind the NUWSS decision to run a candon in a letter that appeared in The Times on May 9, 1907. On May 17, 1907, The Times printed a letter from Bertha Mason which also discussed the reasons behind the NUWSS decision to sponsor Russell's candidacy.

[42]The NUWSS executive committee decided that it wanted its candidate to be a suffragist, a Liberal, and a Free Trader. Russell was chosen because he met these qualifications. NUWSS, Ex. com. mins., May 1, 1907, in minutes of the executive committee of the Central Society for Women's Suffrage, Fawcett Library, London. Russell's Liberalism was a handicap in a Conservative constituency like Wimbledon, and the NUWSS would have been wiser to run a Conservative, protectionist suffragist, as this would have been a more dramatic way of showing that it opposed Chaplin only because of his views on women's suffrage. The women's suffrage issue was overshadowed by the candidates' disagreements over protectionism versus free trade. One of the lessons learned at Wimbledon was to select candidates who held the same political views, and belonged to the same political party as their antisuffragist opponents.

its candidate, the NUWSS hoped to attract the votes of the Liberals in the constituency, and even to receive official support from the Liberal Party. The Liberal Party declined to assist, however, and the NUWSS was left to bear the whole effort. In a period of ten days it sent 328 workers into the constituency, and it spent nearly £1,400 on the campaign.[43] Russell polled a respectable 3,299 votes but Chaplin was returned by a majority of 6,964.[44]

The Wimbledon election garnered considerable national publicity for the suffrage cause, and it created a spirit of élan within the organization, but the cost was enormous, considering the society's limited resources, and one cannot but feel that part of the reason for this departure from the policy of by-elections for education was the urge to draw some of the limelight away from the WSPU and get the attention of being an "innovator" in the suffrage movement. Apparently the NUWSS itself questioned the wisdom of sponsoring women's suffrage candidates, for it did not venture into such a campaign again until the General Election of 1910.

Throughout 1908 and 1909 the NUWSS continued its policy of participating in by-elections, conducting campaigns to publicize the women's cause and gather new recruits for the suffragist ranks. From the modest start in 1907, the NUWSS went on to take part in thirty-one by-elections in the next two years—doing propaganda work in twenty-six of those and actively campaigning in five.[45] It acquired a staff of

---

[43]London Society for Women's Suffrage, Annual Report, 1907 (London, 1907), p. 8; National Union of Women's Suffrage Societies, Annual Report, 1907, p. 52. The NUWSS had come to an agreement with the WSPU that it would stay out of the Stepney by-election if the WSPU would agree to stay out of the Wimbledon election. See NUWSS, Ex. com. mins., May 3, 1907, in minutes of the executive committee of the Central Society for Women's Suffrage, Fawcett Library, London. The NUWSS raised a special Wimbledon Election Fund to cover the cost of the election. National Union of Women's Suffrage Societies, Annual Report, 1907, pp. 38-39, 52.

[44]The Times, May 16, 1907.

[45]National Union of Women's Suffrage Societies, Annual Report, 1908 (London, 1909), pp. 14-17, and Annual Report, 1909 (London, 1910), pp. 16-19. These by-elections were: West Hull, Ashburton, Worcester, South Leeds, Hastings, Peckham, West Derby, N. W. Manchester, Sheffield-Dewsbury, Wolverhampton (Shrops.), Newport, Pudsey (Yorks), Pembroke, Shoreditch, Haggerston, Newcastle-upon-Tyne, Chelmsford, Taunton, Forfar, Central Glasgow, South Edinburgh, Hawick, Croydon, East Edinburgh, Sheffield-Attercliffe, Stratford-on-Avon, Cleveland, Mid-Derby, East Edinburgh, Dumfries, Derby-High Peak, and Bermondsey.

paid organizers--six in 1908, ten in 1909--and began compiling information about the various parliamentary constituencies.[46] This information was put into divisional books so that organizers could set to work on a by-election campaign at a moment's notice without having to ask questions about party organizations, employment conditions, and so on.[47]

Though the concentration in 1908 and 1909 was on by-elections, the NUWSS also organized mass meetings and processions along the lines of the successful "Mud March" of February 1907. On June 13, 1908, for example, it sponsored a procession in London in which 10,000 women representing forty-two organizations participated.[48] The member societies held similar, though smaller, gatherings in towns and cities

---

The NUWSS did propaganda work at fifteen by-elections in 1908. It supported W. R. Warren (Lib.) at Haggerston; he was defeated by the Hon. R. Guinness (Cons.). It opposed Sir George Bartley (Cons.) at West Hull; he was defeated by the Hon. Guy Wilson (Lib.). In 1909 the NUWSS did propanganda work at eleven by-elections. It supported G. Falconer (Lib.) at Taunton; he was defeated by the Hon. W. R. Peel (Cons.). It supported J. W. Gulland (Lib.) at Dumfries; he defeated J. B. Duncan (Cons.).

[46]See National Union of Women's Suffrage Societies, Annual Report, 1908, p. 8, and Annual Report, 1909, p. 13. In some cases the member societies employed their own organizers. For example, in 1909, the North of England Society employed an organizer and an assistant organizer. North of England Society for Women's Suffrage, Annual Report, 1909 (Manchester, n.d.), p. 10.

[47]The idea originated with the North of England Society's secretary, Kathleen Courtney. Many of these divisional books are contained in the Correspondence of the London Society for Women's Suffrage, Fawcett Library, London.

[48]London Society for Women's Suffrage, Annual Report, 1908 (London, 1909), pp. 8-9.

throughout England.[49] Besides the public gatherings, there were also countless drawing room meetings throughout the country, and speakers were sent to mothers' meetings, church groups, women's organizations, and political associations.[50] Some of the local societies sponsored caravan tours in support of women's suffrage, and members of the executive and NUWSS organizers went on speaking tours to publicize their demand; Fawcett even debated the suffrage issue at the Oxford Union, becoming the first woman ever to address this group.[51] The aim of all these marches, meetings, and speeches was the same: to publicize the women's demand and to use public opinion to pressure Parliament to enact a measure for women's suffrage.

Throughout this period, even though the NUWSS was actively seeking public support for women's suffrage by holding meetings and demonstrations and participating at by-elections, its attention, like that of the WSPU, was focused on the House of Commons and the Government. As the year 1908 began, the NUWSS was still hopeful that the Liberals would come to the aid of the women's suffrage movement. In February, Henry York Stanger (Lib., N. Kensington) introduced a women's suffrage bill which passed its second reading by a majority of 179 votes.[52] Further progress on the bill was blocked, but this was the first time since 1897 that the House of Commons had acted favorably on a measure enfranchising women and the NUWSS regarded it as an indication that all the efforts to publicize and to propagandize the women's cause were beginning to have an impact on Members of Parliament. Moreover, because a majority of those who voted for the bill were Liberals--many of them in the Government--the NUWSS felt that its faith in the Liberal Party had not been misplaced and that its

---

[49]On October 23, 1908, for example, the North of England Society held a huge meeting in the Free Trade Hall, and on the following day it sponsored a procession. Manchester Guardian, October 24, 1908.

[50]Women's Franchise and Common Cause give a brief weekly summary of the meetings sponsored by the member societies of the NUWSS. The Annual Reports of the NUWSS also list, although by no means completely, the meetings sponsored by the local societies.

[51]The Times, November 21, 1908. Students at Newnham College, Cambridge, originated the idea of the "caravan tours." National Union of Women's Suffrage Societies, Annual Report, 1908, p. 17.

[52]H. C. Deb. 4s, vol. 185, February 28, 1908, cc. 212-87. The provisions of the bill were much the same as those of Dickinson's bill of March 1907. The NUWSS had taken the usual steps to secure a successful reading on the bill, and the societies had been asked to write to their MP's about supporting the bill.

decision not to adopt an anti-Liberal by-election policy had been the correct one.[53]

Nonetheless, although the division on the Stanger Bill re-affirmed the NUWSS hope that the Liberal Government might introduce a women's suffrage bill, it should not have been looked upon quite so optimistically—since one of the most powerful men in the Government, Herbert Asquith, the Chancellor of the Exchequer, had again placed himself clearly as being opposed to any Government approval of the suffragist cause.

Asquith's biographer, Roy Jenkins, terms Asquith's attitude to women's suffrage "bizzare" and maintains that Asquith was never "happy" as an antisuffragist.[54] Asquith's opposition to women's suffrage certainly does not seem consistent with some of his other views. He invariably supported measures which enabled women to participate in local government, and, as Home Secretary, he was responsible for the first women factory inspectors; yet when the parliamentary vote was at stake, he was the women's most ardent opponent.[55] In some ways his logic seemed to agree with that of many other prominent antisuffragists in that he believed women to have a limited political capacity and to be unsuited to participate in national affairs.[56] He had an old-fashioned appreciation of women and feared that the rough-and-

---

[53]Only 29 Conservatives voted for the measure, as opposed to 191 Liberals. Those Members of the Government who supported the Bill included Sir Edward Grey (Foreign Secretary), David Lloyd George (president of the Board of Trade), John Morley (Secretary for India), R. B. Haldane (Secretary for War), John Burns (president of the Local Government Board), Sydney Buxton (Postmaster-General), and Herbert Gladstone (Home Secretary). Gladstone even spoke in support of the bill. The Members of the Government who opposed it included Herbert Asquith (Chancellor of the Exchequer) and Lewis Harcourt (First Commissioner of Works). H. C. Deb. 4s, vol. 185, February 28, 1908, cc. 283-87.

[54]Roy Jenkins, Asquith: Portrait of a Man and an Era (New York, 1964), pp. 247-48.

[55]Asquith had made his first important speech opposing women's enfranchisement in 1892. On April 27, 1892, he spoke against Sir Albert Rollit's (Cons., Islington, S.) Parliamentary Franchise (Extension to Women) Bill. H. C. Deb. 4s, vol. 3, April 27, 1892, c. 1510.

[56]Interview with Dame Margery Corbett-Ashby, December 4, 1974, London. Asquith argued that women "operate by personal influence, and not by associated or representative action, and that their natural sphere is not the turmoil and dust of politics, but the circle of social and domestic life." H. C. Deb. 4s, vol. 3, April 27, 1892, c. 1513.

tumble of parliamentary politics might "unsex" them and rob them of their feminine charms and decorative qualities. He wondered why women even wanted the vote, or how they might benefit from it; the excitement and mystique surrounding "votes for women" completely eluded him.[57]

There was more to his opposition than these somewhat superficial views, however. Asquith was a Liberal of the twentieth century who had broken with Mill's nineteenth-century tradition of liberal individualism, and unlike Mill—and the women of the NUWSS—he looked at reform pragmatically rather than abstractly, in terms of the rights of the individual. Reform was a question of "social and imperial efficiency," and the enfranchisement of women would not facilitate such efficiency.[58] Liberalism, Asquith believed, "had become excessively dominated by the policy of political and religious emancipation which it had followed in the past," and he considered it "doubtful whether further franchise reform would benefit the Liberals."[59] In a sense, Asquith's disagreements with the NUWSS and other proponents of women's suffrage were a clash between the radical liberalism of the nineteenth century and the more collectivist liberalism of the twentieth.

In the winter of 1908, it was rumored that Asquith would succeed Campbell-Bannerman—who was ailing—as Prime Minister, and that the change would come about in the not very distant future. Although Asquith's views on women's suffrage were well known, no one, including the leaders of the NUWSS, had any conception of the lengths to which he would go to oppose the enactment of a measure for women's suffrage. At the end of January, the NUWSS sent a deputation to discuss the suffrage issue with Asquith. The future Prime Minister told the suffragists that he was not convinced that the country was in favor of women's suffrage and that, until he had proof that women wanted to vote, he would not support such a reform. Still, he did not convey the impression of being adamantly opposed to the enfranchisement of women, and he assured the suffragists that he was not "a sinister figure who is exercising with disastrous results a maleficent influence upon the fortunes of your cause."[60] Thus, although the representatives of the

---

[57]Jenkins, p. 247.

[58]As quoted in H. C. G. Matthew, The Liberal Imperialists: The Ideas and Politics of a Post-Gladstonian Elite (Oxford, 1973), p. 140.

[59]Ibid., p. 134.

[60]Women's Franchise, February 6, 1908.

NUWSS left the interview discouraged because the Chancellor had not agreed to help their cause, they did not feel his opposition to women's suffrage was insuperable; not unreasonably, they were confident that if a majority of the party and a majority of the Government favored women's suffrage, Asquith would have no choice but to sponsor such a reform.[61]

The interview with Asquith was only the first of many disappointments for the NUWSS. On February 20, the executive committee of the NUWSS met with the officers of the Labour Party to ask them to press the Government for full facilities for a women's suffrage bill. Arthur Henderson, the party chairman, would not agree to such an undertaking.[62] Henderson's views reflected those of the Labour Party Conference which had, for the past three years, opposed any women's suffrage measures that merely abolished sex disqualification and extended the franchise to women on the basis of a property qualification.[63] The Labour Party feared that the enfranchisement of women on such a limited basis would increase the political power of the propertied classes; thus, it favored giving votes to all men and all women—that is, adult suffrage.[64]

The specter of adult suffrage appeared again on May 20, when Asquith, now Prime Minister, received a deputation of suffragist MP's.[65] He promised that the Government would, before the end of Parliament, introduce a scheme of electoral reform; it would be possible to attach a women's suffrage amendment to this reform if such an amendment were democratic. If the amendment fulfilled this condition he would not oppose it, since his colleagues were in favor of such a reform.[66]

---

[61]Even Jenkins finds it amazing and incomprehensible that Asquith was willing to oppose both the majority of his Cabinet and the majority of his party over the suffrage issue (Jenkins, p. 248). This contravened normal political practices.

[62]Women's Franchise, February 27, 1908. Isabella Ford, a former member of the ILP executive, was a principal speaker for the NUWSS.

[63]Philip Viscount Snowden, An Autobiography (London, 1934), vol. 1, pp. 282-93.

[64]The Times, January 23, 1908.

[65]Ibid, May 21, 1908. Asquith had become Prime Minister in April 1908.

[66]In theory the term "adult suffrage" meant votes for all male and female adults. Asquith's proposal for adult suffrage really

Asquith's and Henderson's pronouncements made it very evident that both the Government and the Labour Party would consider women's suffrage only as part of a larger scheme of electoral reform. Unlike the NUWSS, neither the Liberals nor Labour could look at women's suffrage primarily as a moral or philosophic issue but had to take into consideration how the enfranchisement of women would affect the party standing. Large segments of both parties believed that the enfranchisement of women on the same terms as men were enfranchised would duplicate the class biases and the anomalies of the existing male franchise, and thereby benefit the Conservatives.[67]

Asquith's announcement caused a good deal of consternation within the NUWSS because it indicated that the Government intended to entangle women's suffrage in the complications of comprehensively reforming the franchise laws. Bertrand Russell thought the Prime Minister was offering a great opportunity to the women by promising to make women's suffrage a part of a Government Bill. He urged Fawcett to accept this offer in good faith: "I do not, of course, know what you know about the tricks of official Liberalism but surely, no Prime Minister has hitherto made any promise on the subject to a body of members."[68]

Fawcett herself did not have much confidence in Asquith's good intentions. To her, "democratic amendment" meant votes for all women, and she thought the Prime Minister knew very well that neither the nation nor the House of Commons supported such a radical reform; in other words, Asquith's promise was a bogus offer. The Government wanted to secure the passage of an electoral reform bill that would

---

amounted to full adult male suffrage: he wished to enfranchise some four and a half million men who, either because they could not meet one of the seven franchise qualifications of the Act of 1884, or who could not register because they had not resided continuously in the same place for twelve months, could not vote. Asquith intended to introduce a Government bill which would enfranchise all adult males. The bill could be amended to include females, but the Government would do nothing to promote such an amendment. In fact, given Asquith's opposition to women's suffrage, it was certain he would work against such an amendment.

[67] For a discussion of the connection between women's suffrage and electoral reform see David Morgan, Suffragists and Liberals: The Politics of Woman Sufrage in England (Totowa, N.J., 1975), pp. 35-50.

[68] FLAC, vol. 1, C, Bertrand Russell to Millicent Garrett Fawcett, May 21, 1908, Fawcett Library, London.

abolish plural voting and enfranchise more men, but it did not care what happened to the women: "In offering this 'concession' it appears to me that he has contrived to do as much harm as possible to the Women's Suffrage Movement, and refrained completely from identifying his party with it. . . . His Government is now pledged to give more enfranchisement to the already enfranchised men, but is wholly unpledged to give any enfranchisement to the wholly unenfranchised women."[69]

Fawcett was quite right in thinking that, in the absence of official Government support, there was little likelihood that a "democratic" amendment for women's suffrage would ever pass the House of Commons if there was a free vote on the issue. Conservatives as well as many Liberals were reluctant to enfranchise even a small number of women, much less to accept such a sweeping reform; in addition, many Members of Parliament were confirmed antisuffragists who would oppose any measure that gave votes to women. Fawcett knew very well that Asquith was asking the suffragists to commit themselves to a particular type of reform which would alienate the Conservatives and identify the suffrage movement with the Liberal and Labour parties; though he wanted a suffrage amendment with a strong Liberal-Labour bias, he was unwilling to give it Government support until after it had passed the House of Commons.[70] Fawcett believed it would be harmful to tie the suffrage movement to a political party until the party had given official support to the reform. The NUWSS goal was to prevail upon the Liberal Government to support women's suffrage, but there was no point in exchanging its nonparty status for what was equivalent to an alliance with the Liberals if the Government was unwilling to commit itself unequivocally to women's suffrage.[71]

In March 1909, the introduction of an adult suffrage bill confirmed the NUWSS suspicions that forces within the Liberal Party were attempting to tie the women's suffrage movement to the demand for adult suffrage; the subsequent vote on the bill verified the NUWSS conviction that the women had nothing to gain, and much to lose, by

---

[69]Women's Franchise, June 4, 1908.

[70]The Queen, August 1, 1908.

[71]Other women's suffrage societies shared the NUWSS reaction to Asquith's announcement. In October 1908 the women's suffrage societies sent a joint appeal to Asquith which stated their objections to his plan for electoral reform and asked him to include women's suffrage in any proposed Reform Bill. The Times, October 10, 1908.

such a move.[72] The NUWSS had, from the outset, opposed this bill
which, "in the alleged interest of women's suffrage," gave votes to
more men and embroiled women's suffrage in the controversy of
comprehensive electoral reform.[73] Although the NUWSS had made a major
concession to the Liberals by agreeing to amend the Stanger Bill to
include married women, it would not sponsor a measure which would
alienate many of those who were prepared to vote for a moderate measure
of women's suffrage.[74] As Fawcett noted in a letter to The Times, not
one of the women's suffrage societies supported Howard's Adult Suffrage
Bill, nor could they do so as long as there was "no active demand for
universal adult suffrage" in the country.[75]

The NUWSS predictions proved correct, and many of those who in
the past had supported less comprehensive women's suffrage measures
cast their votes against the Howard Bill; whereas the House of Commons
had passed the Stanger Bill by a majority of 179, the majority on the
Howard Bill was only 35.[76] In the debate Philip Snowden, who, as a
member of the Labour Party, was committed to adult suffrage, frankly
admitted that there was little demand for adult suffrage in the

---

[72]On March 19, 1909, Geoffrey Howard (Lib., Cumb. N.)
introduced an Adult Suffrage Bill for its second reading. The bill,
which abolished plural voting, would have given votes to all men and
women who met a short residential qualification. Howard was the son of
Rosalind, Countess of Carlisle, who was prominent in temperance reform
and in Liberal politics; he was the first cousin of Bertrand Russell.
H. C. Deb., 2nd vol. of session 1909, March 19, 1909, cc. 1360-1429;
The Amberley Papers, edited by Bertrand and Patricia Russell (London,
1937), vol. 1, pp. 26-27.

[73]FLAC, vol. 1, D, Circular from the NUWSS, February 23, 1909,
Fawcett Library, London.

[74]Ibid. If the Stanger Bill were amended in this manner,
married women would be enfranchised as joint occupiers and would not
have to meet a separate property qualification. This in itself was a
major concession on the part of NUWSS, which had always been reluctant
to tamper with qualifications. The existing qualifications were
unfavorable to most married women because they could not qualify as
joint occupiers with their husbands. The NUWSS felt that once the
qualification requirements were changed, two separate issues were being
dealt with: women's suffrage and qualification laws. It felt this
would complicate an already difficult situation, and diffuse the focus
of the suffrage movement. Additionally, it might detract Conservative
support, since the Conservatives were most reluctant to alter the laws
relating to qualifications.

[75]The Times, March 14, 1909.

[76]H. C. Deb., 2nd vol. of session 1909, March 19, 1909, c. 1429.

country, and he conceded that the largest measure that all suffragists could safely support would give women the same voting rights that men now exercised.[77] Not surprisingly, the Conservative suffragists voted solidly against the measure. In this case, the loss of Conservative votes was not compensated for by an increase in Liberal support.[78] Prophetically, Asquith, who had been so adamant in demanding a "democratic" measure of women's suffrage, abstained on the Howard Bill.[79]

The vote on the Howard Bill vindicated the NUWSS assertion that it would be pointless to press for a comprehensive, "democratic" measure of women's suffrage if the Government refused to give such a bill its official support. Asquith's abstention confirmed Fawcett's suspicion that although he was happy to have the suffragists commit themselves to working for a measure of women's suffrage which would most benefit the Liberals, he had no intention, at this stage, of throwing the weight of his party behind such an effort.

By the summer of 1909, the NUWSS was pessimistic about the immediate prospects of the suffrage movement. In June 1909, Fawcett wrote to Maud Arncliffe-Sennet: "I agree with you in thinking the immediate outlook for our cause gloomy in the extreme."[80] The NUWSS policy of courting the Liberals seemed to be making little progress. Asquith, showing his true antisuffragist colors, only temporized and offered excuses to the women. Within the rank and file of the Liberal Party, many suffragist MP's now appeared to be defecting to the adult suffrage movement. Moreover, the Conservative Party did not look like an encouraging alternative. As Lady Frances Balfour wrote to Fawcett, the Conservatives were unwilling to do more than enfranchise rate-paying women, "which is not practical politics."[81] Although women's suffrage had gained a hearing in the House of Commons, no party was willing to endorse this reform. In a very real sense the suffragists' efforts had failed: demonstrations, processions, meetings, letters,

---

[77]Ibid., c. 1384.

[78]The majority included: 109 Lib., 28 Lab., 20 Nat. The minority included: 46 Lib., 74 Cons., 2 Nat. The vote on Stanger's Bill in 1908 had been as follows: For--191 Lib., 29 Cons., 21 Nat., 29 Lab., 1 Soc. Against--49 Lib., 28 Cons., 14 Nat., 1 Lab. An Analysis of Voting on Women's Suffrage Bills in the House of Commons Since 1908, NUWSS pamphlet (n.p., n.d.).

[79]H. C. Deb, 2nd vol. of session 1909, March 19, 1909, c. 1429.

[80]British Museum, Arncliffe-Sennett Collection, vol. 7, Millicent Garrett Fawcett to Maud Arncliffe-Sennett, June 16, 1909.

[81]FLAC, vol. 1, D, Lady Frances Balfour to Millicent Garrett Fawcett, February 4, 1909, Fawcett Library, London.

by-election campaigns had attracted attention to the suffrage movement, but they had not convinced any political party to give official support to the women's cause.

The failure of women's suffrage to make any progress in the House of Commons affected the NUWSS attitude toward the WSPU; by 1909, the NUWSS felt that the militants were partly responsible for the parliamentary troubles of the movement. Irritated by the actions of the militants, MP's frequently told the NUWSS that women's suffrage would never be a matter of practical politics while militancy existed. Although the NUWSS did not condone the Government's treatment of the suffragettes, it was increasingly less sympathetic to the actions of the militants. Thus, the NUWSS found itself in an unenviable middle position, squeezed between the militants on one side and the politicians on the other. The militants would not cease their activities until the Government brought in a suffrage bill, and the Government would not bring in a suffrage bill until militant activities ceased.

Until the summer of 1908, relations between the NUWSS and the WSPU had been fairly cordial. Militancy, still in rather mild forms, was of immense propaganda value to the whole suffrage movement, and the NUWSS readily acknowledged that it owed the WSPU a great debt of gratitude for rekindling the fires of the suffrage movement. The NUWSS sensed that a large segment of the public and a substantial portion of Parliament sympathized with the militants and gave them support because the punishments meted out to the women were ridiculously severe in relation to the comparative mildness of the militancy; moreover, the martyrdom suffered by the imprisoned women caused an outpouring of public sympathy for the women's movement.

Vandalism was another matter. The rock throwing in June 1908 followed by a rushing of the House of Commons in October horrified the NUWSS.[82] In the eyes of the constitutional suffragists, the militants were no longer martyrs, but criminals. Fawcett, greatly perturbed, complained that militant methods threatened to create anarchy, and would certainly destroy any chance for the enactment of a women's suffrage measure:

. . . on the reassembling of Parliament, the well-known attempt to "rush the House of Commons" was made and in anticipation of this handbills were distributed among the lowest classes of London toughs and the dangerous hordes of

[82]On June 30, 1908, Edith New and Mary Leigh threw stones through the windows of No. 10 Downing Street. This was the first act of damage committed by members of the WSPU. E. Sylvia Pankhurst, p. 286. By October, the WSPU felt that it had exhausted the possibilities of peaceful protest. See Rosen, pp. 105-6, 110.

unemployed containing the invitation to "rush the House of Commons." I have never said in public and to very few people in private what I thought of that proceeding; but I tell you in confidence that I considered it a [sic] immoral and dastardly thing to have done. The House of Commons, with all its faults, stands for order against anarchy, for justice against brutality, and to overcome it and to invite others to endeavor to overcome it by brute force of the lowest ruffians in London was in my opinion the act either of a mad woman or of a dastard. It became evident to me that our organization must separate itself entirely from all cooperation with people who would resort to such weapons. . . . It is not by such weapons as these that we stand to win. They have helped the antis and discouraged our friends. The crimes committed in Ireland by Home Rulers stopped Home Rule and if Women Suffragists embark on crime as propaganda, they will stop Women's Suffrage.[83]

Fawcett's criticism of militant suffragism, though rather dramatically stated, got to the heart of the matter: the Irish had been successful in forcing the Home Rule issue upon Parliament because they had been able completely to disrupt political authority in Ireland; but the suffragettes did not have any political hold on Parliament, and their stones and "rushes" would only antagonize the Members into opposing women's suffrage.

In the autumn of 1908, the NUWSS began to hear frequent complaints about the behavior of the suffragettes. Lloyd George maintained that the conduct of these women was making the advocacy of their cause impossible,[84] and Herbert Gladstone, whom the NUWSS regarded as a friend of the cause, showed signs of withdrawing his support from the movement. Lady Frances Balfour, describing a conversation she had with the Home Secretary, wrote to Fawcet: "He was a rather keen suffragist, but I see his trials with the militants have

---

[83]Archives, Manchester Public Library, M/50, Box 10, Millicent Garrett Fawcett to Miss Blackwell, February 22, 1909.

[84]Women's Franchise, October 8, 1908. At a meeting of the Women's Liberal Federation on December 8, 1908, Lloyd George declared that only a reaction against the militants' actions could prevent the enactment of a measure for women's suffrage. An Account of David Lloyd George's Speech to the Women's Liberal Federation, December 5, 1908, NUWSS pamphlet (n.p., n.d.).

a good deal upset him."[85] Undoubtedly many members of the House of Commons used militancy as a convenient excuse for opposing women's suffrage.[86] Yet, many MP's were shocked by the behavior of the suffragettes: it was not only unlawful and un-English, it was unwomanly.[87] Many politicians could accept and sympathize with the militants as martyrs and sufferers, but they suspected and disliked the spectacle of women behaving as aggressors: this violated the Victorian teachings which shaped their conception of women. In deciding to use violence to retaliate against the authorities, the WSPU abandoned its role as innocent sacrificial victim; at the same time it forfeited the moral authority which had been instrumental in helping the militants to win support for the suffrage movement.

But beyond these moral qualms, the NUWSS was dismayed by the political insensitivity of the new militancy, and felt that it must firmly and publicly disavow the militants in order to save the suffrage cause. To this end, in November 1908, the NUWSS sent all MP's and the press a letter which stated its disapproval of militant methods. The NUWSS, while strongly objecting to the violent actions of the suffragettes, noted that delays and disappointments had encouraged militancy. It made a plea for reason: "The justice and expediency of our cause is not defeated by the unwisdom of its advocates; nor should the steady, argumentative agitation of 40 years be now ignored because,

---

[85]FLAC, vol. 20, 2, Lady Frances Balfour to Millicent Garrett Fawcett, November 11, 1908, Fawcett Library, London. This was probably particularly galling to the NUWSS, because Gladstone was one of its best contacts in the Cabinet. Lady Frances Balfour was a friend of the Home Secretary's, and frequently talked with him about the suffrage movement. In the autumn of 1908 (before the "rush" on the House of Commons), she had persuaded him to talk to Asquith about receiving a deputation from the NUWSS. Undoubtedly, the NUWSS feared that the militants' actions had ruined these delicate negotiations. FLAC, vol. 1, 6, Lady Frances Balfour to Millicent Garrett Fawcett, October 3, 1908, Fawcett Library, London. See also British Museum, Papers of Herbert, Viscount Gladstone, Add. Mss. 46066, Lady Frances Balfour to Herbert Gladstone, November 6, 1908.

[86]Even before the militants had begun to retaliate against the Government, the House of Commons had allowed the phenomenon of militancy to distract its attention from the issue of women's suffrage. The discussion of tactics threatened to overwhelm the discussion of the principle of women's suffrage. See, for example, H. C. Deb. 4s, vol. 170, March 8, 1907, c. 1102, and vol. 185, February 28, 1908, c. 219.

[87]The Daily Mail coined the term "suffragette" on January 10, 1906. The word quickly became public property and was used to distinguish the militants from the constitutionalists. The latter were referred to as "suffragists."

in the disappointment of long-deferred hopes, methods of anger and impatience and even of violence, have been resorted to."[88]

At this time many members of the WSPU were also members of the NUWSS. Apparently such a practice was not regarded as inconsistent, and both the militant and constitutional societies gladly accepted these "dual members." In November 1908, the antagonisms that emerged at the annual meeting of the London Society for Women's Suffrage (LSWS) drastically altered this policy. At that meeting, four members of the LSWS who were also members of the WSPU presented resolutions urging the NUWSS to adopt the anti-Liberal by-election policy and also requesting the LSWS not to allow members of its executive committee to hold office in party organizations. The executives of the NUWSS and LSWS interpreted these resolutions as an attempt on the part of the WSPU to capture the LSWS. The meeting was stormy. Fawcett, speaking against the resolution, declared that if the members could not be loyal to the NUWSS policies, they should resign: "If you have not any confidence in this society leave it. If we cannot command your confidence we do not ask for your money. I say this simply 'erring sisters depart in peace,' but we are not going to be dragged into unlawful methods which the great majority disapprove of."[89]

Both resolutions were defeated, but the incident, which was covered in the press, engendered hostility on both sides of the suffrage movement. Emmeline Pethick-Lawrence resigned her membership in the LSWS in protest against Fawcett's criticisms of the suffragettes: "I cannot but be glad to think that the Women's Social and Political Union has shown the example of sex loyalty and of honour to opponents that I think all other societies would do well scrupulously to observe."[90] The meeting signaled that the policy of mutual toleration was at an end, and that a period of mistrust and recrimination had begun.

In the months that followed this meeting, the division between the NUWSS and the WSPU deepened. The militants' actions in September

---

[88]The Times, November 12, 1908.

[89]The "erring sisters" were Dr. Flora Murray, Mrs. Henry Nevinson, Mrs. Hylton Dale, and Dr. Louisa Garrett Anderson. Correspondence of the London Society for Women's Suffrage, Account of the Annual Meeting, November 10, 1908, Fawcett Library, London. Anderson, who was Fawcett's niece, had for some time been trying to persuade Fawcett to amalgamate the NUWSS with the WSPU. Archives, Manchester Public Library, M/50, Box 9, Louisa Garrett Anderson to Millicent Garrett Fawcett, January 22, 1908. See also Correspondence of the London Society for Women's Suffrage, Account of the Annual Meeting, November 10, 1908, Fawcett Library, London.

[90]FLAC, vol. 20, 2, Emmeline Pethick-Lawrence to Miss McKee, November 20, 1908, Fawcett Library, London.

1909 brought matters to a crisis. On September 5, three members of the
WSPU accosted Prime Minister Asquith as he was leaving church, and
later that same day the same women pursued Asquith and Gladstone on the
golf course. That evening, stones were thrown through a window of a
house in which Asquith was dining. Twelve days later, in Birmingham,
while Asquith was speaking at Bingley Hall, Mary Leigh and Charlotte
Marsh, members of the WSPU, who had positioned themselves on a roof
near the hall, interrupted the meeting by chopping up slates from the
roof and hurling them down on the police and then on Asquith's motor
car.[91] Asquith was not injured, but Parliament was outraged. (The
incident also resulted in the policy of forcible feeding.) York
Stanger, an ardent suffragist, told the NUWSS that the militants'
actions were "most seriously imperiling" our cause.[92] Gladstone,
noting that the WSPU'S tactics were "intensely exasperating without
being effective," said that these actions were destroying any chance
for settlement of the women's suffrage question: "All these militant
tactics, at any ràte in their later development, are not only lost
labour, but now are most seriously putting obstacles in the way for a
solution. I am afraid the outlook is thoroughly bad."[93]

For both moral and political reasons, the NUWSS was appalled by
the Birmingham violence. It appeared that there was no limit to the
damage which the militants were prepared to inflict on persons and on
property. The suffragettes' actions had already stiffened many MP's'
spines against women's suffrage and if, as seemed possible, a member of
the Government were hurt, there would be no chance of votes for women.
Lady Frances Balfour, in a letter to Fawcett, commented, "I begin to
understand what Parnell felt when his followers murdered Lord
Frederick."[94] Other members of the executive shared her sentiments.
Editorials in Common Cause lamented that violence was damaging the
suffrage movement: the WSPU was seeking notoriety, but it was not
working for the good of the cause.[95]

The NUWSS did all it could to make public its disapproval of
militant methods and to remind the public and the Government that the
majority of those who worked for women's suffrage were not militant.

---

[91]For a description of these incidents see Rosen, pp. 122-23.

[92]FLAC, vol. 1, F, York Stanger to Philippa Strachey, October
5, 1909, Fawcett Library, London.

[93]British Museum, Papers of Herbert, Viscount Gladstone, Add.
Mss. 46067, H. Gladstone to Mrs. Richmond, September 22, 1909.

[94]FLAC, vol. 1, F, Lady Frances Balfour to Millicent Garrett
Fawcett, October 4, 1909, Fawcett Library, London.

[95]C. C., September 16 and October 14, 1909.

The NUWSS Council passed a resolution which condemned the use of violence and distributed copies of the statement to all Members of Parliament and to the press: "The Council of the National Union of Women's Suffrage Societies strongly condemns the use of violence in political propaganda and, being convinced that the way of advancing the cause of women's suffrage is by energetic, law-abiding propaganda, reaffirms its adherence to constitutional principles."[96] At the 1909 annual meeting of the LSWS, the suffragists again emphasized their determination to separate themselves from the WSPU by passing a resolution which required all members of the society to pledge to support only "lawful and constitutional methods" and to accept the NUWSS by-election policy.[97]

By the end of 1909 all semblance of tolerance and goodwill between the NUWSS and the WSPU had vanished. The alliance had never been based on very solid ground, and disagreements over tactics and issues of morality were inherent in the fundamentally different political outlooks of the two organizations, as well as in their different attitudes toward the male establishment and, not the least, their temperaments.

The WSPU was skeptical of the NUWSS' faith in the Liberal party and of its close ties to, and reverence for, the political establishment. The roots of the WSPU lay in the industrial North, far distant from the Houses of Parliament; in a sense the Pankhursts, unlike Fawcett and her colleagues, always remained "outsiders" in parliamentary circles.[98] It was always clear that the leaders of the WSPU were much less cautious, less patient, less amenable to Parliament—and to the standards of society—than were the leaders of the NUWSS. Among many of the suffragettes, there seemed to be an almost religious, single-minded devotion to the cause, a devotion which in their eyes would justify both militancy and outrageous, unfeminine behavior. Emmeline Pethick-Lawrence's letter welcoming Lady Constance Lytton into the WSPU is a good example of the tendency:

I do not know, and am quite content not to know, what is it that you have to do. But the ruler of human destiny knows. . . . you have been led to us, for the fulfillment of your own life, for the accomplishment of your destiny and for the working out of a new deliverance for humanity. . . . you have been appointed, just as the little working girl Annie Kenney

---

[96]FLAC, vol. 1, F, Resolution of the Cardiff Council sent by Philippa Strachey to H. York Stanger, October 8, 1909.

[97]London Society for Women's Suffrage, Annual Report, 1909, p. 16.

[98]Interview with Dame Margery Corbett-Ashby, December 4, 1974, London.

in the factory was appointed just as we have each with our
various experiences and powers been appointed to work out the
divine will with regard to a new stage in the evolution of the
human race--as I realize this, I am filled with worship and
wonder and thanks and joy--for the song of Mary the Mother of
the Messiah has been put into our mouths. What does the pain
and the sorrow and the labour and the weariness matter? How
little it weighs in the sum of things.[99]

The NUWSS could not understand the millenarian zeal which the
WSPU brought to the suffrage cause, nor could it understand the
militants' antipathy toward men. Fawcett and her colleagues--and many
of the members of the affiliated societies--had grown up with liberal-
minded men who had no wish to degrade women. They welcomed the backing
of men like Bertrand Russell and encouraged men to join their
organization. The WSPU, and particularly its leaders, Christabel and
Emmeline Pankhurst, distrusted men and were convinced of their
"deliberate oppression and sexual exploitation of women."[100] They did
not welcome men into the WSPU, and they made sexual separatism one of
the prominent characteristics of the organization.[101] This attitude
clearly had a great deal to do with their mistrust of Parliament and,
in particular, the desire to oppose it rather than try to work with it.

Thus, although a mutual goal for a time brought the two groups
together in apparent harmony, differences of opinion on basic issues
were inevitable. Up until 1908, even though some differences were
already evident, the NUWSS, partly because it needed the support of the
WSPU and partly also because it felt a genuine admiration for the way
in which the WSPU had resuscitated the suffrage movement and shaped the
policies and development of its own organization, hesitated to
criticize. The security of increased membership (see Table 1) and an
established national identity gave the NUWSS the confidence to pursue
an independent policy and disown tactics which it not only disapproved
of from a moral point of view but also believed to be politically
damaging.

---

[99]FLAC, vol. 20, 2, Emmeline Pethick-Lawrence to Lady Constance
Lytton, October 28, 1908, Fawcett Library, London. For other examples
of this millenarianism within the WSPU see Rosen, pp. 196-200.

[100]Claus, p. 111.

[101]Ibid., pp. 87-89. Fawcett's views were quite different: "I
never believe in the possibility of a sex war. Nature has seen after
that; as long as mothers have sons and fathers daughters there can
never be a sex war. What draws men and women together is stronger than
the brutality and tyranny which drive them apart." As quoted in
Strachey, Millicent Garrett Fawcett, p. 232.

Table 1[a]

Growth of NUWSS, LSWS, and NESWS, 1907-1909

	1907	1908	1909
National Union of Women's Suffrage Societies[b]			
Number of societies	31	70	130
Annual income	£1,194-1-6	£2,738-6-11	£3,385-13-9
Total membership	5,836	8,291	13,429
London Society for Women's Suffrage[c]			
Number of societies	36	44	34
Annual income	£1,031-1-2	£1,307-15-6	£2,275-0-6
Total membership	Unknown	2,563	3,111
North of England Society for Women's Suffrage[d]			
Number of societies	4	8	13
Annual income	£209-9-10-½	£1,102-0-5	£1,099-2-0-½
Total membership	219	1,060	1,740

[a] Information contained in this table is compiled from the Annual Reports for the years 1907, 1908 and 1909 of the NUWSS, the LSWS, and the North of England Society for Women's Suffrage.

[b] The annual income of the NUWSS included only those funds directly received at headquarters, and did not include any of the incomes of the branch societies. In 1909, for example, the income of the branch societies was estimated to be £8,000-10,000. This was only an estimate, as not all the societies sent their financial returns to headquarters. Only those societies that were directly affiliated to the NUWSS were listed as belonging to the NUWSS. The London Society for Women's Suffrage, for example, had thirty-four branches in 1909; yet, only the London Society was listed as belonging to the NUWSS.

[c] The decline between 1908 and 1909 in the number of societies belonging to the LSWS is accounted for by the fact that these societies had become directly affiliated with the NUWSS.

[d] Other affiliates of the NUWSS also grew in size. For example, between 1908 and 1909 the Edinburgh Society increased in membership from 400 to 700, and the Brighton Society grew from 95 to 450 members. National Union of Women's Suffrage Societies, Annual Report, 1909, p.12.

Although the NUWSS had become increasingly critical of the WSPU's tactics, disapproval of militant methods did not signify that the NUWSS approved of the Government's handling of the militants. The NUWSS consistently maintained that the Government's delays and evasions had brought about the militants' actions. As Lady Frances Balfour wrote to Herbert Gladstone: "Asquith always thinks he can have a day-to-day hand-to-mouth policy in this matter. Every time it [the enfranchisement of women] is put off the strength of the movement grows."[102]

The NUWSS criticized the Government for treating the suffragettes as second-class misdemeanants.[103] It believed that the Government should recognize that these women were fighting for a political goal, and as such, should be treated as political protestors and put in the first class of prisoners. Fawcett noted the irony of the spectacle of a Liberal Government doing battle with the women, when it had managed to turn its back on the outrages in Ireland: "There is a certain element of humour afforded by the spectacle of those who condoned every kind of ferocity and crime in pursuit of Irish Home Rule being driven almost beside themselves by the much milder degree of criminality which has been perpetrated by the suffragettes."[104] She felt that the Liberals should have learned that punishment and coercion could offer no final solution to the suffrage problem.

In placing itself between the Government and the militants, and not siding with either of the concerned parties, the NUWSS acted very astutely. Although Members of Parliament and the public at large could condemn the militants' actions, it was impossible to praise the Government's treatment of the suffragettes. In an age in which women were still put on a pedestal, it was difficult for many people to stomach the idea of a woman, particularly a "respectable" woman of middle or upper class background, suffering the indignities of prison. The institution of forcible feeding made it even more difficult to defend the Government's handling of the situation.[105] On the other hand, the militants were destroying property, disrupting public order, and, in some cases, inflicting personal injury. Did women deserve the

---

[102]British Museum, Papers of Herbert, Viscount Gladstone, Add. Mss. 46066, Lady Frances Balfour to Herbert Gladstone, November 6, 1908.

[103]C. C., July 15, 1909. CAB 41/32/29, August 4, 1909, noted that: "If they [the suffragettes] are made first class misdemeanants, the prisons would soon be full of them."

[104]Millicent Garrett Fawcett, "The Women's Suffrage Movement: Statesmanship or Coercion?" Englishwoman, 4, no. 11 (December 1909):147.

[105]See Rosen, pp. 123-24.

vote if they behaved in such a manner? The NUWSS answer was to cry a plague on both their houses. Its policy was to depict the militants as a minority group whose actions, although reprehensible, were in no way characteristic of the mainstream of the suffrage movement. Its message was simple: by refusing to give votes to women until militancy stopped, Parliament was paying too much attention to the suffragettes and was unfairly punishing the constitutional suffragists for the deeds committed by their militant sisters. With good reason, the NUWSS saw itself as the representative of solid, upstanding, law-abiding women who desired the vote and were innocent victims caught in the cross-fire between the militants and the Government.[106]

By the autumn of 1909, the prospects for the enactment of women's suffrage appeared to be very bleak; under the pressure of events, much of the optimism which, in 1906, had infused the NUWSS had faded. Within three years the political fortunes of the suffrage movement had, in many respects, taken a turn for the worse: the Prime Minister was hostile to women's suffrage, and both the Liberal Party and the Labour Party seemed inclined to press for adult suffrage, if they were going to consider any sort of franchise reform at all.[107] In addition, the Government had begun to do battle with the House of Lords, and under the circumstances a Government-sponsored franchise bill seemed unlikely before the next election.[108]

Militancy, too, had begun to exert an adverse effect on the fortunes of the suffrage movement. Whereas in 1906 the actions of the WSPU had abetted the cause of women's suffrage, by 1909 the increasingly violent behavior of the suffragettes had begun to alienate many former supporters, particularly in Parliament, which in December 1909 passed a Public Meetings Bill purposely designed to control militancy.[109] Equally important, the issue of militancy had divided the suffrage movement itself and vitiated its strength.

The only consolation that the NUWSS could draw from this generally unencouraging state of affairs was the realization that, as an organization, it had made considerable gains between 1906 and 1909. It was larger, stronger, and more centralized than ever, and its operations were more diversified and efficient. It had its own offices, an administrative staff, a staff of organizers, a literature department, and a newspaper. Much of the growth had been indirectly stimulated by the WSPU, and this growth had made it possible for the

---

[106]Fawcett, "The Women's Suffrage Movement," gives an argument along these lines.

[107]Asquith's refusal to see a deputation from the NUWSS in the autumn of 1909 was another indication that the Prime Minister had no intention of dealing with the suffrage question. C. C., October 7, 1909.

[108]Morgan, pp. 5–56.   [109]Ibid.

NUWSS to stand on its own against the WSPU. Furthermore, it did appear that women's suffrage, as an issue, had begun to make an impact on the nation. Still, the fact remained that, by the end of 1909, neither the NUWSS nor the WSPU had found a way of convincing the Liberals to sponsor a measure to enfranchise women. The extraparliamentary activities of the suffrage organizations had not secured the passage of a measure of women's suffrage, and it now appeared unlikely that women's suffrage could ever be rescued from this parliamentary impasse.

CHAPTER III

1910: THE CAMPAIGN FOR THE CONCILIATION BILL

Just as 1909 was drawing to a close, the announcement of a General Election to be held in January, promised to improve the prospects for women's suffrage and release the suffrage issue from its parliamentary limbo. Before the year 1910 was over, another General Election would give the suffrage societies the chance to show that they could help to elect Members who would support their cause in the House of Commons. More important, the formation in the House of Commons that year of an all-party Conciliation Committee for Women's Suffrage, and the subsequent appearance of a Conciliation Bill to enfranchise women, made many suffragists, both inside and outside Parliament, guardedly optimistic that the House of Commons would soon enact a measure for women's suffrage. To Fawcett and her colleagues it seemed as if a reversal had at last come about in the fortunes of the suffrage movement; the opportunities that 1910 promised overshadowed the frustrations and disappointments of the preceding years.

In December 1909, Asquith, Grey, and Churchill opened the election campaign with significant statements on the suffrage issue and implied that the new Parliament should have a mandate to act on the question.[1] The NUWSS interpreted these statements as an indication that women's suffrage was of some political importance as an issue to the Liberal Party, and it made up its mind to use the election to lobby for women's suffrage and to show the Liberals that the electorate desired votes for women.

As in previous elections, the NUWSS concentrated much of its energy on working to secure the return of MP's who favored the enactment of women's suffrage.[2] The local affiliates worked to obtain pledges of support from candidates and canvassed for those who favored women's suffrage, and as in previous elections they used the campaign

---

[1]On December 10, at a meeting in the Albert Hall, Asquith stated that the Government had no desire to "burke" the women's suffrage question, and that accordingly, the House of Commons ought to have an opportunity to express its views on the subject. On the same day Grey, speaking at Alnwick, reiterated his support for women's suffrage. A few days earlier, Churchill had made a similar statement.

[2]The election manifesto of the NUWSS appeared in The Times, December 18, 1909.

to publicize the aims of the society and educate the constituencies about women's suffrage.[3] The executive committee itself directed propaganda campaigns in certain constituencies represented by prominent politicians, including the constituencies of Asquith and Churchill. Hoping to capture the attention, if not the support, of the Liberal and Labour Parties, it also took an active part in promoting the candidacy of Arthur Bulley, who was contesting Rossendale on a women's suffrage platform. In all these campaigns the aim of the NUWSS was to force the women's suffrage issue upon both the general public and the parliamentary candidates, as well as the parties generally.[4]

At the election one of the main objects of the NUWSS activity was to collect signatures for a "voters" petition. The NUWSS hoped that the signatures of actual electors would have an impact upon MP's which those of voteless women had not achieved. Furthermore, because MP's were bound, by parliamentary rules, to lay every petition from constituents before the House, the Government would be repeatedly confronted by the voters' demand for women's suffrage. The petitions, which called upon the House of Commons "without delay to pass into law a measure for the enfranchisement of women," were collected in over 290 constituencies, and totaled more than 280,000 signatures.[5] The presentation of the petitions to the House of Commons in March gave the

---

[3]C. C., February 10, 1910; Neal Blewett, The Peers, the Parties, and the People: The British General Elections of 1910 (Toronto, 1972), p. 335; London Society for Women's Suffrage, Annual Report, 1910), pp. 6-7.

[4]C. C., December 9 and 16, 1909. The constituencies were Dewsbury (Walter Runciman, Lib., president of the Board of Education); Blackburn (Philip Snowden, Lab.); Barnard Castle (Arthur Henderson, Lab.); Dundee (Winston Churchill, Lib., president of the Board of Trade); Cleveland (Herbert Samuel, Lib., Chancellor of the Duchy of Lancaster); East Fife (Herbert Asquith, Lib., Prime Minister); East Lothian, Haddingtonshire (Richard Haldane, Lib., Secretary for War). Bulley, a member of the Fabians and of the Social Democratic Party, was put up against Lewis Harcourt (Lib., First Commissioner for Works), a noted antisuffragist, by the Lancashire and Cheshire Women's Textile and Other Workers' Representation Committee. In his campaign Bulley coupled a Labour appeal to the suffrage cause; he polled only 639 votes. See Blewett, p. 335.

[5]Englishwoman's Review, 41 (April 15, 1910): 112. This was approximately 4 percent of those who voted in the election. David Butler and Jennie Freeman, British Political Facts, 1900-1968 (3rd ed.; London, 1969), p. 141.

voters, and the politicians as well, a fresh reminder of the women's demands.[6]

The NUWSS was well pleased with the results of their election work: according to its own perhaps too optimistic estimate, 323 members of the new House of Commons were in favor of some form of women's suffrage.[7] Altogether, expenses for questioning, canvassing, and petitioning by the NUWSS came to some £1,460; additional funds were expended by local societies.[8] Although the NUWSS tended to inflate the actual role that the women's suffrage issue played in the election—it was, in fact, only one of a host of other issues, and prominent politicians maintained that the issue of women's suffrage was not one on which votes were won or lost—there were nonetheless significant ramifications to the NUWSS' role in the January election.[9] In important, though somewhat intangible, ways, the election activity of the NUWSS abetted the fortunes of the suffrage movement—not the least of which was that of reminding the electorate, and the parties, that the women's issue was still very much alive, and was in the hands of a large force of dedicated, law-abiding women, who were working through

---

[6]In March "blue papers" in the House of Commons contained daily references to the voters' petitions. At this time the petitions were being presented at the rate of betwen 10 and 20 per day. Englishwoman, (April 1910):245.

[7]C. C., February 10, 1910. The NUWSS thought it had the support of 185 Liberals, 85 Conservatives, 32 Labourites, and 21 Nationalists. The League for Opposing Woman Suffrage, basing its calculations on the July 12, 1910, vote on the Conciliation Bill, estimated that there were 283 suffragists in the House of Commons: 146 Liberals, 83 Conservatives, 37 Labourites, and 17 Nationalists. Martin Pugh, Electoral Reform in War and Peace, 1906-1918 (London, 1978), p. 187.

[8]See National Union of Women's Suffrage Societies, Annual Report, 1910, p. 45. According to the Annual Report, 1910 of the North of England Society, it spent, for example £260-6-8-1/2. See p. 67.

[9]Neal Blewett notes (pp. 330-33) that the January election was charactereized by an unprecedented amount of activity on the part of pressure groups, and that they spent vast amounts on propaganda. Although Blewett considers that the women's issue was peripheral to the election debate, he does note that the women's movement had a considerable number of dedicated workers at its disposal, and that it also commanded large financial resources. See also, for example, Archives, Manchester Public Library, M/50, Box 9, Rt. Hon. Walter Runciman to Millicent Garrett Fawcett, July 10, 1910.

normal channels to obtain the vote.[10] Under these circumstances, it became more difficult to write off women's suffrage as an issue espoused only by a few militant members of the lunatic fringe. Additionally, the NUWSS' advocacy of the women's issue must have pricked many voters' consciences. Many Liberals in particular were extremely unhappy that the party had turned its back on what was often regarded as a Liberal cause. Especially after the Government gave its approval to forcible feeding late in 1909, many Liberals wondered how long Asquith would ignore the wishes of the party rank and file. If such staunch and "respectable" Liberals as Lady Frances Balfour and Eva McLaren opposed the Government's handling of the suffrage issue, how much longer could the Liberal Party continue to depend on the support of other Englishwomen?

While the NUWSS election work was still in progress, plans were under way for a scheme by which the women's cause could be more effectively promoted in the new Parliament. In January 1910, Fawcett began to correspond with H. N. Brailsford about the formation of an all-party committee which would draft a measure for women's suffrage and guide it through Parliament; this correspondence inaugurated an association that was to have an impact on the women's suffrage movement for the next four years.

Brailsford had long been a staunch advocate of women's suffrage, and, since the summer of 1909, he had been doing his best to try and convince the Liberal Government either to give time for the passage of a moderate suffrage bill which would get the support of all parties or to seek an electoral mandate to extend the franchise to women.[11] He had resigned his position as leader-writer for the Daily News in October 1909 in protest against the paper's acquiescence in the Government's decision to implement forcible feeding. The arrest of Brailsford's wife, Jane, a WSPU member and a former member of the NUWSS, that same month further strengthened his sympathies with the suffrage movement. He was appalled by the Government's brutal treatment of those arrested and full of admiration for the courage and determination of the militants: "I am not a woman's man. I am indeed

---

[10]The LSWS, in approaching candidates, emphasized that it had no connection with the WSPU, and stated that all NUWSS affiliates "have invariably worked by peaceful methods only and deeply regret the lawless actions of a section of the advocates of women's suffrage." Circulars of the London Society for Women's Suffrage, Circular to Parliamentary Candidates, December 1909, Fawcett Library, London. The NUWSS believed that militant methods and women's suffrage had become inextricably confused in the public mind; it emphasized the need to change this perception. C. C., February 3, 1910.

[11]Fred Leventhal, "The Conciliation Committee," unpub. ms., pp. 122-23.

quite absurdly unsusceptible save in my wife's case. But towards all of these twelve, from the brave little mill girl to Lady Constance Lytton--a saintly woman--I feel a reverence I could not exaggerate."[12] Although Brailsford was closer to the militant wing of the suffrage movement, his reputation as an advocate of women's suffrage had spread to constitutionalist circles, and in December 1909 the Scottish Women Graduates had invited him to contest Dundee as a women's suffrage candidate.[13]

By January 1910, Brailsford had abandoned hope that he could, either on his own, or through the Men's League for Women's Suffrage, of which he was a member, do anything to end the impasse over women's suffrage. Accordingly, he began to formulate a plan to work through the political system for a nonpartisan solution to the suffrage problem: his idea was to form a "conciliatiton committee" to promote the settlement of the women's suffrage question.[14] Though he was not yet certain about the exact organization of this committee, he realized that if it was to have any success, it would need the support of the leading suffrage societies. Brailsford did not know Fawcett personally, but he thought that her parliamentary contacts and her political experience would make her a desirable ally and a natural sounding board for his ideas.[15]

On January 18 Brailsford wrote to Fawcett, outlining his plan for the new parliamentary committee:

I have some thought of attempting to found a Conciliation Committee for Women's Suffrage. My idea is that it should undertake the necessary diplomatic work of promoting an early settlement. It will not be large, and should consist of both

---

[12]British Museum, Papers of Herbert, Viscount Gladstone, Add. Mss. 46067, H. N. Brailsford to Mrs. Byles, [October 1909]. Jane Brailsford was arrested for chopping a barricade with an ax. For a full account of the incident see Andrew Rosen, Rise Up, Women!, p. 125.

[13]Bodleian Library, Nevinson Journals, e615, December 20, 1909. This committee wanted to obtain the parliamentary vote for women graduates of the Scottish universities. Chrystal MacMillan, the hon. secretary and treasurer of this organization, was a member of the NUWSS executive.

[14]Leventhal, p. 127.

[15]Apparently Brailsford had not had any communication with Fawcett prior to January 1910. Professor Fred Leventhal, who is writing a biography of Brailsford, has said that he thought Brailsford wrote to Fawcett about the formation of the committee only because she was influential in the suffrage movement, not because she was a personal friend. (In conversation, Boston, November 1, 1974.)

men and women--the women in touch with the existing societies,
but not their more prominent leaders, the men as far as
possible not identified officially with either party.[16]

Brailsford went on to say that he thought the committee should
work for a limited bill the first session and he asked Fawcett for her
advice. Fawcett, though delighted by Brailsford's scheme, expressed
doubts whether members of militant and nonmilitant societies could
happily co-exist on such a committee, and the militants concurred with
Fawcett's diagnosis.[17] Accordingly, in a letter dated January 25,
Brailsford scrapped the idea of having women on the committee and went
on to give his thoughts as to how the present political situation
affected the women's cause. He was by no means overconfident. The
prospect of the militants' declaring a truce undoubtedly paved the way
for accord with the Government and heightened the chances for success
within Parliament.[18] Additionally, the even balance of political
parties within the House of Commons was favorable to a bipartisan
compromise which would bring some limited form of women's suffrage:
the Liberals had lost their majority in the House of Commons, and any
women's suffrage measure would need the backing of members of all
parties if it were to pass.[19] But though the timing seemed right,
Brailsford was uneasy about the grumblings of the adult suffragists:

> The principle in my mind is a "settlement by consent," i.e.,
> by the good will of all political parties. The relatively
> nice balance in the new House seemed to me to favour this, and
> I know that a few men in the front benches desire it. . . .
> The new situation seems to me excessively difficult. There
> can be no reform Bill. Yet I fear that the drift towards
> Adult Suffrage has gone so far that the absurdly named

---

[16]Archives, Manchester Public Library, M/50, Box 10, H. N.
Brailsford to Millicent Garrett Fawcett, January 18, [1910].

[17]Leventhal, pp. 127-28.

[18]Brailsford was able to persuade the militants to announce a
truce on January 31, 1910. Christabel Pankhurst had agreed to this
truce because she felt mild militancy was "played out" and that the
pause would strategically benefit the militants. Christabel Pankhurst,
Unshackled: The Story of How We Won the Vote (London, 1959), pp. 153-
54. Throughout January, Brailsford and Lord Lytton had negotiated with
the Pankhursts to call a halt to militancy. Public Record Office,
London, Papers of Edward, Viscount Grey of Falloden, FO 800/90, H. N.
Brailsford to Augustine Birrell, [1910], enclosed in a letter from
Augustine Birrell to Sir Edward Grey, November 2, 1910.

[19]The Liberals held 275 seats, the Conservatives 273, the
Nationalists 82, and Labour 40.

"limited" Bill stands no chance unless a resolute concerted effort is made to force it through.[20]

By February the prospects for a "settlement by consent" looked more promising, and Brailsford's plans had begun to materialize. He wrote Fawcett informing her that Lord Lytton had assumed the chairmanship of the newly formed Conciliation Committee, which now included a dozen members from all parties: "At the start the M.P.'s wish to act alone, not to invite more outsiders or women—the idea being that what is needed is private negotiations among the various parties and their leaders. It is on this we are concentrating."[21] Brailsford, now secretary of the Committee, gave Fawcett a lengthy analysis of the parliamentary situation and asked her to use her political influence to gain support for the committee: he particularly wished her to convince Sir Charles McLaren, a prominent Liberal, to give his backing to the newly formed group.[22] Brailsford felt, correctly, that women's suffrage had become something of an embarrassment to the Government and was one issue which all parties wished to settle, one way or the other. In addition, the party distribution in the House of Commons favored a nonparty solution of the women's suffrage question; all parties in the House had a suffragist wing, but no one party was in a position to dictate a settlement on the issue. Therefore a nonpartisan "conciliation" bill for women's suffrage, introduced by a private member, might prove the best and most acceptable way to end the controversy over women's suffrage. The main drawback to the plan appeared to be the intransigence of the Liberals:

Our chief obstacle is the decision of the Liberals to work on party lines, or rather not to work on them. For though they won't join with others, they don't propose to do anything

---

[20]Archives, Manchester Public Library, M/50, Box 10, H. N. Brailsford to Millicent Garrett Fawcett, January 25, [1910].

[21]Ibid., H. N. Brailsford to Millicent Garrett Fawcett, February 28, [1910]. Like Brailsford, Lord Lytton had close ties with the women's suffrage movement. His grandmother Rosina, Lady Lytton, was an early suffragist and a close friend of Lydia Becker. One of his sisters, Lady Constance Lytton, was active in the WSPU, and another sister, Lady Betty Balfour, was a moving spirit in the Conservative and Unionist Women's Franchise Association. In March 1910, Lord Lytton became president of the Hitchin Women's Suffrage Society, a branch of the NUWSS.

[22]For the McLarens (like the Lyttons), suffrage was a family affair, and the family's ties to the NUWSS were particularly strong. Priscilla Bright McLaren, Sir Charles's mother, had been active in the suffrage movement since the 1860's and had been a member of the first NUWSS executive committee. Sir Charles's brother, Walter McLaren, was chairman of the NUWSS executive committee, and his sister-in-law, Eva McLaren, was a former member of the NUWSS executive.

themselves. I saw Mr. Geoffrey Howard about this, and he
assured me that their women advisors were agreed in
recommending party action, or as I prefer to call it,
inaction. He said that a deputation from the NUWSS had
attended their meeting and given this advice—or acquiesced in
this decision (I am not sure which). I hope he misrepresented
the advice given him. But it is very difficult to argue with
reluctant Liberals when they produce as an excuse for doing
nothing, that the women themselves want nothing done.[23]

Brailsford was anxious to find out whether Fawcett had, in fact,
supported the Liberals' position, and he hoped to try and persuade her
and the organization she represented to convince Liberal suffragists to
cooperate with the Conciliation Committee.

Fawcett and her colleagues were only too glad to give
Brailsford any assistance possible. For the NUWSS Brailsford's scheme
came as a godsend: the Conciliation Committee seemed to promise a way
out of the parliamentary impasse. By 1910 the NUWSS had grown weary of
trying to persuade the Liberal Government to introduce a women's
suffrage bill and was pessimistic that it would ever convince Asquith
to sponsor such a measure; moreover, given the antisuffragist component
in the Liberal Party, the election results of 1910 made it unlikely
that any private member's bill for women's suffrage, if framed in the
interests of Liberalism, would pass the House of Commons. Thus the
idea of a compromise bill, backed by members of all parties, was very
appealing.

Having secured Fawcett's blessing, Brailsford went ahead with
plans for the nascent Committee. By March the difficulties with the
Liberals seemed to have been overcome and MP's of all parties were
slowly joining the Committee.[24] Brailsford was optimistic that the
Government would give facilities for his bill, and he informed Fawcet
that Grey and other ministers were supporting the Committee's
efforts.[25] The problem now was to devise a bill that would be

---

[23]Archives, Manchester Public Library, M/50, Box 10, H. N.
Brailsford to Millicent Garrett Fawcett, February 28, [1910].

[24]At the end of March the Conciliation Committee had twenty
members. Ibid., H. N. Brailsford to Millicent Garrett Fawcett, March
21, [1910]. By May 1910, the committee had grown to include 36
members: 16 Liberals, 11 Conservatives, 5 Nationalists, and 4
Labourites.

[25]Although Brailsford did not name the other ministers, he was
probably referring to Birrell and Churchill, who, in April 1910,
allowed Brailsford to announce that they welcomed the formation of the
Committee. Ibid., Circular of the Conciliation Committee for Women's
Suffrage [May 1910].

acceptable to suffragists of all partiies. Brailsford thought that a bill modeled on Stanger's 1908 measure to extend the franchise on the basis of the existing male qualifications offered the simplest and most acceptable solution. The Liberals, however, balked at this suggestion because they feared "the property vote in the Counties".[26] They were convinced that they would meet with electoral defeat if women were given the vote according to the existing franchise. An adult suffrage measure had some appeal for both the Liberals and Labour, but it, too, had severe drawbacks: the House of Lords would undoubtedly reject it, and the Irish Nationalists, who feared that it would involve redistribution of seats, would probably oppose it. With their majority dependent on the Irish, the Liberals could not afford to incur their hostility.[27] In addition, many Liberal suffragists were not prepared to support a measure that established an electorate in which women outnumbered men. Furthermore, there was no Conservative support for adult suffrage. If the Liberals feared the votes of wealthy women, the Tories disliked the prospect of working men and women going to the polls to vote for socialist legislation.[28]

Taking all these considerations into account, Brailsford decided that the best chance for success was to offer a bill based on the municipal qualification. The Liberals would accept it because "it omits the freeholder and the 'property' and the Plural vote," and the Conservatives would accept it because it "does not enfranchise married women."[29] The question was whether the suffrage societies would accept it: it was limited in scope and did not fulfill the suffragists' demand that women be enfranchised on the same basis as men.

At the end of March, Brailsford wrote to Fawcett to ask her support for the proposed bill: "I am now nearly sure that most of the Liberals, including even the Adultists, would support a Bill on the basis of the present municipal qualification. I know of course that would not satisfy you, and it ought not to satisfy you, but I think you

---

[26]Ibid., H. N. Brailsford to Millicent Garrett Fawcett, March 21, [1910].

[27]At the time Brailsford was drafting the Bill, the Irish were very critical of the Government. See, for example, CAB 41/32/50, February 22, 1910, and CAB 41/32/51, February 25, 1910.

[28]The vote on Geoffrey Howard's Adult Suffrage Bill in March 1909 had shown that Conservatives would not support an Adult Suffrage Bill. It had also shown that Liberal support for such a measure was weaker than for a more limited women's suffrage measure such as the Stanger Bill. See Chapter 2, note 78.

[29]H. N. Brailsford to Lord Lytton, March 17, [1910], as quoted in Leventhal, p. 131.

will be glad to welcome it as an installment of justice."[30] Very much
the pragmatist, Fawcett quickly replied that she would warmly welcome
any bill that had a reasonable chance for success. From the NUWSS
point of view, the most important criterion for a bill was not how many
women it would enfranchise, but how many votes it would receive in the
House. The proposed bill was not ideal. It withheld the vote from
women lodgers, women owners, and women university graduates, and also
from most married women, because husband and wife could not qualify
with respect to the same property. Furthermore, Fawcett pointed out,
the municipal basis for the parliamentary franchise had the drawback of
not being uniform for England, Scotland, and Wales, or for London and
the country. Nonetheless, she believed the Bill was a step in the
right direction and she gave her approval.[31] Brailsford replied with
thanks for her approval and her criticism, and asked her to see that
the NUWSS adopted a resolution giving its support to the proposed
measure. The NUWSS backing would be of great value to the Conciliation
Committee. He added that he was having trouble convincing Arthur
Balfour, the Conservative leader, to make public his support for the
measure. Although Balfour had privately stated that he favored the
proposal, he was now showing signs of indecision, "a state of mind with
which I imagine his friends are rather familiar."[32] Acting on
Brailsford's request, the NUWSS executive committee quickly passed a
resolution in support of the proposed Conciliation Bill; at the same
time it firmly stated that it was not abandoning its ultimate goal of
votes for all women.[33]

Having secured the blessing of the NUWSS, and the more grudging
acquiescence of the WSPU, the Conciliation Committee went ahead with
its plans to introduce a suffrage bill based on the municipal
franchise. On May 27, The Times announced that a Conciliation
Committee composed of thirty-six MP's belonging to all parties planned
to introduce a women's suffrage bill under the ten-minute rule. A few
weeks before this the Committee had issued the text of the proposed
bill:

1. Every woman possessed of a household qualification, or of
a ten pound occupation qualification, within the meaning of
The Representation of the People Act (1884), shall be entitled
to be registered as a voter, and when registered to vote for
the county or borough in which the qualifying premises are
situate.

---

[30]Archives, Manchester Public Library, M/50, Box 10, H. N.
Brailsford to Millicent Garrett Fawcett, March 21, [1910].

[31]Ibid.

[32]Ibid., H. N. Brailsford to Millicent Garrett Fawcett,
March 27, [1910].

[33]Ibid., E. Dimock to H. N. Brailsford, April 9, 1910.

2. For the purposes of this Act, a woman shall not be disqualified by marriage for being registered as a voter, provided that a husband and wife shall not both be qualified in respect of the same property.

The memorandum that accompanied the bill noted that it represented a "working compromise," and as such, tried to conciliate all those who were to some degree favorable to women's suffrage. It was a cautious, moderate measure which recommended it to Conservatives; yet, it excluded the ownership and lodger qualifications which the Liberals and Labourites disliked. The provisions of the bill were simple, so that no great demands would be made on parliamentary time. Since all householders would be given the vote, the bill would enfranchise working, as well as middle and upper class, women.[34] Moreover, the one million women who would receive the parliamentary vote were not neophytes in matters of government, since for the most part they already enjoyed the municipal franchise. The Committee admitted that the bill was not ideal, but it made a first step in giving votes to women; more important, it stood a good chance of winning approval in the House of Commons: "Its single merit is that, in a way which no party can consider objectionable or unfair, it breaks down the barrier which at present excludes all women from citizenship rights."[35]

For the next month members of the NUWSS executive closely followed the progress of the bill. At the end of May, Lady Frances Balfour informed Fawcett that such prominent politicians as Alfred Lyttelton (Cons., St. George's, Hanover Square), Birrell, and Churchill had agreed to speak in its support.[36] Fawcett replied that she was optimistic about the bill, and felt it was "a big step in the direction of a practical settlement."[37] Brailsford encouraged her hopes for success. Late in May, he wrote her a glowingly optimistic letter, saying the bill was being received with unexpected enthusiasm and that he was confident that it would pass its second reading. He cautioned

---

[34]The contention that the bill would enfranchise working women was based on the ILP survey of 1904 and on a canvass conducted in 1904 which revealed that 91 percent of registered women occupiers belonged to the working class. For a defense of the democratic aspects of the Conciliation Bill see H. N. Brailsford, "Mr. Lloyd George and Women's Suffrage," NUWSS leaflet (n.p., n.d.).

[35]Archives, Manchester Public Library, M/50, Box 15, Circular of the Conciliation Committee for Women's Suffrage [May 1910].

[36]FLAC, vol. 1, Hi, Lady Frances Balfour to Millicent Garrett Fawcett, May 26, 1910, Fawcett Library, London.

[37]Ibid., Millicent Garrett Fawcett to Lady Frances Balfour, May 29, 1910.

her, however, that the suffrage societies would have to manifest their enthusiastic support for the bill to ensure its success in the House. They would have to show a united front to the Government, and, "in the interests of the Bill," the militants and the nonmilitants would have to put aside their differences.[38] Both Brailsford and Lytton were convinced that the key to success lay in bringing public opinion to put pressure upon the Government, and they both urged the NUWSS to do everything possible to win support for the bill. Brailsford was particularly anxious that the NUWSS should try and convince the Women's Liberal Federation to press the Government to give time for the bill.[39] Lytton wanted Fawcett and her colleagues to lobby for the bill in any manner they thought would be effective: ". . . any help wh. you or any of the members of your society could give in the next few days to induce the Govmt. to consider favourably our demand for time would now be invaluable. . . . Will you do what you can both privately and publicly to impress upon the Govt. that our Bill is weightily supported."[40]

Acting on Lytton's and Brailsford's request, Fawcett began to marshall the NUWSS organization behind the Conciliation Bill. On June 6, she sent out a circular to all NUWSS branches, urging the local societies to do everything possible to demonstrate support for the all-important bill. This was, she said, the most promising opportunity for women's suffrage since 1884, and she urged the societies to hold meetings, organize deputations, and pass resolutions to show their local MP's and the Prime Minister how widely the bill was supported.[41]

The NUWSS branches responded quickly to Fawcet's prompting—reiterated by similar appeals from members of the executive—and began putting on pressure. The London Society for Women's Suffrage contacted some three hundred influential male supporters and asked them to interview or write to MP's; it sent circulars to all its members requesting them to write letters on behalf of the bill to members of the Government. It also sponsored meetings, organized deputations to

---

[38]Archives, Manchester Public Library, M/50, Box 10, H. N. Brailsford to Millicent Garrett Fawcett, May 27, [1910].

[39]Ibid., H. N. Brailsford to Millicent Garrett Fawcett, June 2, [1910]. The Women's Liberal Federation (WLF) had arranged to hold its Annual Council in London in mid-June. The Federation was influential with the Liberal Party, as it had a membership of around 90,000. Fawcett had a very good relationship with the WLF: many members of the NUWSS executive were also on the WLF executive.

[40]Ibid., Box 9, Lord Lytton to Millicent Garrett Fawcett, June 3, 1910.

[41]FLAC, vol. 1, Hii, Circular from Millicent Garrett Fawcett, June 6, 1910, Fawcett Library, London.

MP's, and on June 8, hired fifty sandwichmen to picket Whitehall with placards in support of the bill.[42] In Tunbridge Wells the local NUWSS affiliate canvassed all those who had signed the voters' petition and asked them to request their MP's to vote for the bill. The Newcastle Society for Women's Suffrage sent a barrage of letters to all the MP's in Northumberland and Durham begging their support for the measure. At Portsmouth the NUWSS branch contacted temperance groups and party organizations and urged them to lobby for the bill.[43] On the whole, the NUWSS staged a very effective and persuasive campaign; but on June 14, the efforts of the suffragists were rewarded when the Conciliation Bill at long last passed its first reading.[44]

The first hurdle had been overcome: the NUWSS was now concerned that the Government would refuse to grant further facilities to the bill. Brailsford, who remained in close touch with the NUWSS throughout this period, shared the suffragists' anxiety. He was eager for the NUWSS to continue lobbying for the bill and wanted the organization to devote special attention to the mercurial Lloyd George. Lloyd George had not given his benediction to the bill, and, according to Emily Davies, Brailsford was worried that his opposition might prove fatal: "Mr. Brailsford said that our great enemy in the Cabinet is Mr. Lloyd George, who declares that he will not look at anything but Adult Suffrage, and that pressure brought to bear on him would be more useful than anything else."[45] Both the NUWSS and Brailsford felt that there was no reason that the Government should not give facilities for the bill: the militants were quiet, the constitutional crisis was in abeyance, and there was no real pressure of business. There would probably not again arise so favorable an opportunity for the House of Commons to consider a women's suffrage bill.[46]

Although supporters of women's suffrage desired a promise of full facilities for the Conciliation Bill, the immediate problem was to secure the bill's second reading. To this end, with the assistance of the Women's Liberal Federation (some of whose executive were active members of the NUWSS), the NUWSS prevailed upon Asquith to receive a

---

[42]C. C., June 16, 1910; Circulars of the London Society for Women's Suffrage, Circular from Philippa Strachey, June 1910, Fawcett Library, London.

[43]C. C., June 16 and 23, 1910.

[44]H. C. Deb. 5s, vol. 17, June 14, 1910, cc. 1202-7.

[45]Papers of Emily Davies, Emily Davies to Philippa Strachey, June 12, 1910, Fawcett Library, London.

[46]C. C., June 2, 1910.

deputation to discuss the future of the Conciliation Bill.[47]
Brailsford was delighted by this turn of events and was anxious for
Fawcett and her colleagues to make the most of the interview. He wanted
the suffragists to concentrate on extracting a promise for a second
reading and, for the moment, to skirt the issue of further facilities
for the bill. Brailsford assured Fawcett that if the suffragists
proceeded "stage-by-stage," the Government might, eventually, be
pressured into giving full facilities: "We need at the start get no
more than a Second Reading. I count on the interest and pressure
rising in volume as people begin to realize that there really is a
chance now. If we can delay a hasty refusal, it may in a few weeks be
morally impossible for any Government to say no at the final stage."[48]

On the eve of the deputation, Brailsford's chief worry was that
the suffragists would show their impatience with the Government's
handling of the Conciliation Bill. He feared that any display of
aggressiveness on the part of the women would only cause Asquith to
deny their request for a day for the second reading. Brailsford
recognized that Asquith would not be pushed by the women, and he
counseled Fawcett to proceed warily and tactfully with the Prime
Minister:

> Above all we must not allow him to give an advance decision
> hastily. All we need at once is a second reading, and all we
> propose to ask for now is a second reading free from
> conditions.
>   For these reasons may I suggest that while your deputation
> state the case for facilities this year as strongly as it can
> be put, you might also add that so far from pressing him for
> an answer now, you ask him to watch the feeling of the country
> and the House before coming to any final decision.[49]

The interview with Asquith took place on June 21. Fawcett,
leading a delegation of twenty-one extremely distinguished members of
the NUWSS, calmly requested Asquith to give the House of Commons the
opportunity to discuss and vote on the Conciliation Bill. The Prime
Minister, however, was unwilling to make any such commitment; the

---

[47]Bertha Mason, parliamentary secretary of the NUWSS, requested
the interview, and Asquith acceded to this request. See National Union
of Women's Suffrage Societies, Annual Report, 1910, p. 18. Mrs.
Broadley Reid, Mrs. Walter McLaren, the Hon. Mrs. Bertrand Russell, and
Lady Bamford-Slack, members of the executive of the Women's Liberal
Federation, were also active members of the NUWSS.

[48]Archives, Manchester Public Library, M/50, Box 10, H. N.
Brailsford to Millicent Garrett Fawcett, June 2, [1910].

[49]Ibid., H. N. Brailsford to Millicent Garrett Fawcett, June
20, [1910].

interview ended with the opposing opinions aired but no promise or hints of future promises.[50] Yet, the deputation, coupled with other pressure, both parliamentary and public, may have brought about a slight shift in Asquith's position. On June 23, he announced in the House that the Government would give time, before the close of the session, for a full debate and division on the second reading of the Conciliation Bill; he added very firmly, however, that the bill would not be given any more facilities that session.[51]

The members of the NUWSS, although discouraged by the interview with Asquith, did not accept this as the last word on the Conciliation Bill; they believed that if Asquith had been pushed this far, he could be pressured into giving the bill full facilities. The immediate task was to obtain an early date for the second reading, since a postponement of the debate until August would not leave time for the bill to pass on to subsequent stages. During the last week of June, the members of the Conciliation Commitee and their suffragist colleagues in Parliament lobbied to secure an early date for the second reading.[52] While this agitation was going on in parliamentary circles, the NUWSS was busy organizing extraparliamentry support for the bill as another means of bringing pressure to bear on the Prime Minister. On June 28 it sponsored a huge meeting in Queen's Hall in support of the bill.[53] Fawcett had been worried that the meeting might be

---

[50]National Union of Women's Suffrage Societies, Annual Report, 1910, p. 18. The deputation included Emily Davies, the founder of Girton College; Eleanor Rathbone, Liverpool town councillor; Clementina Black, a member of the executive of the Women's Industrial Council; Isabella Ford, a former member of the executive of ILP; Sophie Bryant, headmistress of the North London Collegiate School; and Ethel Snowden, a leading figure in the Labour Party.

[51]H. C. Deb. 5s, vol. 18, June 23, 1910, c. 488. The Cabinet made this decision on June 23, reversing the position it had taken on June 8 and on June 15. CAB 41/32/63, June 23, 1910; CAB 41/32/61, June 8, 1910; CAB 41/32/62, June 15, 1910.

[52]One hundred ninety-six MP's signed a memorial to the Prime Minister in support of the bill. C. C., July 7, 1910; The Times, June, 29, 1910.

[53]The NUWSS invited a number of its most noted supporters to sit on the platform at the meeting. Among these was George Bernard Shaw, who refused this invitation in his own inimitable manner: "My presence on the platform would be of no use unless I were labelled; and if I were, the audience would be so irritated at seeing me sitting there without hearing a speech from me that it would probably move an amendment in opposition to the Bill and carry it. Besides, I shall not be in town that Tuesday." FLAC, vol. 1, Hii, G. B. Shaw to Philippa Strachey, June 23, 1910, Fawcett Library, London.

vituperative toward the Government. She felt that the suffragists, as
supplicants, were in a vulnerable position, and would have to couple
determination with tact; like Brailsford, she believed that supporters
of the Conciliation Bill would have to deal very gingerly with the
Prime Minister while they waited patiently for him to bow to the
pressure of opinion:

> I feel that quite our best line for tomorrow is to emphasize
> what we have gained thus far and make the most of it. We must
> be very careful not to say anything irritating to the
> Government or to the Liberals in the House. Don't give them
> an excuse for throwing us over. Place an implicit and
> childlike faith in their vague promise. Above all we must not
> charge Asquith for being squeezable. It is the very way to
> prevent successful squeezing.[54]

Under Fawcett's careful control, the meeting went as planned, and it
raised £1,500 for the NUWSS war chest.[55] Two days later Fawcett
received a telegram from Walter McLaren announcing the good news that
the suffragists had won another partial victory.[56] Asquith had once
again bowed before the combined forces of the suffragists and had given
the Conciliation Bill an early date for its second reading: the House
of Commons would hold a debate and division on it July 11 and 12.
Brailsford's and Fawcett's strategy of proceeding slowly and using
pressure, both parliamentary and extraparliamentary, to wring
concessions from Asquith seemed to be working. Fawcett, not
unreasonably elated over this success, exclaimed jubilantly, "The walls
of Jericho have not gone down, but they are beginning to tremble.[57]

But even as the agitation on behalf of the Conciliation Bill
appeared to be making some headway with the Government, the very thing
that Brailsford had warned against—a split in the suffrage ranks—was
rapidly developing. Brailsford had cautioned Fawcett that the
Government would rejoice at any signs of disunity and would use those
dissensions as an excuse to postpone the bill. Now, at the end of
June, a series of disagreements and misunderstandings between the NUWSS
and the WSPU threatened to lead to a complete breakdown in
communications between the two societies.

[54]FLAC, vol. 1, Hii, Millicent Garrett Fawcett to Lady Frances
Balfour, June 27, 1910, Fawcett Library, London.

[55]National Union of Women's Suffrage Societies, Annual Report,
1910, p. 19.

[56]FLAC, vol. 1, Hii, Walter McLaren to Millicent Garrett
Fawcett, June 30, 1910, Fawcett Library, London.

[57]Millicent Garrett Fawcett, "The Parliamentary Situation on
Mr. Shackleton's Bill," Englishwoman, 6 (July 1910): 243.

The immediate cause of the squabble was the NUWSS decision to hold a demonstration in July in support of the Conciliation Bill. Prompted by Brailsford's plea for a show of unity, the NUWSS executive decided to abandon, for this one occasion, its policy of "clear separation between the two wings of the movement" and to extend the olive branch to the WSPU.[58] On June 27 Fawcett met with Emmeline Pethick-Lawrence and Christabel and Emmeline Pankhurst and invited their organization to participate in the NUWSS procession, on the condition they would agree to abstain from violence until after it was held. The WSPU, impatient with the Government's procrastination over fixing a date for the second reading of the Conciliation Bill, would not guarantee to prolong the truce, and Fawcett abandoned the idea of a joint demonstration.[59]

The very next day, June 28, Fawcett received a letter from Emmeline Pethick-Lawrence regretting the fact that the NUWSS would not cooperate with the WSPU in a public demonstration, and asking her to reconsider the matter. Fawcett was angered by the implication that it was the NUWSS and not the WSPU that had been uncooperative, and she immediately sent out a circular to all the branch societies which described her conversation with the WSPU's leaders and charged them with being intransigent and duplicitous: "No offer of joint action of a peaceful character has been made by the Social & Political Union. An offer of this kind had been made by the National Union and rejected emphatically by Mrs. and Miss Pankhurst and Mrs. Pethick-Lawrence, who stated on the 27th that in their opinion the time for peaceful demonstrations was over and the last word had been said."[60]

Fawcett must have taken her grievances against the WSPU to Brailsford, for on June 30 he wrote to her, obviously trying to calm her and to soften her attitude toward the WSPU. Brailsford, caught between the two parties, was in the unenviable situation of having to try and make the peace. All the women involved were extremely strong-minded and could be intractable, and a petty disagreement could very well turn into a full-scale and possibly a public dispute. For the sake of the Conciliation Bill, Brailsford had to try and smooth the

---

[58]Circulars of the London Society for Women's Suffrage, Circular from Philippa Strachey, May 19, 1910, Fawcett Library, London.

[59]Archives, Manchester Public Library, M/50, Box 10, Circular issued by the National Union of Women's Suffrage Societies and signed by Millicent Garrett Fawcett, June 28, 1910. On June 27, the day of the meeting, Asquith had not yet announced his intentions regarding the Conciliation Bill.

[60]Ibid.

troubled waters. In his letter to Fawcett he attempted to convince her of the good intentions of the WSPU's leaders:[61]

> They are really most generous and large-minded women, from whom any tactics of the kind you suspect are entirely foreign. Mrs. Lawrence's fault (as it is her virtue) is a kind of spiritual exhaltation, a wholly sincere if somewhat meridional absorption in the subjective beauty of big brave actions. Miss Pankhurst is all for frontal attacks and for a sort of Lancashire "fannoch" directness, which I have often found a little rough though I like and respect her. Mrs. Pankhurst in the gentlest and most self forgetful way was for going herself on the spot to call on you to make her explanation. . . . They are thinking of nothing but the vote, and they value as much as any of us the need for absolute unity at this moment. Their attitude to the National Union—it would be foolish to deny it—was often critical in the past though never, so far as I saw it, bitter or unsisterly. It was simply the inevitable attitude of eager, self-confident people, who felt absolutely sure that they had invented a better strategy than yours. Of late, ever since we came together to work for this Bill, all of this has changed into a hopeful confident friendly sense that we are all good allies.

He went on to say that he was sure Fawcett had misunderstood their intentions regarding violence, and he made a final plea for unity:

> Assume that you are just in your judgment and think as ill of these women as you please. Still they control a great organization. We need it to carry our Bill. We can succeed only by unity now and in the future. Ought we not to set the personal factors aside and as statesmen consider solely what use we can make of all our forces?

Fawcett was not easily appeased, nor were the WSPU leaders ready to compromise. Fortunately the disagreement did not become public, but tensions remained high and neither group seemed to be able

---

[61]Ibid., H. N. Brailsford to Millicent Garrett Fawcett, June 30, [1910].

to give up any part of its basic principles for the sake of unity within the movement as a whole.[62]

   In retrospect the disagreement between the WSPU and the NUWSS over the proposed demonstration seems very petty and highly exaggerated. Yet, this apparently trivial squabble is important because it illustrates the tensions which were present within the women's suffrage movement--tensions which, however latent, had the potential to jeopardize the whole campaign for votes for women. Part of the problem was, of course, a matter of tactical differences, or, as one member of the NUWSS executive committee put it, "the old antithesis between those who 'know no argument but force' and those who 'know no force but argument.'"[63] It would be simplistic, however, to imagine that tactical considerations alone ignited the controversy between the two societies. As in the past, in its dealings with the militants, the NUWSS was torn between a desire for unity and a desire to establish its own pre-eminence in the suffrage movement. It recognized the services which the WSPU had performed for the suffrage movement, but it felt that militant enthusiasm might endanger the very future of the suffrage cause. Additionally, there seemed to be a complete lack of rapport between the leadership of the two organizations. The executive of the NUWSS, and particularly Fawcett, resented the WSPU attitude as being both self-righteous and condescending. The NUWSS prided itself on its democratic principles and it was very impatient with the Pankhursts' high-hands manipulation of the WSPU.[64] And while the NUWSS was doing everything it could to help the Conciliation Committee win support for the bill, the WSPU was capturing the headlines and getting the attention of the nation. With some justification, the NUWSS felt that it received none of the credit for the advances made in the suffrage

---

[62]On July 16 Fawcett sent a confidential memo to all NUWSS branches informing them that Emmeline Pethick-Lawrence had asked the NUWSS to participate in a WSPU demonstration scheduled for July 23. She said she had accepted the invitation provisionally on condition that the WSPU agreed to abstain from militancy until after that time but that the WSPU had refused to make such an agreement. FLAC, vol. 1, Hii, Circular from Millicent Garrett Fawcett, July 16, 1910, Fawcett Library, London.

[63]Helena Swanwick, I Have Been Young [London 1935], p. 189.

[64]Dame Margery Corbett-Ashby, a former member of the NUWSS executive committee, repeatedly emphasized the point that the NUWSS was a completely democratic body. The executive committee, which was elected by representatives from the NUWSS branches, made its decisions collectively, and no individual, including Fawcett, ever completely dominated it. By contrast, Dame Margery spoke of the autocracy of the WSPU, and referred to it as "pure tyranny." (In conversation, December 4, 1974).

movement and yet was always penalized for the militants' mistakes:[65] "Like all moderate parties, we were kicked on both sides and, while we had to endure the stones and offal which were frequently hurled at us on their account, we were constantly told by wobbly politicians that they could no longer support us unless we somehow stopped the militants." As the NUWSS role in the suffrage movement became more prominent, the NUWSS attitude to the WSPU became less conciliatory and by June 1910, cooperation between the two societies had become increasingly difficult. This lack of communication, verging on rivalry, between the two wings of the suffrage movement, was a major weakness in the movement; moreover, it was a weakness which those who opposed women's suffrage could easily exploit. *as also peace m/meal*

Meanwhile, as the NUWSS was involved in this dispute with the WSPU, it continued its efforts on behalf of the Conciliation Bill. Brailsford and others on the Conciliation Committee had told Fawcett how effective the NUWSS had been in lobbying for the bill thus far, and Fawcett urged the affiliates to work diligently to obtain a large majority on the bill's second reading:

> We have been assured that at this particular juncture it is of great importance for the Conciliation Committee to have at their back the great constitutional movement represented by the National Union. This is absolutely the case, and every member of the Conciliation Committee will tell you so. The point we have now reached could not have been reached but for the exertions and influence exercised by the National Union, therefore I feel it is absolutely necessary for us to continue in our line of movement. . . . I know we shall have great difficulty in keeping certain men to their pledges. You must leave no stone unturned to make them feel they risk a great deal in their constituencies if they do not keep to their pledges.[66]

---

[65]Swanwick, p. 192. It must be emphasized that, except on rare occasions, the NUWSS hostility to the militants did not extend to the Women's Freedom League. Like the NUWSS, the Women's Freedom League (WFL) was a democratic organization. It was a much smaller organization than the WSPU, and its activities were much less publicized. Although it engaged in militancy, it never went to the extremes of the WSPU; to a large extent, it lived in the shadow of the WSPU. The NUWSS executive felt great admiration and respect for Charlotte Despard, the leader of the WFL, and her sister, Katherine Harley, was in fact a member of the NUWSS executive committee.

[66]Correspondence of the London Society for Women's Suffrage, Report of Proceedings of the Council Meeting Held at the Victoria Rooms, Bristol, on Friday, July 1st, 1910, pp.1-2, Fawcett Library, London.

The NUWSS was very conscious that if the bill did not receive a substantial majority on the second reading, there would be no question of further facilities, and during the first part of July it lobbied energetically. The affiliates sent deputations to MP's, organized letter-writing campaigns, and sent whips to the MP's urging them to vote for the bill on July 12.[67] On July 9 the NUWSS sponsored a huge demonstration in Trafalgar Square, in a last effort to convince the House of Commons to act favorably on the bill. The branch societies sent deputations to the event, and large contingents of suffragists came from as far away as Manchester and Edinburgh. Over 10,000 people gathered in the square, festooned with the red, white, and green banners of the NUWSS, to listen to the speakers.[68] The demonstration was a fitting climax to the NUWSS activities on behalf of the bill. Working closely with the Conciliation Committee, the organization had neglected no possibility in its search for support for the bill; the NUWSS had been told that its activities had influenced some MP's to look favorably on the suffrage measure.[69] The true test of all these long months of lobbying would come in two days' time when the House of Commons would begin debate on the Conciliation Bill.

The attention of all suffragists was fixed on Parliament on July 11, when David Shackleton (Lab., Lancs., N. E., Clitheroe) introduced the Conciliation Bill for its second reading.[70] The first day of debate was only a sparring session between those who supported and those who opposed the measure; on July 12, the arguments became much more heated and the opponents of the Conciliation Bill placed their heavy artillery in the field. Churchill, whom the suffragists had regarded as a friend, made perhaps the most damning, and the most

---

[67]Circulars of the London Society for Women's Suffrage, Circular to the local committees, July 1, 1910; Circular to MP's, July 5, 1910; Fawcett Library, London.

[68]FLAC, vol. 1, Hii, K. D. Courtney to Philippa Strachey, July 2, 1910; Elsie Inglis to Philippa Strachey, July 7, 1910; Fawcett Library, London. The Times, July 11, 1910; North of England Society for Women's Suffrage, Annual Report, 1910, p. 17.

[69]See, for example, Correspondence of the London Society for Women's Suffrage, Sir Samuel Scott to H. M. Phipson, July 8, 1910, Fawcett Library, London.

[70]H. C. Deb. 5s, vol. 19, July 11, 1910, cc. 41-48.

articulate, attack on the bill.[71] He brought forth a battery of
arguments against it, calling it undemocratic and accusing it of
discriminating against wives and mothers.[72] He also attempted to scare
the Liberals with the specter of plural and faggot votes which would
benefit the Tories: "I also see a grave danger in creating without
great consideration a vast body of privileged and dependent voters, who
might be manipulated and manoeuvered in this direction or that. . . .
It is not merely an undemocratic Bill it is worse. It is an anti-
democratic Bill. It gives an entirely unfair representation to
property as against persons."[73] Lloyd George, also a supposed friend
of the suffrage movement, joined his colleague in speaking against the
bill. His arguments were similar to Churchill's--that the bill was
undemocratic, and that it did not go far enough in enfranchising large
numbers of women. He emphasized that the bill could not be amended,
and declared that this constituted "an attempt to dictate to the House
of Commons the way in which the question should be solved."[74]

The Prime Minister joined in the fray, and, in a speech which
both opponents and supporters of the bill termed one of the best of his
political career, he forcefully reiterated his opposition to this

---

[71]The suffragists exaggerated Churchill's support for their
cause. Churchill, as his biographer notes, was at best ambivalent
toward the movement. Randolph S. Churchill, Winston S. Churchill, vol.
2 (Boston, 1967), p. 379. The saga of Churchill and the Conciliation
Bill is fully told in Randolph S. Churchill, Winston S. Churchill,
Companion vol. 2, part 3 (Boston, 1967), pp. 1427-56.

[72]Under the provisions of the bill, most married women could
not receive the vote since they could not qualify as joint-occupiers.
The Committee had framed the bill in this manner because it felt that
the House would not consent to the enfranchisement of between six and
seven million women.

[73]H. C. Deb. 5s, vol. 19, July 12, 1912, cc. 221-24.
Brailsford had told Churchill, before the debate, that if he was really
worried about large-scale faggot voting, the Committee would be willing
to amend the bill so that a husband and wife could not be qualified in
respect of premises situated in the same constituency. Churchill
opposed the bill, not for the reasons he stated in the debate, but
because he feared his party's interests would be hurt by the Bill. See
Winston S. Churchill, Companion vol. 2, part 3, pp. 1444 and 1453.

[74]H. C. Deb. 5s, vol. 19, July 12, 1910, c. 308. The bill had
been committed with a restricted title so that it would take up as
little of the House's time as possible. Lloyd George's objections,
like Churchill's, were, in truth, based on considerations of party
advantage. Lewis Harcourt, who organized the antisuffragist opposition
to the bill, had persuaded Lloyd George to speak against it. Brian
Harrison, Separate Spheres, p. 165.

"half-hearted and unstable compromise." In a remarkable statement, Asquith, a stalwart opponent of women's suffrage, criticized the bill precisely because it did not enfranchise enough women: "For my part I should not regard any measure of woman suffrage as satisfying my conceptions of equality which did not confer the suffrage on precisely the same grounds as, for the time being, it is enjoyed by man."[75] Like Churchill, he appealed to the Liberals' fears of votes for the propertied, and he expressed his doubt that the House of Commons would ratify a bill that was so undemocratic, and had so little public support: "In the first place there should be the fullest and clearest proof that it was in accordance with the wishes and desires of the women themselves, and in the second place, it must be democratic in its character and scope. Neither of these propositions is satisfied by the measure before us."[76]

With the exception of Philip Snowden, supporters of the bill were not nearly so effective in their arguments as those who opposed it. Snowden, however, was brilliant in his defense of the measure, and he brought the debate to a close with an impassioned, yet reasoned speech on behalf of the Bill. He was furious over Lloyd George's and Churchill's defections, and accused them of trying to kill the bill: "They are quite in favour of the principle, but it would pass the wit of man to put that principle into a Bill which would meet the approval of the Chancellor of the Exchequer and the Home Secretary. . . . They think they can take shelter and hide their opposition to the enfranchisement of women by pretending to be more democratic than those in favour of women's suffrage."[77] Snowden heatedly refuted the criticism that the bill was undemocratic, quoting statistics that showed that 94 percent of women occupiers in London belonged to the working class. Yet, if Lloyd George persisted in calling the bill undemocratic, Snowden promised that its sponsors would be happy to recommit it in respect of the title, provided the Government would guarantee to give the time necessary to discuss the amended bill. In a succinct phrase he pointed out the one reason why all suffragists should support the bill, regardless of its imperfections: "For the best of all possible reasons—namely, that it is the only Bill which can unite the various sections of opinion which are in favour of the extension of the suffrage to women."[78]

When the bill was at last put to a vote, it passed its second reading by the large majority of 299 to 189.[79] Yet, the suffragists' victory was once again Pyrrhic; by an even more decisive majority—320

---

[75]H. C. Deb. 5s, vol. 19, July 12, 1910, c. 249.

[76]Ibid., c. 251.   [77]Ibid., c. 323.   [78] bid., c. 318.

[79]The Times, July 14, 1910. The vote was as follows: For—161 Lib., 87 Cons., 31 Lab., 20 Nat. Against—60 Lib., 113 Cons., 2 Lab., 14 Nat.

to 175--the House voted to send the bill to a Committee of the Whole House.[80] It appeared that the House of Commons had chosen to prevent the bill from proceeding any further.[81] The Times commented wryly that the division lists constituted a "pleasing subject of study for all those who are interested in political gyrations, and care to note how members who made impassioned speeches on the suffragist side promptly dashed suffragist hopes by swelling the majority for the extinction of the Bill."[82]

The NUWSS' official reaction to the events of July 11 and 12 was restrainedly enthusiastic, but privately members of the organization were fearful about the future fate of the bill. The Liberals had not responded to Brailsford's efforts to gain a compromise, and the opposition of Churchill and Lloyd George, in particular, did not bode well for the measure.[83] Fawcett was well aware that the bill's supporters inside the House predicted that the bill would not proceed any further that session. Lady Frances Balfour wrote her the details of a conversation she had had with her brother-in-law, Arthur Balfour, about the bill:

> . . . he thought the best speaking was against us and that he had never heard Asquith speak so well or with more seriousness. He understood the Cabinet had taken the matter very seriously, all the more as they were so divided. I said I believed it would make both parties put off the day of

---

[80]The decision to send the bill to a committee of the Whole House instead of to a standing committee meant the Government would have to find time and grant special facilities for the committee stage on the floor of the House. Normally when a bill passed its second reading, it was sent to a Grand Committee, which sat while the House of Commons was transacting other business; thus, the committee stage could proceed without special facilities. The vote to refer the bill to a Committee of the Whole House was as follows: For--125 Lib., 175 Cons., 5 Lab., 15 Nat; 118 MP's who voted for the bill also voted to refer it to a Committee of the Whole House: 59 Lib., 55 Cons., and 4 Lab.

[81]Some members maintained that they voted to refer the bill to a Committee of the Whole House, not because they wished to bury it but because they believed franchise bills were too important to be sent to a Grand Committee. See H. C. Deb. 5s, vol. 19, July 29, 1910, c. 2599.

[82]The Times, July 14, 1910.

[83]The NUWSS dubbed Lloyd George "the wrecker" and Churchill "the contortionist." C. C., July 28 and August 4, 1910.

extending the franchise. He said, "that is a very true and pertinent observation." By implication the talk implied the Bill was dead.[84]

Within the House it soon became apparent that enthusiasm for the Conciliation Bill was on the wane. Liberal adult suffragists, fearing that the passage of the measure would damage their cause, were making moves to overthrow it, and Lloyd George, who had emerged as the suffragists' archopponent, was doing his best to dissipate Liberal support.[85] On July 20 Lloyd George flatly told a meeting of Liberal suffragists that the Government could not afford to be embarrassed by the suffrage issue at a time when it was engaged in a struggle with the House of Lords.[86] A week later John Redmond indicated that his party concurred with the Chancellor of the Exchequer: he announced that the Nationalists would not press for further facilities for controversial bills until the constitutional question was settled.[87] Soon after this the fate of the Conciliation Bill was publicly sealed. On July 28 Lloyd George announced in the House of Commons that the Government would not give further facilities to the bill that session.[88] Three days later Parliament was prorogued until November. The suffragists would have to await Parliament's return in the hope that the Government would prove more conciliatory about facilitites for the bill in the autumn.

Although all these auguries indicated that the Conciliation Bill was "dead" for that session, the NUWSS went ahead with its plans to marshall support for the bill; throughout the summer and autumn of 1910 it continued to lobby for the measure. To a large extent tactical considerations influenced the NUWSS decision. The Conciliation Bill gave the NUWSS a focus around which it could organize, and it placed the suffrage cause, in a concrete fashion, before the nation. Equally important, the NUWSS feared that if the bill were dropped, and it acknowledged the bill was dead, the WSPU would end its truce and once again wage war on the Government. The NUWSS believed such a move would be suicidal: the Government would not even consider granting

---

[84]FLAC, vol. 1, Hii, Lady Frances Balfour to Millicent Garrett Fawcett, July 14, 1910, Fawcett Library, London.

[85]The Times, July 14 and 16, 1910. Brailsford commented icily: "It has apparently escaped the notice of our Liberal critics that our Bill was expressly framed to meet their objections to the old Suffrage Bill." H. N. Brailsford, "The Tactics of Woman Suffrage," The Nation, July 23, 1910, p. 596.

[86]The Times, July 21, 1910.

[87]Ibid., July 28, 1910.

[88]H. C. Deb. 5s, vol. 19, July 28, 1910, c. 2339.

facilities to a women's suffrage bill while the WSPU persisted in its militant campaign. Thus, the specter of militancy encouraged the NUWSS to behave as if the Conciliation Bill were very much alive.[89]

Besides these tactical considerations, the NUWSS still harbored a faint hope that Asquith, who had, in the past, made concessions to the suffragists, might again prove "squeezable if only we can squeeze hard enough."[90] This perception greatly underestimated the depth of Asquith's opposition to women's suffrage, and it also tended to ignore the degree to which the Liberal Party was split over women's suffrage. Brailsford and other members of the Conciliation Committee shared the NUWSS misconceptions, however, and to a large extent, the NUWSS took its political cues from this Committee; it saw itself as the working partner of this parliamentary body of suffragists and felt strongly that it must support these men. The Conciliation Committee had refused to accept or to admit defeat, and the NUWSS followed its lead. At the end of July, the NUWSS executive passed a resolution, "That until the promoters of Mr. Shackleton's Bill decide to drop it, the National Union shall not consider the Bill destroyed."[91] The Conciliation Bill had given the women's suffrage movement its most promising opportunity since the 1880's. If there was any chance at all for the bill, the suffragists could not concede defeat.

Influenced by these factors, the NUWSS continued throughout the summer and autumn of 1910 to campaign for the Conciliation Bill. The aims of the suffragists were to keep the issue alive in the constituencies, to enlist public support for the suffrage cause, and to convince MP's to press for further facilities for the bill. The local societies cooperated enthusiastically, sending deputations to MP's, canvassing women municipal electors to support the measure, holding weekly meetings to explain the bill, and, on occasion, sponsoring impressive demonstrations.[92] At the request of Bertha Mason, parliamentary secretary of the NUWSS, the affiliates also contacted women's organizations, such as the Women's Cooperative Guild and the British Women's Temperance Association, and tried to stir these groups to give active support to the bill. The NUWSS was particularly eager to reach women who were active in party politics, notably in the Women's Liberal Association and the Women's Liberal Federation; it felt that these women could be particularly useful in "squeezing" Asquith to

---

[89]The WSPU was, indeed, at this time hinting that it intended to end the truce. See Leventhal, p. 139.

[90]Archives, Manchester Public Library, M/50, Box 9, Helena Swanwick to Millicent Garrett Fawcett, June 22, 1910.

[91]C. C., August 4, 1910.

[92]C. C., September 22 and October 20, 1910; North of England Society for Women's Suffrage, Annual Report, 1910, p. 17.

grant further facilities to the bill.[93] Members of the NUWSS executive, who were making speaking tours during the parliamentary interim, were very impressed by all the work of the branches. Lady Frances Balfour, describing to Fawcett her suffrage "progress," declared that her audiences were larger and more sympathetic than ever before.[94]

Throughout these months the NUWSS remained in close contact with the Conciliation Committee. Brailsford was extremely appreciative of the information the NUWSS supplied to him regarding shifts in Parliamentary opinion. He was particularly concerned about the possible defections of Liberal adult suffragists, and at his suggestion, an affiliate of the NUWSS, the North Western Federation for Women's Suffrage, conferred with Geoffrey Howard and Richard Denman (Lib., Carlisle) and secured a promise that they would not introdudce a wider suffrage bill.[95] Also at Brailsford's request, the NUWSS arranged deputations to Cabinet ministers who were friendly to women's suffrage, solicited MP's for their opinions on the Conciliation Bill, and persuaded city councils to petition Parliament on behalf of the bill.[96] Acting on Brailsford's suggestion, the NUWSS also began to collect statistics on women municipal electors, so that the Conciliation Committee could use this information to refute the charge that its bill was "undemocratic."[97] Brailsford depended on the NUWSS, with its large network of affiliates, to lobby for the Conciliation Bill during the parliamentary recess. The NUWSS, for its part, was eager to show the Government that the Conciliation Bill had strong

---

[93]FLAC, vol. 1, Hii, Circular from the Bertha Mason, [September 1910], Fawcett Library, London; C. C., August 11, 1910.

[94]FLAC, vol. 1, Hii, Lady Frances Balfour to Millicent Garrett Fawcett, October 18, 1910, Fawcett Library, London; see also Correspondence of the London Society for Women's Suffrage, Fawcett Library, London, passim.

[95]Papers of Catherine Marshall, Cumbria County Record Office, Carlisle, Cumberland, H. N. Brailsford to Catherine Marshall, August 12 and August 20, 1910 (hereafter cited as Marshall Papers); National Union of Women's Suffrage Societies, Annual Report and Rules of the North Western Federation, 1910–1911 (Carlisle, 1911), p. 8. Catherine Marshall, chairman of the North Western Federation, came from a staunchly Liberal family and thus enjoyed good relations with the Women's Liberal Association. Howard had introduced an Adult Suffrage Bill in 1909.

[96]Correspondence of the London Society for Women's Suffrage, Philippa Strachey to H. N. Brailsford, September 20 and October 21, 1910, Fawcett Library, London; North of England Society for Women's Suffrage, Annual Report, 1910, p. 18, C. C., October 20, 1910.

[97]C. C., October 20, 1910.

support both in Parliament and in the constituencies; Bertha Mason emphasized this objective to the affiliates:

> The Conciliation Committee do not regard Mr. Shackleton's Bill as dead, but intend before Parliament reassembles to lay before the Prime Minister further evidence of the urgency of the demand for the passage into law of the Bill this year. The clear duty then of the National Union is to strengthen in every possible way the hands of the Conciliation Committee in their work, and they beg that your society will do its utmost to gain further support for the Bill.[98]

Nonetheless, there were clear indications, throughout the parliamentary interim, that Asquith intended to stick to his guns and that the Government had no intention of granting further facilities to the bill. Lloyd George continued his attacks on the measure, claiming it would add "hundreds of thousands" to the plural vote; he admitted, however, that the battle with the House of Lords colored his views on the bill and that the Government intended to settle the constitutional question before it became embroiled in women's suffrage.[99] Other Cabinet ministers echoed Lloyd George's sentiments: Runciman and Birrell both informed the NUWSS that it would be impossible to give facilities to the Conciliation Bill that session.[100] Even more disappointing and disheartening to the suffragists was the position of Sir Edward Grey. Early in November the Foreign Secretary, viewed as one of the most staunch supporters of women's suffrage in the Cabinet, announced that the Government would neither give facilities for the

---

[98]FLAC, vol. 1, Hii, Circular from Bertha Mason, August 3, 1910, Fawcett Library, London.

[99]The Times, September 29, 1910. Brailsford was irate at these accusations and accused Lloyd George of being blatantly insincere in his protestations of friendship for women's suffrage. He declared that, if given the chance, Lloyd George would indefinitely postpone women's suffrage: "His alternative is to wait first until the constitutional question is settled, then until the Welsh Church is disestablished, and at that distant date to bring in a Bill for which there is in the House no majority, and from the suffrage societies no backing." Manchester Guardian, October 3, 1910.

[100]C. C., November 3, 1910. Brailsford had urged Birrell to come out with a strong statement in favor of granting full facilities to the bill, if not this session, next session. He told Birrell that the Committee was prepared to open the title of the bill, although this might mean that Lloyd George would so amend it that all Tory support would be lost. PRO, Papers of Edward, Viscount Grey of Falloden, FO 800/99, H. N. Brailsford to Augustine Birrell [1910], enclosed in a letter from Augustine Birrell to Sir Edward Grey, November 2, 1910.

bill that year, nor make any promises for the coming year.[101] Clearly, the Conciliation Bill was in trouble if Cabinet support for the measure was beginning to wither. The constitutional crisis provided a convenient pretext for blocking the Conciliation Bill, but the real problem was that even those ministers who favored women's suffrage were not committed to this particular measure.

Parliament reconvened on November 15. The week before the session opened the NUWSS began a series of meetings and demonstrations in support of the bill which culminated in a procession to Westminster Abbey.[102] But "suffrage week" was a rather hollow pageant, for by mid-November the NUWSS executive committee had abandoned hope that the Government would give facilities to the bill that session. The collapse of the constitutional conference and the prospect of imminent dissolution had sealed the fate of the measure.[103] On the day the House of Commons reassembled, Bertha Mason visited No. 10 Downing Street to make one last plea for facilities for the bill. Vaughan Nash and Geoffrey Howard, who acted as Asquith's spokesmen, confirmed the pessimism of the suffragists; they would make no guarantee that the Government would give facilities to the bill even in the next parliamentary session.[104]

Both the NUWSS and the Conciliation Committee reluctantly acknowledged that the Conciliation Bill was dead for 1910; their aim now was to obtain full facilities for the bill in the next session of Parliament. Brailsford, however, was not sanguine about the future prospects for the bill.[105] He informed Fawcett that a General Election would be held soon and gloomily predicted that if, as he expected, the Liberals were returned with an increased majority, the Government would not agree to grant facilities to the bill in 1911:

> This greatly diminishes our chances of getting a pledge for next year. And if the Liberals improve their majority (as

---

[101]The Times, November 14, 1910.

[102]C. C., November 17, 1910.

[103]FLAC, vol. 1, Hiii, Circular from T. G. Whitehead, November 5, 1910, Fawcett Library, London.

[104]National Union of Women's Suffrage Societies, Annual Report, 1910, pp. 22-23.

[105]On November 17 Asquith informed Lytton that, owing to lack of time, no further facilities would be granted to the bill that session. The Conciliation Committee took Asquith at his word and declared the bill dead for 1910. The Times, November 18, 1910.

they expect) they will be less inclined than ever to take a
limited Bill.

We shall continue to negotiate, and shall probably get
something but not good enough, I'm afraid, to satisfy the
Liberals.[106]

There was not enough support for women's suffrage within the Liberal
Party to carry a "democratic bill," unless the bill had the official
support of the Government. This was unlikely to be forthcoming, and
therefore any bill for women's suffrage would need the support of some
Conservative MP's if it were to be successful. And since the
Conservatives, both because they were philosophically opposed to any
wide extension of the franchise and because they feared such a change
would hurt their party at the polls, would not support a "democratic
bill" for women's suffrage, it seemed best to stick with the
Conciliation Bill instead of jettisoning it in favor of a more
comprehensive measure.

Brailsford's worries were compounded by his fear that the WSPU
was about to end its truce with the Government—since any revival of
militancy would make it impossible to bargain with the Government about
facilities for the bill.[107] Lytton shared Brailsford's pessimism and
was desperately negotiating with Asquith for some assurance that he
would give facilities to the bill next year. On November 17 Lytton
wrote Fawcett that he was "sanguine of success" that he could obtain
the desired guarantee, provided the militants did not jeopardize his
diplomatic efforts by resorting to violence:

I may tell you confidentially that I have already received
private assurance from Mr. Balfour that if the Prime Minister
will give an undertaking on this point he will be prepared to
do the same in the event of his being in office. . . . The
only danger is that the raid which the WSPU are preparing
tomorrow may spoil everything. I have reasoned with them as
strongly as I can, explained to them what I am working for and
my reasons for expecting success—but it is useless and they
will not listen to me. . . . It will be deplorable if their
impatience prevents us from getting the assurance wh. wd. be
really valuable.[108]

---

[106]Archives, Manchester Public Library, M/50, Box 10, H. N.
Brailsford to Millicent Garrett Fawcett, November 11, [1910].

[107]Bodleian Library, Nevinson Journals, e616, November 9, 1910.

[108]FLAC, vol. 1, Hiii, Lord Lytton to Millicent Garrett
Fawcett, November 17, 1910, Fawcett Library, London. The Nevinson
Journals indicate that Lytton had arranged a meeting with Asquith and

Lytton's worst fears were realized. On November 18--"Black
Friday"--the militants stormed into Parliament Square and battled with
the police. The clash resulted in the arrest of 115 women.[109]
Brailsford was furious at the WSPU and claimed that the raid "wrecked
his diplomacy with Asquith."[110] As Lytton predicted, the revival of
militancy only harmed the women's cause. Asquith refused to make any
commitment to give facilities to the bill in the next session of
Parliament,[111] and on November 22, the militants again vented their
wrath, this time mobbing Asquith and injuring Birrell; they also threw
rocks at the houses of Churchill, Grey, Harcourt, and Burns. As a
result of these rampages, 180 women were arrested.[112]

Grimly, the NUWSS and the Conciliation Committee went on with
plans for the coming General Election. Asquith had at least promised
to give facilities to a women's suffrage bill sometime in the new
Parliament.[113] The Times declared that Asquith's pledge, though vague,
had made women's suffrage an issue at the election: "if the election
confirms the Government in power, the new Parliament will be considered
to have received a mandate on the subject of women suffrage."[114]
Sharing The Times' interpretation of the Prime Minister's promise, the
Conciliation Committee issued a resolution which called on all women to
campaign for the return of MP's who were pledged to support the
Conciliation Bill.[115]

The NUWSS concurred with the Conciliation Committee and adopted
the position that it was more fruitful to worry about the suffragist

---

other Liberal MP's to discuss facilities for the Conciliation Bill next
year. Owing to the actions of the WSPU on November 22, this meeting
never took place. Bodleian Library, Nevinson Journals, e616, November
29, 1910, and January 2, 1911.

[109]Rosen, pp. 138-39.

[110]Bodleian Library, Nevinson Journals, e616, November 29, 1910.

[111]H. C. Deb. 5s, vol. 20, November 22, 1910, cc. 272-73.

[112]The Times, November 23, 1910.

[113]H. C. Deb. 5s, vol. 20, November 22, 1910, cc. 272-73.

[114]The Times, November 23, 1910.

[115]Ibid., November 24, 1910.

component in the new Parliament than to bemoan the failings of the past Parliament. Fawcett blamed the militants for much of the coolness in Parliament. Lady Frances Balfour had lunched with Asquith the day after the militants mobbed him, and she reported to Fawcett that the Prime Minister had barely escaped harm, while Birrell had injured his knee.[116] Fawcett's reply was blunt:

> The PM's statement of the 22nd was not just exactly what we wanted, but it was better than anything that had ever been offered us before and was at any rate good enough to make The Times say the next day that it had made w. s. [women's suffrage] a question definitely before the country at the election and that if there is a Liberal majority it will be a mandate to "grant suffrage to women." And then those idiots go out smashing windows and bashing ministers' hats over their eyes.[117]

In Common Cause, she made her criticism of the militants' political stupidity even stronger:

> I deeply deplore the futile silliness and want of political instinct which led, at such a moment, to window smashing and assaults on Cabinet Ministers. . . . But for this folly the Conciliation Committee might have entered into negotiations with the Prime Minister. . . . No one can negotiate with a man and "bash" his hat over his eyes at one and the same moment. The sane suffragists will have to suffer these absurdities.[118]

However, there was an immediate task at hand--the General Election--, and on November 26 the NUWSS held a special council to map out its electioneering strategy. As in the past, the NUWSS would support proponents of women's suffrage and oppose antisuffragist candidates; in addition, in certain selected constituencies where the sitting member was a staunch opponent of women's suffrage, the NUWSS would sponsor candidates to run on a women's suffrage platform. Taken as a whole, the policy of the NUWSS was to secure the return of as many MP's as possible pledged to support women's suffrage. The NUWSS evidently still believed that a Liberal Government, led by Asquith, would have to give full facilities to a Conciliation Bill if the House of Commons were firmly behind it, and it was up to the NUWSS to see

---

[116]FLAC, vol. 1, Hiii, Lady Frances Balfour to Millicent Garrett Fawcett, November 24, 1910, Fawcett Library, London.

[117]Ibid., Millicent Garrett Fawcett to Lady Frances Balfour, November 28, 1910.

[118]C. C., December 1, 1910.

that those elected to the new Parliament would back the Conciliation Bill.[119]

During the election campaign the NUWSS focused its main energy on three constituencies where it sponsored women's suffrage candidates. The South Salford Women's Suffrage Association, an affiliate of the NUWSS, persuaded Brailsford to run as a women's suffrage candidate against Hilaire Belloc, an archopponent of women's suffrage. The local Liberal organization thereupon withdrew Belloc's name and nominated the Hon. Charles Russell, a suffragist, as its official candidate. After some negotiations, the South Salford Committee agreed to withdraw Brailsford after Russell had promised to send out a letter to the electors of South Salford in support of the Conciliation Bill.[120] Fawcett was triumphant at what she felt was a victory over the Liberal party machine and claimed, "The Liberals came crawling on their knees" at South Salford.[121] Unfortunately, the NUWSS met with less success in the other two constituencies in which it sponsored women's suffrage candidates, and its candidates came in miserably last: at Camlachie the NUWSS candidate, William Mirlees, polled only 35 votes, and at East St. Pancras Herbert Jacobs polled 22 votes.[122] Something was no doubt won in the realm of propaganda, but all the effort expended in sponsoring women's suffrage candidates had no effect on decimating antisuffragist ranks in Parliament.

---

[119]FLAC, vol. 1, Hiii, Copy of the resolutions passed at the Special Council of the NUWSS, November 26, 1910, Fawcett Library, London.

[120]Manchester Guardian, September 26, 1910; C. C., November 24, 1910; North of England Society for Women's Suffrage, Annual Report, 1910, pp. 20-21; The Times, November 28 and 30, 1910. Belloc's biographer contends that Belloc's withdrawal had nothing to do with women's suffrage, but the fact that the Liberal machine replaced Belloc with a candidate who was very conciliatory to the suffragists indicates that the suffrage issue did influence the selection of candidates at South Salford. See Robert Speaight, Hilaire Belloc (New York, 1957), pp. 293-95.

[121]FLAC, vol. 1, Hiii, Millicent Garrett Fawcett to Lady Frances Balfour, November 28, 1910, Fawcett Library, London.

[122]C. C., December 8 and 15, 1910. The poll at Camlachie was as follows: Halford Mackinder (Cons.), 3,479; James Hogge (Lib.), 3,453; James Kessack (Lab.), 1,439; and William Mirlees (W.S.), 35. Thus, Mackinder, the antisuffragist, won the election by only 26 votes. The poll at East St. Pancras was as follows: Joseph Martin (Lib.), 3,891; John Hopkins (Cons.), 3,038; and Herbert Jacobs (W.S.), 22. The full particulars of the East St. Pancras election are contained in the Correspondence of the London Society for Women's Suffrage relating to the East St. Pancras Election, Fawcett Library, London.

More real gains were made in the twenty-two constituencies in which the NUWSS aided party candidates—most of them Liberals—by supplying organizers, volunteer workers, and money, though here, too, the gains were mainly valuable as propaganda. The contests did give the suffragists an opportunity to educate the public about the Conciliation Bill and promoted the NUWSS as an organization, but the outcomes were determined by local factors, competing issues, and local party standing rather than by positions on women's suffrage, and only eight of the candidates whom the NUWSS supported were victorious.[123]

Even so, the results of the second General Election of 1910 were better than expected in that the Liberal landslide that Brailsford had dreaded had not come about, and the new House of Commons was almost as evenly balanced as the old:

	January, 1910	December, 1910[124]
Liberals	275	272
Conservatives	273	272
Irish Nationalists	82	84
Labour	40	42

The Government had been returned to power, and the new Parliament had received its "mandate" on women's suffrage; in addition, there were more supporters of women's suffrage in the newly elected House than there had been in the old.[125]

The outcome of the election was the one bright ray in an otherwise clouded horizon; in December 1910 it appeared the NUWSS was only a little closer to its goal of securing votes for women than it

---

[123]See H. C. Sessional Papers, 1911 (lxii) (272).

[124]David Butler and Jennie Freeman, British Political Facts, 1900–1968, p. 141.

[125]Millicent Garrett Fawcett, "The Political Outlook for Women's Suffrage," Englishwoman, 9 (January 1911): 2; C. C., February 9, 1911; Daily Chronicle, February 25, 1911. The NUWSS estimated there were 323 supporters of women's suffrage in the old House of Commons. In the new House of Commons it estimated there were 246 "resolute supporters" of women's suffrage, 120 "less reliable" supporters, 42 adult suffragists, 65 neutrals, and 193 opponents.

had been in 1909. In the annual report for 1910 the NUWSS summed up a year of great achievement, and great failure. The gains in income and membership were striking:[126]

	Number of Societies	Annual Income	Membership
1909	130	£3,385-13-9	13,429
1910	207	£5,503- 7-1	21,571

The growth of the affiliates paralleled that of the central organization: in 1909, their total income was estimated to be, at most, £10,000, and by 1910 it had risen to £14,000.[127] The NUWSS thought these statistics proved that it had been successful not only in popularizing the women's suffrage cause but also in strengthening the

---

[126]National Union of Women's Suffrage Societies, Annual Report, 1909, pp. 42-43; National Union of Women's Suffrage Societies, Annual Report, 1910, pp. 44-45. Because of the tremendous growth which it had sustained, the NUWSS restructured its organization in 1910 and established federations composed of all its affiliated societies within a given area. Each federation was headed by a committee consisting of one representative from each society in its area, and one representative from the NUWSS executive. The federation committees were instructed to promote the formation of new societies, and to secure cooperation among the branch societies in their respective areas. Twice a year conferences were held between representatives of all the federation committees and members of the NUWSS executive. The federation scheme strengthened the ties between societies within a given area, and enabled them to coordinate their activities. The formation of federations improved and consolidated the local organization of the NUWSS, and it enabled the NUWSS executive to discharge its supervisory and directorial duties more efficiently. Councils of the National Union of Women's Suffrage Societies, Report of the Annual Council of the National Union of Women's Suffrage Societies, March 19, 1910, Fawcett Library, London. By the end of 1910, there were fifteen federations in the NUWSS. National Union of Women's Suffrage Societies, Annual Report, 1910, p. 13.

[127]National Union of Women's Suffrage Societies, Annual Report, 1909, p. 40; National Union of Women's Suffrage Societies, Annual Report, 1910, p. 44. The London Society for Women's Suffrage and the North of England Society for Women's Suffrage had greatly increased their incomes:

	1909	1910
LSWS	£2,275-0-6	£3,358-2-2
NESWS	£1,099-2-0-½	£1,925-18-3-½

London Society for Women's Suffrage, Annual Report, 1909, p. 18, and Annual Report, 1910, pp. 16-17; North of England Society for Women's Suffrage, Annual Report, 1909, p. 51, and Annual Report, 1910, p. 67.

conviction that the vote could be won by legal means. Each additional shilling, each new member, made the NUWSS more confident that both its cause and its tactics were beginning to make an impact on the country and to win new advocates.

The darker side of the picture was that the prospects for the Conciliation Bill, which had once appeared so bright, now seemed dim. In summing up the NUWSS activities for 1910, one member correctly noted: "The history of the National Union has been in the main the history of the Conciliation Bill, every effort being directed to backing the self-sacrificing and arduous efforts of Mr. Brailsford."[128] The NUWSS had presided over the birth of the bill and had paved the way for its acceptance by the House of Commons; yet, despite all its work on the Conciliation Bill's behalf, the NUWSS had once again witnessed the familiar but painful sight of a suffrage bill being prevented from going beyond a second reading. At the close of 1910, it seemed probable that, despite Asquith's November pledge, the suffragists would never celebrate the passage of the Conciliation Bill. Brailsford, writing to Fawcett, gave a most somber prediction:

Since the Conciliation Committee met I have been able to ascertain direct from the Prime Minister (and Lord Lytton has news from Sir Edward Grey) what the "pledge" means. It is not a pledge for our Bill, even implicitly, and we are frankly warned that it must not be so interpreted. The Government holds itself free to judge what Bill will meet with the largest support in the House! . . . I think we shall get time for some Bill and then every conceivable dodge will be used to defeat it.[129]

With the additional threat of a renewal of militancy, it appeared the agitation for women's suffrage could indeed "go scuffling on for years."[130]

As of December 1910, the NUWSS was pessimistic about the future of the women's cause. In the immediate sense all its work had been a failure. But as a lesson in practical politics, the NUWSS work on the Conciliation measure had been valuable, and it was to have a great impact on the organization's future development. The Liberal Government's handling of the Conciliation Bill had caused both disappointment and rancor. The suffragists felt, with justice, that the ministers' criticisms of the bill were unfounded and that the Government could have found time for full facilities for the bill had

---

[128]North of England Society for Women's Suffrage, Annual Report, 1910, p. 31.

[129]Archives, Manchester Public Library, M/50, Box 10, H. N. Brailsford to Millicent Garrett Fawcett, December 3, [1910].

[130]Bodleian Library, Nevinson Journals, e616, January 2, 1911.

they been so inclined. The Government's unwillingness to respond to
the women's pleas left the NUWSS both angered and disillusioned.
Unlike the WSPU, however, the NUWSS as an organization was given to
long deliberations and was not quick to translate anger into action.
Furthermore, many members of the NUWSS still continued to have faith in
the notion that women's suffrage was a Liberal cause and that
eventually the party would come round. In December 1910, with the
Liberals again in power, the NUWSS could see only two possibilities of
action: to continue to cooperate with the Conciliation Committee, in
hopes that a Liberal Government would grant full facilities to the
committee's bill, or to make war on the Government and work for the
Liberals' ouster. Continued cooperation might not ever bring results,
but the NUWSS regarded militancy as suicidal, so cooperation it would
have to be. Yet this decision did not mean that the experience with
the Conciliation Bill had left no impression on the NUWSS. In January
it had appeared that 1910 would be a banner year for supporters of
women's suffrage. By December, the Liberal Government had dashed this
hope. In retrospect it appears that the fate of the Conciliation Bill
in 1910 caused the NUWSS to become seriously disappointed for the first
time with the Liberals, and propelled it in the direction of an
alliance with the Labour Party.

CHAPTER IV

1911-1912:   THE CAMPAIGN CONTINUES

From January 1911 to March 1912, the NUWSS continued the long, slow task of pushing the Conciliation Bill. The close alliance with the Conciliation Committee, the intransigence and procrastination of the Government, and the disagreements with the militants—all that had been part of the struggle in 1910—were to be repeated again in 1911 and 1912. But there were changes. The NUWSS, severely tried by the Government's duplicitous attitude to the Conciliation Bill, lost all confidence in the Liberal Party. And as the antics of the militants grew wilder, the NUWSS and the Conciliation Committee finally had to abandon any hope that the unity of the suffrage movement could be preserved.   During this period the NUWSS came of age as an organization. It firmly established its leadership in the suffrage movement and developed the confidence to break away from its own past and forge a new strategy for winning the vote.

As 1911 opened, it was clear to the NUWSS that the prospects for the Conciliation Bill in the new year were at best uncertain.[1]   On the positive side, there were more suffragists in the new House than there had been in the old, and the distribution of seats continued to favor a nonparty measure along the lines of the Conciliation Bill.[2] Asquith had pledged that facilities would be given in the new Parliament for effectively proceeding with a bill for women's suffrage. The promise was vague, but the suffragists hoped they could convince the Prime Minister to honor it this session: the Parliament Bill would be out of the way by summer and time would be available for facilities for the Conciliation Bill.   There was even a good chance that Asquith might resign because of difficulties with the Parliament Bill, and that Haldane or Grey, both suffragists, would replace him.[3]   If that were to happen, the outlook for the Conciliation Bill would improve dramatically.

Although loath to admit it, the NUWSS recognized that the liabilities of the Conciliation Bill far outweighed its assets.   In

---

[1]Millicent Garrett Fawcett, "The Political Outlook for Women's Suffrage," Englishwoman, 9 (January 1911): 2; NUWSS, Ex. com. mins., February 2, 1911, Fawcett Library, London.

[2]C. C., February 9, 1911; Daily Chronicle, February 25, 1911.

[3]Fawcett, "The Political Outlook for Women's Suffrage," p. 6.

January 1911 Cabinet support for women's suffrage was on the wane. Both Grey and Lloyd George had refused to promise to work for facilities for any women's suffrage bill in 1911 and confidently predicted that other issues would fully occupy the Government for the next two years.[4] Uncertainty about the intentions of the militants compounded the suffragists' worries about the Cabinet. The WSPU had not yet agreed to extend its truce with the Government, and a resumption of militancy would only arouse antagonism within the Cabinet and endanger the Conciliation Bill. Augustine Birrell, a suffragist, claimed that the WSPU's November raids had incensed Liberal suffragists and admitted to C. P. Scott, the editor of the Manchester Guardian, that he was so enraged by their actions that he was "quite prepared to see the suffrage question shelved in this Parliament and indefinitely postponed."[5] If the Conciliation Bill was to be successful in the House of Commons, it would need the support of a large block of Liberal MP's; thus, the suffragists could not risk the alienation of Liberal votes.

Within the Liberal Party the adult suffragists were encouraging their suffragist colleagues to jettison the Conciliation Bill. Led by W. H. Dickinson, a cabal of Liberals agitated for a women's suffrage bill that would enfranchise married women as joint occupiers with their husbands; such a measure would add some 6,000,000 women to the electorate.[6] Not surprisingly, this proposal appealed to many Liberal and Labour MP's who considered the Conciliation Bill too narrow and feared that the women whom it would enfranchise would vote for the Tory Party. The NUWSS and the Conciliation Committee opposed the Dickinson plan because they thought it was too extreme to pass the House of Commons: moderate suffragists would never support such a sweeping measure, and most Conservatives would regard it as anathema. Yet, if such a measure was available as an alternative to the Conciliation Bill, many members of the Liberal and Labour parties would favor the more radical proposal.[7]

Added to the machinations of the adult suffragists, the indifference of Liberal ministers, and the threat of renewed militancy,

---

[4]Fred Leventhal, "The Conciliation Committee," p. 142.

[5]British Museum, Scott Papers, Add. Mss. 50901, Diary of C. P. Scott, February 2, 1911 (hereafter cited as Scott diary).

[6]Dickinson introduced this bill, entitled the Women's Enfranchisement (No. 2) Bill, for its first reading on April 5, 1911. H. C. Deb. 5s, vol. 23, April 5, 1911, c. 2279.

[7]Both Brailsford and the NUWSS continued to believe that the House of Commons would not pass any measure for women's suffrage which was more comprehensive than the Conciliation Bill. For this reason they continued to favor the "limited" measure.

the Conciliation Bill was also, it appeared, being threatened by the possibility of a referendum on the subject of women's suffrage. The National League for Opposing Woman's Suffrage (NLOWS) was urging Asquith to adopt this course, and supporters of the Conciliation Bill feared that the Government were almost unanimous in agreeing that women's suffrage was a good subject for such a test.[8] The NUWSS was very pessismistic about the outcome of a referendum, and it realized that an adverse vote on the question would kill the Conciliation Bill.[9]

Assessing the balance sheet on the Conciliation Bill, the NUWSS recognized that there was little hope for the measure in 1911. The suffragists were reasonably confident that the measure would be given a second reading, but doubted that it would get any further facilities. They decided that they must continue their partnership with the Conciliation Committe nonetheless and lobby for the bill—hoping, as before, that a show of public enthusiasm for the measure combined with a substantial majority on the second reading might be enough to persuade the Government to give the bill full facilities. This logic may have underestimated Asquith's perfervid opposition to the women's cause and overrated Liberal support for the Conciliation solution, but since the Conciliation Bill, as the Labour Leader pointed out, still offered the only hope for solving the suffrage question, it would have to be tried once again. "Obviously the Bill is a compromise," the Labour Leader noted, "—an honourable compromise—but it is a measure not in the clouds but on the table of the House of Commons, and is the only measure of Women's Suffrage likely to become law for some time."[10] There were also no indications that force, rather than persuasion, would "squeeze" the Government to look more favorably on the women's cause: neither the stick of the militants nor the carrot of the constitutionalists provided the key to the tactical dilemma of how, in 1911, the women could wrest women's suffrage from the House of Commons.

Throughout the first weeks of 1911, preparations went ahead for the first reading of the Conciliation Bill. Unfortunately, none of the MP's who were pledged to bring in the bill had been successful in the ballot, but through a comic twist of fate, the member who had won first place in the ballot withdrew, and Sir George Kemp (Lib., N.W. Manchester), who had won second place, was prevailed upon by the NUWSS,

---

[8]The Times, February 13 and 21, 1911. The NLOWS was confident that women's suffrage would be defeated in such a referendum. Brian Harrison, Separate Spheres, p. 160.

[9]FLAC, vol. 1, Hii, Eleanor Rathbone to Helen Ward, July 23, 1910, Fawcett Library, London.

[10]Labour Leader, February 24, 1911. By this writing, however, relations between Brailsford and the Pankhursts had improved and the WSPU had agreed to extend the truce. Leventhal, p. 142.

and its affiliate, the Manchester Society for Women's Suffrage, to introduce the bill.[11] In an effort to appease the bill's critics and to obtain wider support for the measure, the Conciliation Committee had made some not insignificant modifications in the original bill: the £10 qualification had been dropped, and, with an eye to Asquith and Lloyd George, the Committee had altered the title so that the bill could be amended; also, to eliminate Churchills' bogy, the faggot vote, the new bill prohibited a husband and wife from registering in the same parliamentary borough or county constituency. As Brailsford noted, the Conciliation Bill of 1911 embodied the simplest, most widely accepted franchise—the household qualification. Describing the virtues of this qualification, he wrote: "It is better understood than any other. It was the great gift of Conservatives and Radicals in 1867. It will give a vote to every woman, rich or poor, who is the head of her house, and the mistress of her own offices—to every woman who is the tenant even of one room over which she can prove that she has full control."[12]

The first reading of the Conciliation Bill took place on February 9.[13] As the suffragists expected, the bill passed this test and was scheduled to be read a second time on May 5. The NUWSS was confident that the bill would pass its second reading as well, but it wanted it to do so with such a large majority that the Government would seriously have to consider granting additional facilities to the bill that session. Thus, from February to May, the NUWSS lobbied to win support for the bill.

As in 1910, the NUWSS worked in close cooperation with the Conciliation Committee and used its own large network of affiliates to propagandize for the bill in the constituencies. At Brailsford's behest the NUWSS also directed all its affiliates to obtain resolutions in support of the Conciliation Bill from town, county, and district councils, the object being to convince the councils "to petition for

---

[11]NUWSS, Ex. com. mins., February 16, 1911; National Union of Women's Suffrage Societies, Annual Report, 1911 (London, 1912), p. 32. According to one journalist, an Irish Member "who thought he was balloting for tickets for the Ladies' Gallery" won first place and later withdrew when he discovered his mistake. B. F. Cholmeley, "The Parliamentary Situation", Englishwoman, 9, no. 27 (March 1911): 241.

[12]C. C., February 9, 1911. These changes met most of the criticisms which had been leveled at the bill in 1910, and, as the debate on May 5 was to show, they effectively silenced some of the more persuasive and eloquent arguments formulated by the critics.

[13]H. C. Deb. 5s, vol. 21, February 9, 1911, c. 452.

facilities for the Bill."[14]   The affiliates attacked this challenge with great enthusiasm and persuaded 146 councils to support the bill.[15] The London Society for Women's Suffrage maintained that the resolutions pressured MP's into supporting the bill and produced statistics which showed a direct correlation between the council resolutions and the votes of MP's.[16]

The NUWSS also directly confronted Members of the House and asked their support for the bill.[17]   In this work, as with the council resolutions, the NUWSS kept in close touch with the Conciliation Committee and put its organizational resources at the Committee's disposal. Brailsford supplied the NUWSS with the names of MP's whose vote on the second reading was in some doubt, and the NUWSS in turn sent on information about the attitudes of MP's to the affiliates, asking them to give special attention to those who seemed to be wavering in their support for the bill. The affiliates then painstakingly courted MP's, by both letter and deputation, duly reporting the results of these labors to headquarters.[18] When the vote came on the second reading of the bill, many of the affiliates claimed that their work had directly influenced the votes of MP's.[19]

To capture the attention of the House of Commons and win public support for the bill, the NUWSS sponsored a variety of suffrage activities in the winter and spring of 1911—public meetings, garden

---

[14]Correspondence of the National Union of Women's Suffrage Societies, 1911, Circular from Kathleen Courtney, February 9, 1911, Fawcett Library, London.

[15]National Union of Women's Suffrage Societies, Annual Report, 1911, pp. 19-20.

[16]London Society for Women's Suffrage, Annual Report, 1911 (London, n.d.), pp. 8-9.

[17]NUWSS, Ex. com. mins., February 16, April 27, and May 4, 1911, Fawcett Library, London.

[18]See Correspondence of the National Union of Women's Suffrage Societies, 1911, Kathleen Courtney to Philippa Strachey, February 9, 1911, and Philippa Strachey to T. G. Whitehead, February 14, 1911; Correspondence concerning the Conciliation Bill, 1911, Circular from the London Society for Women's Suffrage, May 4, 1911; FLAC, vol. 1, Ji, J. Sidney Buxton to Miss Deverall, April 28, 1911; Correspondence of the London Society for Women's Suffrage with its branch societies, passim; all in the Fawcett Library, London.

[19]See, for example, Correspondence concerning the Conciliation Bill, 1911, Philippa Strachey to Millicent Garrett Fawcett, November 30, 1911, Fawcett Library, London.

parties, at-homes, and suffrage plays—and it also sponsored a National Convention in London to dramatize support for the measure.[20] The convention, attended by 268 representatives from the affiliates, drafted a resolution demanding full facilities for the bill.[21] In addition to these activities, the NUWSS participated in seven by-elections, using these occasions to work for the return of candidates who supported the bill.[22] It sent speakers to women's organizations, such as the Women's Liberal Association and the Women's Co-Operative Guild, to enlist their support for the measure, and it took particular pains to strengthen its ties with the Irish Women's Suffrage and Local Government Society.[23] The NUWSS recognized that the Nationalists could prove influential in persuading the Prime Minister to give full facilities to the bill, and it hoped to work through the Irish suffrage organization to secure the support of Irish MP's.[24] During the spring of 1911, the NUWSS not only worked to promote the bill but also tried to subvert the strategems of the NLOWS, which was promoting its referendum scheme and, using the argument that women did not want the vote, was urging MP's to vote against the Conciliation Bill. The NUWSS' counterargument was that it was unfair to make women's suffrage a "legislative experiment."[25] Through all these various activities the NUWSS tried to strengthen the hand of the Conciliation Committee in negotiating with the Liberal Government. It continued to work right up to the eve of May 5, the day that had been set for the second reading.

---

[20]For an idea of the number and variety of functions that the NUWSS organized during this period see the following: C. C., March and April 1911, passim; Manchester and District Federation, Annual Report, 1911 (Manchester, n.d.), pp. 15-40; North Eastern Federation of Women's Suffrage Societies, Annual Report, 1912 (Newcastle-upon-Tyne, n.d.), pp. 12-18.

[21]Manchester and District Federation, Annual Report, 1911, p. 12; London Society for Women's Suffrage, Annual Report, 1911, p. 12.

[22]National Union of Women's Suffrage Societies, Annual Report, 1911, p. 16. The by-elections were Horncastle, Cambridge Univ., Western Wilts. (Westbury), N.E. Lanark, Bootle, Haddington, and Cheltenham.

[23]See, for example, Correspondence concerning the Conciliation Bill, 1911, Circular regarding Miss Deverall's speech to the East St. Pancras W.L.A., May 2, 1911, Fawcett Library, London.

[24]Correspondence of the National Union of Women's Suffrage Societies, 1911, Resolutions of the Annual Council of the NUWSS, January 26, 27, 28, 1911, Fawcett Library, London.

[25]Ibid., Circular from Edith Palliser, March 2, 1911, Fawcett Library, London; The Times, May 1 and 3, 1911.

In contrast to July 1910, the debate on May 5 was almost dull. When Sir George Kemp presented the Conciliation Bill for its second reading, the front benches were nearly empty because, in the interests of saving time, the leaders of the Liberal and Conservative parties had decided not to participate in the debate.[26] Looking at the empty benches, Lord Hugh Cecil (Cons., Oxford Univ.) drily observed: "From the appearance of the Front Benches it would seem that the Olympians have determined to leave the contest and to let the Greeks and the Trojans fight it out themselves."[27] But there was no fight and it seemed as if the MP's were so certain of the outcome of the debate that they were disinclined to exert themselves. Supporters of the bill continued to emphasize its democratic aspects; in a play for Liberal votes, they promised that if the bill passed, neither its sponsors nor the women's suffrage societies would demand an immediate dissolution but would be prepared to wait until the next General Election to bring in the new register.[28] Representing the suffragist camp, Lord Hugh Cecil sternly warned the Government that many Members would be extremely displeased if the bill passed its second reading only to be denied further facilities: ". . . the House of Commons, to which the Government are always offering incense, though they offer very little besides, and to which they show the utmost respect in words, should be allowed a full and fair opportunity of deciding upon this great issue."[29] On the antisuffragist side, opponents of the bill devoted much time to expatiating on "the role of women" but, unlike 1910, made few damaging criticisms of the provisions of the bill.[30]

When the vote came, the optimism of the Conciliation Committee and the NUWSS proved more than justified; 255 MP's voted for the bill,

---

[26]Papers of Millicent Garrett Fawcett, A. J. Balfour to Millicent Garrett Fawcett, May 3, 1911, Fawcett Library, London. Philippa Strachey sarcastically commented that it was not the consideration of parliamentary time, but the Parliamentary Golf Handicap, which prompted the leaders' decision not to participate in the debate. Correspondence of the London Society for Women's Suffrage, 1911, Philippa Strachey to Lady de la Warr, May 1, 1911, Fawcett Library, London.

[27]H. C. Deb. 5s, vol. 25, May 5, 1911, c. 805.

[28]The normal procedure was to have an immediate dissolution the moment the new register was brought in. David Morgan, Suffragists and Liberals, p. 53.

[29]H. C. Deb. 5s, vol. 25, May 5, 1911, c. 806.

[30]Sir Maurice Levy (Lib., Leicester, Loughborough), for example, claimed women "prefer the sovereignty and authority of men" and thus had no desire to vote. Ibid., c. 755.

while only 88 voted against it.[31] Analyzing the vote, the NUWSS noted there were 108 MP's whom it considered suffragists who did not vote or pair on May 5, and 11 MP's who it thought favored the suffrage cause but voted or paired against the bill; in the future the NUWSS would pay particular attention to those 119 MP's.[32] The affiliates of the NUWSS were delighted by the successful vote and felt that their work had helped produce the large majority.[33] Brailsford shared their jubilance and declared that the "superb division" was "the fruit of all the unremitting work which women all over the country had been doing."[34] Fawcett was equally exuberant and wrote Lady Frances Balfour, "Yes, it really is quite glorious and I feel we are nearing the end of our long fight."[35]

Both Brailsford and Fawcett, for all their delight at the victory, were very aware that the successful division did not guarantee that the Government would give time to the bill; a re-enactment of 1910 was entirely possible. Brailsford was anxious to persuade Cabinet ministers to support the demand for facilities--particularly the Chancellor of the Exchecquer, Lloyd George, whose well-known powers of persuasion would be very useful. Brailsford urged the NUWSS to do everything possible to cajole their old opponent Lloyd George into their camp and suggested that flattery and praise for the insurance scheme might beguile him into working for facilities for the Conciliation Bill: "He is sore at all the treatment he has received from suffragists both militant and nonmilitant. That phase was inevitable and even salutory. But I see the chance of ending it. I

---

[31]Ibid., c. 806. The breakdown on the vote, including the pairs, was as follows: For--170 Lib., 78 Cons., 31 Nat., 31 Lab. Against--48 Lib., 86 Cons., 9 Nat. The bill received a larger majority than any Government measure obtained in the same session.

[32]In the first category there were 42 Lib., 40 Cons., 17 Nat., 9 Lab.; in the second category there were 6 Lib., 4 Cons., 1 Nat. Correspondence concerning the Conciliation Bill, 1911, List of Miss Edith Palliser analyzing the vote of May 5, 1911, Fawcett Library, London.

[33]Correspondence concerning the Conciliation Bill, 1911, Philippa Strachey to Millicent Garrett Fawcett, November 30, 1911; Surrey, Sussex, and Hants Federation, Annual Report, 1912 (Southsea, n.d.), p. 6.

[34]Archives, Manchester Public Library M/50, Box 10, H. N. Brailsford to Millicent Garrett Fawcett, May 7, [1911].

[35]FLAC, vol. 1, Ji, Millicent Garrett Fawcett to Lady Frances Balfour, May 6, 1911, Fawcett Library, London.

think the insurance scheme is the golden opportunity. The moment he thinks he can be the hero of the women of England our Bill will pass."[36]

Like Brailsford, Fawcett was determined to do everything possible to press the Government for facilities for the bill; she was concerned that if the Conciliation Bill did not pass through all its stages this session, it would not receive the protection of the provisions of the Parliament bill before the next dissolution.[37] At her direction NUWSS headquarters ordered the affiliates to try and persuade MP's to lobby for parliamentary time for the bill. Edith Palliser, parliamentary secretary of the NUWSS, urged the branches to pay special attention to Liberal MP's, and she asked them to work through both Men's and Women's Liberal Associations to press for facilities. The NUWSS predicted that the more "pressure we can bring to bear from the constituencies upon the Prime Minister and the MPs," the greater the likelihood that time would be given to the Conciliation Bill.[38]

Throughout May the pressure on the Government to grant facilities to the Conciliation Bill increased. Such diverse groups as the London University Convocation, the Dublin Corporation, and the Women's Liberal Federation urged the Government to give time for the bill.[39] Suffragist MP's convincingly argued that there was time available, and one such MP, Lord Robert Cecil, pointed out that this was the ideal moment for Parliament to enact a women's suffrage bill:

Everyone knows that it is inconceivable that any better opportunity than the present will be found for giving effect to that pledge. Will the Government act up to their promises, or are we to be met by further evasions? We heard much recently about the difference between the male and female sense of honour. If facilities for the Bill are again withheld, women may rightly thank God that such a difference exists.[40]

The Committee of Liberal Suffragist MP's echoed Cecil's sentiments and urged Asquith to grant the time necessary to carry the bill through all

---

[36]Archives, Manchester Public Library, M/50, Box 10, H. N. Brailsford to Millicent Garrett Fawcett, May 7, [1911].

[37]Millicent Garrett Fawcett, "Women's Suffrage: The Political Situation," Englishwoman, 10, no. 30 (June 1911): 243.

[38]Correspondence of the National Union of Women's Suffrage Societies, 1911, Circular from Edith Palliser, May 17, 1911, Fawcett Library, London.

[39]The Times, May 10 and 11, 1911; H. C. Deb. 5s, vol. 25, May 12, 1911, c. 1529.

[40]The Times, May 9, 1911.

its stages. The Conciliation Committee pressed the Prime Minister to receive a deputation to discuss the bill; if Asquith hedged on the question of facilities, the Committee intended to ask for time to put the matter to a division of the House by way of a resolution reaffirming its desire to proceed effectively with the bill this year. Sir Edward Grey had promised that if such a resolution were carried, he would ask that the bill be given a week in August.[41]

Faced by this clamorous demand for facilities, the Government could not indefinitely postpone consideration of the fate of the Conciliation Bill. On May 14 the Cabinet held a long discussion about the bill. Grey, Runciman, Haldane, and Birrell wanted the House to decide by vote whether it wished to proceed with the bill this year, while Loreburn, Lloyd George, and McKenna--supported by a majority of the Cabinet--opposed the suggestion. A final decision on the matter was postponed until the following week.[42] On May 24 the Cabinet again examined the issue and decided to refuse the Conciliation Bill additional facilities in the current session; it agreed, however, "to undertake to give a week for its consideration (after second reading) in next session."[43] The ostensible reason for the Government's decision was lack of time: the Government maintained it could not give facilities to the bill without endangering other legislative proposals. But the real reasons were highly political: divisions within the party, and, more particularly, within the Cabinet, over the question of women's suffrage, as well as reservations about the provisions of the bill and the possible effect of the bill on the fortunes of the Liberal Party. On May 29 Lloyd George announced the Cabinet's decision in the House of Commons: ". . . they could not allot to the Woman Suffrage Bill this year such an amount of time as its importance demands. They will be prepared next session, when the Bill has again been read a second time . . . to give a week (which they understand to be the time suggested as reasonable by the promoters), for its further stages."[44]

Not surprisingly, this announcement infuriated the Conciliation Committee and the NUWSS. At Brailsford's suggestion the NUWSS executive issued a resolution expressing its belief that the Government had once again betrayed the suffragists. The scenario was altogether too familiar to the NUWSS; the Government had given pledges to the suffragists, the bill had passed its second reading, the Government had waffled on its promises, and the Conciliation Bill had once again been

---

[41]Correspondence of the National Union of Women's Suffrage Societies, 1911, Circular from Edith Palliser, May 20, 1911, Fawcett Library, London.

[42]CAB 41/33/15, May 14, 1911.

[43]CAB 41/33/16, May 24, 1911.

[44]H. C. Deb. 5s, vol. 25, May 29, 1911, cc. 703-4.

postponed. The suffragists were uneasy about the "week" promised to the bill next session and wanted the Government to clarify the particulars. Did the Government mean a week for all stages, or only for the committee stage? Would it provide for a closure resolution? Would it give time for the third reading of the bill early in the session so that the bill could go to the House of Lords that session? Until the Government elaborated on these questions, Lloyd George's vague promise would not satisfy the suffragists.[45]

Sir Edward Grey's reply on June 1 was convincing enough to raise the morale of the whole suffrage movement.[46] Grey assured the suffragists that this was not another "bogus offer," and that the week promised to the bill would be "elastic"; the Government had, he declared, given a "real opportunity" to the suffragists.[47] On June 17 the doubts of the suffragists were further allayed and their spirits buoyed by a letter from Asquith to Lytton which substantiated Grey's declaration:

It follows that "the week" offered will be interpreted with reasonable elasticity, that the Government will interpose no obstacle to a proper use of closure, and that if, as you suggest, the Bill gets through Committee in the time proposed, the extra days required for Report and Third Reading would not be refused.

The Government, though divided in opinion on the merits of the Bill, are unanimous in their determination to give effect, not only in the letter, but in the spirit, to the promise in regard to facilities which I made on their behalf before the last General Election.[48]

Thus in the summer of 1911 , the NUWSS was more optimistic about the fate of the Conciliation Bill than it had ever been before: Asquith and Grey had disseminated the "mist of ambiguities" surrounding the question of facilities for the Conciliation Bill and had convinced the suffragists that there was a "real opportunity" for this measure.[49] Although the executive committee had decided to abandon all efforts to gain a further hearing for the bill in the current parliamentary

---

[45]Correspondence of the National Union of Women's Suffrage Societies, 1911, Circular from Edith Palliser and Kathleen Courtney, June 1, 1911, Fawcett Library, London.

[46]Bodleian Library, Nevinson Journals, e616, June 2, 1911.

[47]The Times, June 2, 1911.

[48]Ibid., June 17, 1911.

[49]Millicent Garrett Fawcett, as quoted in ibid., June 3, 1911.

session, its members were confident that the bill would go through all its stages in the first session of 1912.[50] Fawcett declared, "we are higher up on the ladder of success than we have ever been before."[51]

The WSPU was quite as jubilant as the NUWSS. Christabel Pankhurst described Asquith's pronouncement as "a pledge upon which women can base the expectation of taking part as voters in the election of the next and every future Parliament," and the WSPU, "full of hope and joy" and confident of the Government's good intentions, suspended its anti-Liberal by-election policy.[52] The old spirit of unity among the suffragists, for two years so missing, reappeared. On June 17 the suffrage organizations staged a spectacular procession which demonstrated both the magnitude and the new cohesiveness of the movement; 40,000 women, stretched in a procession five miles long, marched from the Embankment to the Albert Hall. The Times commented: "The surprise of the demonstration, however, was the unexpected strength of the constitutionalists which it showed. The Women's Social and Political Union and the Women's Freedom League combined were outnumbered and overshadowed by the National Union of Women's Suffrage Societies."[53] Here was a testimonial to all the work that the NUWSS had done on behalf of the Conciliation Bill.

In a very real sense the suffragists' optimism about the prospects of women's suffrage was justified. Within the Cabinet suffragist sentiment was growing stronger. Although Asquith was still adamantly opposed to the very idea of women's suffrage, he had given a public pledge that the Conciliation Bill would have full facilities next session; it seemed unlikely that the Prime Minister would renege on so explicit a promise. Churchill and Lloyd George were a problem, of course. The NUWSS had given up all hope of converting Churchill, but it had not yet written off Lloyd George and believed it could woo him to support the bill. As Brailsford had pointed out, Lloyd George was perhaps the most influential man in the Liberal Party, and his approval of the bill would carry considerable weight with his colleagues.

As the summer wore on, the NUWSS grew even more hopeful about the prospects of women's suffrage in the next session. In August the Government at last won their battle with the House of Lords. With the passage of the Parliament Act, the Liberals could no longer use the

[50]NUWSS, Ex. com. mins., June 29, 1911, Fawcett Library, London.

[51]Millicent Garrett Fawcett, "Women's Suffrage: The Political Situation," Englishwoman, 10, no. 30 (June 1911): 241.

[52]F. W. Pethick-Lawrence, Fate Has Been Kind, p. 252; Bodleian Library, Nevinson Journals, e616, June 18, 1911; Andrew Rosen, Rise Up, Women!, p. 150.

[53]The Times, June 19, 1911.

constitutional crisis as an excuse to delay women's suffrage; moreover, the Government could now attend to other parts of their program, including electoral reform. The Court of Appeals reversal of the Kent versus Fittall decision, with its redefinition of "the latchkey voter," combined with the Liberals' desire to eliminate the plural voter, virtually guaranteed that the Government would introduce some measure of electoral reform in the next session of Parliament.[54] Given the suffragist sentiment in the Cabinet, it would be difficult for the Government to tackle this issue without considering the claims of the proponents of women's suffrage.

Finally, the NUWSS believed that the militants' decision to continue the truce could not but help the suffrage cause. The suggragettes' violent actions, and their anti-Liberal by-election policy, had outraged many MP's, while providing others with a convenient excuse to oppose the Conciliation Bill. With suffragists and suffragettes joined in a united front, opponents of women's suffrage could no longer play one faction of the suffrage movement against the other nor use militancy as a "red flag" to wave in front of MP's to encourage them to oppose women's suffrage. In the summer of 1911, the NUWSS began, on an unprecedented scale, to cooperate with the militants, working with them at by-elections and staging meetings and processions throughout the country.[55] The divisions of the past were forgotten; the display of unity could only be an asset to the suffrage movement.

From July to October 1911, the NUWSS concentrated its energies on building up parliamentary support for the Conciliation Bill. Although the bill would not come before the House of Commons until 1912, the NUWSS believed that continuous pressure must be applied on MP's to ensure a sucessful vote on the bill: the task before the NUWSS

---

[54]Morgan, pp. 80-82; National Union of Women's Suffrage Societies, Annual Report, 1911, p. 35; Votes for Women, September 22, 1911. The court's decision meant that a lodger with his own door key could be considered a householder. The Government hoped to gain this "householder" vote. There were approximately 500,000 plural voters. The Liberals had for some time wished to eliminate the plural voting system, which benefited the Conservative Party. Martin Pugh, Electoral Reform in War and Peace, 1906-1918, pp. 1-2, 31-32.

[55]For examples of this cooperation see: North and East Ridings Federation, Annual Report, 1911-1912 (Whitby, n.d.), p. 10; West Midland Federation, Annual Report, 1911-1912 (n.p., n.d.), p. 12; North Eastern Federation, Annual Report, 1912, p. 7.

was "the consolidation of the majority for the Conciliation Bill."[56]
As in the past, the local affiliates sent deputations to MP's,
sponsored meetings and lectures, organized suffragist caravan tours,
did propaganda work among a variety of political associations, sent
speakers to social and educational groups, and worked at by-
elections.[57] NUWSS headquarters continued to keep in close contact
with the Conciliation Committee, and Brailsford depended on the
suffrage organization both to lobby for the bill and to act as a
liaison between the commitee and the parliamentary constituencies.[58]

Most of the NUWSS propagandist and lobbying activities in this
period were directed toward the Liberal Party. The July Council of the
NUWSS ordered the affiliates to devote special attention to the local
Liberal associations, particularly the Women's Liberal Federation, and
to persuade them to pressure Liberal MP's to support the Conciliation
Bill.[59] The main threat to the Conciliation Bill would be within the
Liberal Party, notably Liberal MP's who wished to "widen" the bill; by
Brailsford's estimate, the fate of the bill depended on the votes of
seventy to eighty Liberals who were good suffragists, but had qualms
about the narrowness of the Conciliation Bill.[60] The NUWSS realized
that the bill was limited, but continued to feel that, without the
official support of the Liberal Party, no wider suffrage measure would
pass the House of Commons. The Conciliation Bill had been successful
both in 1910 and 1911 because it commanded Conservative support, and
the NUWSS predicted that any attempt to widen the measure would

---

[56]Archives, Manchester Public Library, M/50, Box 1, Circular
from Edith Palliser and Kathleen Courtney, October 3, 1911.

[57]National Union of Women's Suffrage Societies, Annual Report,
1911, pp. 17-18; London Society for Women's Suffrage, Annual Report,
1911, p. 11; Manchester Federation, Annual Report, 1911, p. 14; North
Eastern Federation, Annual Report, 1912, pp. 7, 9, 11.

[58]For evidence of this collaboration see NUWSS, Ex. com. mins.,
September 14, October 19, and November 2, 1911, Fawcett Library,
London.

[59]Correspondence of the National Union of Women's Suffrage
Societies, 1911, Memorandum on the Provincial Council held on July 7
and 8, 1911; NUWSS, Ex. com. mins., August 3, 1911; Fawcett Library,
London.

[60]Archives, Manchester Public Library, M/50, Box 1, H. N.
Brailsford, "Memorandum on the Present Position of the Conciliation
Bill," October 2, 1911.

alienate the Tories.[61] As Brailsford noted, if this happened, "the Bill from that moment is lost."[62]

Doubts about the solidity of Liberal support for the Conciliation Bill had been confirmed on July 19, when the NUWSS received word that the Liberal suffragists were considering adopting a bill that would enfranchise householders and wives of householders, or, if this proved infeasible, would attempt to attach "widening" amendments to the Conciliation Bill. This was a political ploy of Lloyd George's. At Brailsford's request the NUWSS contacted all Liberal MP's, reminding them that the authors of the Conciliation Bill had already made concessions to the Liberals and that there were not enough Liberal suffragists to carry a measure which did not take into account Conservative prejudices; if the Liberal suffragists wished a more comprehensive measure of women's suffrage, they would have the opportunity to secure this when the Government introduced its proposed Reform Bill.[63] Fortunately, the NUWSS arguments proved persuasive and the Liberal suffragists voted to continue their support for the Conciliation Bill.[64]

Lloyd George was a tenacious combatant, however, and the persuasive powers of this "Welsh wizard" seemed endless. His hints that he might be able to convince the Government to give official support to the Conciliation Bill if its provisions were extended were

----

[61]Correspondence of the National Union of Women's Suffrage Societies, 1911, Millicent Garrett Fawcett, "Parliament and the Conciliation Bill: A Plea for Firmness," October 3, 1911; Circular from Edith Palliser, July 25, 1911; Fawcett Library, London. On July 20, the Conservative suffragists met and agreed to resist any amendment that would extend the provisions of the Conciliation bill. The Times, July 21, 1911.

[62]Archives, Manchester Public Library, M/50, Box 1, H. N. Brailsford, "Memorandum on the Present Position of the Conciliation Bill," October 2, 1911.

[63]NUWSS, Ex. com. mins., July 20, 1911, Fawcett Library, London. The NUWSS estimated that within the Liberal and Nationalist Parties there were 65 confirmed antisuffragists, and it felt certain that if the Conciliation Bill were widened, the Conservatives would combine with these antisuffragists to defeat it. The Conciliation Committee shared this opinion. Archives, Manchester Public Library, M/50, Box 1, Circular from the Earl of Lytton, August 10, 1911.

[64]NUWSS, Ex. com. mins., July 20, 1911, Fawcett Library, London.

very alarming.[65] In August the Chancellor of the Exchequer announced in the House of Commons that the Government's promise of facilities did not apply exclusively to the Conciliation Bill, but to any women's suffrage bill which passed a second reading and could be amended.[66] Much to the suffragists' relief, Asquith let it be known that he was standing by his June promise. Lytton wrote Fawcett: "Mr. Lloyd George is quietly put aside and there can no longer be any question that the promise was given to our Bill and will be fulfilled in due course."[67]

But Lloyd George was far from having been "quietly put aside." Ostensibly, Lloyd George opposed the Conciliation scheme because it discriminated against the working class, but his real reason was political: he feared the bill would benefit the Tories. In June 1911, Lloyd George had told C. P. Scott that he favored giving the vote to all joint householders, and that he felt he could rally the party behind such a measure.[68] By September he was considering his women's suffrage scheme within the context of large-scale electoral reform. On September 5 he wrote the Master of Elibank and asked him to ascertain the Liberal agents' opinions on the defects of the present electoral system. Lloyd George was particularly concerned about the Conciliation Bill and complained that it would add "hundreds of thousands of votes" to the Conservative Party:

I think the Liberal Party ought to make up its mind as a whole that it will either have an extended franchise which would put working men's wives on to the Register, as well as spinsters and widows, or that it will have no female franchise at all. . . . we are likely to find ourselves in the position of putting this wretched Conciliation Bill through the House of Commons, sending it to the Lords, and eventually getting it through. Say what you will, that spells disaster to

---

[65]See C. C., August 3, 1911; Manchester Society for Women's Suffrage, Annual Report, 1912, p. 14; Correspondence of the National Union of Women's Suffrage Societies, 1911, Millicent Garrett Fawcett, "Parliament and the Conciliation Bill: A Plea for Firmness," October 3, 1911, Fawcett Library, London.

[66]H. C. Deb. 5s, vol. 29, August 16, 1911, cc. 1913-14.

[67]FLAC, vol. 1, Hii, the Earl of Lytton to Millicent Garrett Fawcett, August 24, 1911, Fawcett Library, London.

[68]Scott diary, June 15, 1911.

Liberalism and unless you take it in hand and take it at once, this catastrophe is inevitable.[69]

Lloyd George's worries were echoed by the Liberal agents, who, according to J. Renwick Seager, head of the Registration Department at Liberal headquarters, were "emphatically adverse" to the Conciliation Bill.[70]

To Lloyd George the issue was clear-cut: either there would be no women's suffrage, or there would be a comprehensive measure of women's suffrage. Lloyd George was certainly not prepared to sacrifice the Liberal Party for the women's cause, but he did have some sympathy for the suffragists and the goal they sought to achieve, and he therefore chose to work for an extensive measure of women's suffrage. He knew that although Asquith would never agree to include women's suffrage as part of a Government Reform Bill, he would allow such a bill to be amended in favor of votes for women and he believed that he could use his influence to push such amendments through the House of

---

[69]David Lloyd George to Alexander Murray, Master of Elibank, September 5, 1911, as quoted in Morgan, p. 82. Pugh, p. 35, indicates there was no factual basis for this assumption. See also Chapter 2, note 34 above.
In 1911 the Conciliation Committee, in order to prove "that the Bill was not a measure for giving 'votes to ladies,'" took a census of women householders in Bangor, Carnarvon, and Dundee. The object of the survey was to ascertain the social position of women householders. In Dundee, 89.1 percent of these women were working class; in Bangor and Carnarvon, 75 percent were working class. On the basis of these findings, the Committee estimated that in these constituencies, eight out of every ten women enfranchised by the Conciliation Bill would belong to the working class. Philip Snowden, In Defense of the Conciliation Bill, NUWSS pamphlet (n.p., n.d.).

[70]CAB 37/108/148, Report of J. Renwick Seager, November 8, 1911. Seager had canvassed the secretaries of twelve Liberal Federations to ask their views on three aspects of the franchise: the value of a simple residential qualification, the impact of current registration laws on the Liberal Party, and the potential consequences of the Conciliation Bill on the electoral fortunes of the Liberals. Seager's report is interesting not only because it shows the Liberal agents' hostility to the Conciliation Bill, but also because it reveals some of the prejudices and suspicions that surrounded women's suffrage. The Liberal agents obviously had mixed feelings about the whole issue of women's suffrage. They declared that "religious bigotry would find a ready response among the women" and that women would vote for "Temperance, Social Reform, and Peace." The agents' attitude to women's suffrage is paradoxical: their analysis of the Conciliation Bill shows they believed women would vote along class lines, yet in other parts of their report they treat the women's vote as a single block and indicate that sex is a more important demarcation than class.

Commons. The task would be to convince the suffragists to jettison the Conciliation Bill and throw their support to his plan of amending the Reform Bill. Accordingly, on October 26 Lloyd George approached C. P. Scott with a "deal": if supporters of the Conciliation Bill would endorse his idea of a Reform Bill which could be amended to enfranchise women, he would agree not to oppose the Conciliation Bill, should such an amendment fail to pass the House of Commons. To make his point clear, he threatened to use every means in his power to defeat the Conciliation Bill if the suffragists rejected his plan; his opposition, he assured Scott, combined with that of Churchill, Harcourt, Chamberlain, Smith, and Long, would kill the Conciliation Bill.

At Lloyd George's request Scott communicated this proposal to the Conciliation Committee and the NUWSS.[71] Brailsford was not enthusiastic about the proposal. He was worried that the militants, who thoroughly distrusted Lloyd George, would oppose any project connected with him; moreover, he feared the Conservatives would desert the Conciliation Bill if the Committee endorsed Lloyd George's scheme.[72] Caught between Scylla and Charybdis, Brailsford assented to Lloyd George's plan, with the proviso that the Chancellor would promise to give active support to the Conciliation Bill if the women's suffrage amendments to the Reform Bill were defeated. Obviously worried about the reaction of the WSPU, Brailsford was determined to keep these negotiations with Lloyd George "absolutely secret" until a firm agreement had been made.[73]

The reactions of the NUWSS were far more enthusiastic than those of Brailsford. Courtney and Swanwick, whom Scott informed of the proposal, "hailed the prospect as opening up a new and far better prospect of success" and were confident that Fawcett would support the plan.[74] The suffragists were cognizant of Lloyd George's immense prestige and felt that his active involvement in the suffrage cause would be a tremendous asset; as Swanwick wrote Maud Arncliffe-Sennett: "We have suffered immensely from the lack of driving force within the

---

[71]Scott diary, November 16, 1911. Scott's diary flatly contradicts Morgan's assertion that "there also exists no evidence that the suffragists expected that the Government was reviving the whole electoral issue." Morgan, p. 83.

[72]According to Nevinson, by the end of October 1911 relations between the WSPU and Brailsford had become strained. (Bodleian Library, Nevinson Journals, e616, October 31, 1911.) Not surprisingly, Brailsford was reluctant to do anything that would further jeopardize his relations with the militants; he knew the Pankhursts hated Lloyd George. Scott diary, November 16, 1911.

[73]Leventhal, p. 148.

[74]Scott diary, November 16, 1911.

House and if anything we can do can help to engage Lloyd George so deeply that he can't get out--why, I want to do it."[75] Whatever reservations some of the suffragists may have had privately about Lloyd George's morals or methods, they could not doubt his influence in the party or in the Cabinet.[76] The NUWSS had tried, unsuccessfully, to persuade prominent suffragists in the Cabinet, such as Haldane and Grey, to be more vocal and active in espousing the cause.[77] They had not expected support from Lloyd George, but they certainly were prepared to look favorably on any proposal which enlisted him in the suffragist ranks.

The women's suffrage issue had forced the Government to "undertake a comprehensive measure at a time when they would not otherwise have done so for lack of parliamentary time"; on November 7 Asquith informed a group of adult suffragists that next session the Government intended to introduce a franchise bill that would give universal manhood suffrage.[78] He assured them that the bill could be amended to include votes for women. The NUWSS had expected this announcement. After conferring with Brailsford, it issued a statement which criticized the exclusion of women from the proposed Reform Bill, and announced that the NUWSS would work to amend the bill in favor of women; it added that the suffragist forces did not intend to abandon the Conciliation Bill until they had seen how women fared in the Reform Bill.[79]

At this time the NUWSS had two immediate goals: to determine the exact terms on which the Government would accept amendments to the Reform Bill, and to enlist Cabinet support for the proposed women's suffrage amendments. On November 17, representatives from the NUWSS participated in a deputation to Asquith, the purpose of which was to elicit information about the Reform Bill. In answer to Fawcett's queries, Asquith promised that the Reform Bill would go through all its

---

[75]British Museum, Arncliffe-Sennett Collection, vol. 15, Helena M. Swanwick to Maud Arncliffe-Sennett, November 10, 1911.

[76]In November, Helena Swanwick made most unflattering comments about Lloyd George to her husband: "I get so horribly depressed at having to use such a man I can't get over the nausea of having to treat him more or less as a friend." Helena M. Swanwick, I Have Been Young p. 215.

[77]Papers of Emily Davies, Emily Davies to Philippa Strachey, October 20, 1911, Fawcett Library, London.

[78]Pugh, p. 36; The Times, November 7, 1911.

[79]NUWSS, Ex. com. mins., November 9, 1911, Fawcett Library, London.

stages in 1912, and that it would be drafted in such a way that women could be enfranchised on different qualifications from those that enfranchised men. He pledged that the Government would not oppose women's suffrage amendments, and said that if such an amendment were carried, the Government would regard it as an integral part of the bill. This last promise was particularly important, because it meant the Government would bear responsibility for piloting women's suffrage through the House of Lords.[80]

The NUWSS delegation left the interview feeling pleased at the way in which Asquith had clarified his intentions in regard to the bill. The next step was to convince members of the Cabinet to come out in strong support of the women's suffrage amendments: the chief targets were Lloyd George and Sir Edward Grey, whom the NUWSS regarded as the linchpins of the suffrage forces in the Cabinet and in the House of Commons. On November 7, the day of Asquith's "bombshell," Brailsford had held a very satisfactory interview with Lloyd George and the Master of Elibank; in the event the amendment scheme failed, they had promised to use all their influence to secure a moderate suffrage bill, such as the Conciliation Bill, and had said they could keep Churchill and Redmond from opposing such a measure.[81] Brailsford had left the interview certain of victory.[82] The NUWSS negotiations with Lloyd George had also gone well. Swanwick had lunched with Scott and Lloyd George on November 15 and had left the meeting convinced that the Chancellor sincerely wished to help the suffragists. She wrote her husband:

He is very anxious to get us on his side, and of course we want him on ours. He strikes me as amazingly quick and adaptable, indiscreet and unscrupulous. I should never feel he wouldn't throw anyone or anything over if he saw something he wanted. But he wants to get this done. He said with curious candour, "It's the Conciliation Bill has done it. I'm bound to confess it set me thinking of a practicable measure to substitute for it. Now it's blown into the air." So I said, "Don't you believe it! It's waiting round the corner

---

[80]National Union of Women's Suffrage Societies, Annual Report, 1911, p. 38; "Echoes," Englishwoman, 12, no. 36 (December 1911): 347-49. The deputation included representatives from the WSPU and the WFL. The NUWSS had arranged a previous conference for all the organizations concerned, in order to map out a common strategy. The WSPU refused to attend, on the grounds it could not adopt the same line as the other societies.

[81]Leventhal, p. 148.

[82]Bodleian Library, Nevinson Journals, e616, November 18, 1911.

for you unless you give us something better," and he answered, "Oh, I know, I'm going to give you something better."[83]

Two days later the Chancellor of the Exchequer told a group of Liberal women that he was prepared to do all in his power to promote a women's suffrage amendment to the Reform Bill and that he would even be willing to move the amendment.[84] Shortly after this he promised the NUWSS that he would speak at a meeting which was scheduled for February in the Albert Hall, and sent a message of encouragement to the suffragists: "I am willing to do all in my power to help those who are labouring to reach a successful issue in the coming session. Next year provides the supreme opportunity, and nothing but unwise handling of that chance can compass failure."[85] On November 23 he intimated that he and other members of the Government were prepared to stump for women's suffrage throughout the country.[86]

Sir Edward Grey echoed many of Lloyd George's sentiments. Since June, Grey, preoccupied with Agadir, had been very quiet on the subject of women's suffrage. Now at last he seemed ready to work for the women's cause. He assured Lytton that women's suffrage had a much better chance of being enacted by the amendment proposal than by the Conciliation Bill, and hinted that he might move such an amendment. Grey added that he favored an amendment which would enfranchise householders and wives of householders, and indicated his willingness to campaign for such a measure.[87]

Grey's pronouncement, combined with Asquith's pledge and Lloyd George's promise of support, elated both the NUWSS and Brailsford.[88] The suffragists felt that they now had two strings to their bow. If the scheme to amend the Reform Bill failed—and they had been assured that the Reform Bill would precede the Conciliation Bill—they would still have the Conciliation Bill; moreover, Lloyd George, the most powerful opponent of the Conciliation Bill, now promised to support

---

[83]Swanwick, p. 211.

[84]National Union of Women's Suffrage Societies, Annual Report, 1911, p. 39.

[85]C. C., November 23, 1911; Swanwick, p. 215.

[86]C. C., November 30, 1911; The Times, November 24, 1911.

[87]The Times, November 21 and December 1, 1911.

[88]Haldane, Runciman, and Birrell had agreed to help Grey and Lloyd George. C. C., November 30, 1911.

it.[89] Brailsford regarded the "whole situation as much more favourable" than it had been before Asquith's announcement.[90] Fawcett echoed his sentiments and wrote her niece, Louisa Garrett Anderson, "We have the best chance of women's suffrage next session that we have ever had, by far."[91]

On December 8 the NUWSS held a special council to map out strategy. A great deal of discussion focused on the proposed amendments to the Reform Bill. Brailsford, a guest at the meeting, informed the audience that there would be a series of amendments to include women in the bill, and that these amendments would be considered in descending order, with the most comprehensive amendment first. He predicted that three amendments would be moved: first, an amendment that would give votes to women on the same terms as men; second, a "Norwegian amendment" which would enfranchise householders and wives of householders; third, a "Conciliation" amendment which would enfranchise women householders.[92] Given Grey's and Lloyd George's support for the Norwegian amendment, Brailsford felt that most Liberals, Nationalists, and Labourites could be persuaded to support this proposal and he seemed confident that it could be carried. He reminded the Council that if all three amendments failed, there still remained the Conciliation Bill to fall back on.[93] Summing up the prospects, Brailsford termed the suffragist position "incomparably more secure than we occupied a month ago" and predicted that "we cannot fail to secure something as substantial as the Conciliation Bill and we may reasonably hope for some intermediate compromise immensely more satisfactory."[94] The council resolved to "keep all options open" and to work for both the Conciliation Bill and the amendments to the Reform Bill. Like Brailsford, the representatives of the NUWSS seemed

---

[89]Lloyd George had told Brailsford the Reform Bill would come up before the Conciliation Bill (Leventhal, p. 148). The NUWSS assumed the Reform Bill would have precedence over the Conciliation Bill because it would have to be passed next session in order to allow time for the Lords' veto. C. C., November 16, 1911.

[90]Bodleian Library, Nevinson Journals, e616, November 8, 1911.

[91]Papers of Millicent Garrett Fawcett, Millicent Garrett Fawcett to Louisa Garrett Anderson, copy, December 3, 1911, Fawcett Library, London.

[92]In Norway all women who qualified as householders, or who were wives of householders, could vote. Manchester Guardian, November 17, 1911.

[93]C. C., December 14, 1911.

[94]H. N. Brailsford, Women and the Reform Bill (London, 1911), p. 7.

confident that some measure of women's suffrage would be enacted next session.[95]

Undoubtedly much of this optimism was inspired by the groundswell of Liberal and Labour support for the suffrage cause. The suffragists had every reason to be pleased by developments in the Liberal and Labour parties. Ramsey MacDonald, chairman of the Parliamentary Labour Party, had promised that the Labour Party would do everything possible to put women's suffrage in the Reform Bill; equally important, the ILP had inaugurated a "political equality campaign" in support of women's suffrage and planned to use its 800 branches to promote the suffrage cause.[96] With the assistance of leading members of the Liberal and Labour parties, the NUWSS and a number of other women's organizations had formed a central committee to coordinate propaganda in support of women's suffrage.[97] Fawcett had also been able to persuade Grey to promise to move an amendment to the Reform Bill, most probably the Norwegian amendment. She was delighted with this pledge, for she felt, quite correctly, that the Conservatives were more likely to support a measure advocated by Grey than one by Lloyd George, whom they detested.[98]

By December 1911 the NUWSS had determined its primary goal: to secure the inclusion of women's suffrage in the Government Reform Bill. The suffragists did, however, intend to keep the Conciliation Bill alive for two reasons. They wanted to make sure that the Liberals, spurred on by fear of the Conciliation Bill, would work hard for a women's suffrage amendment to the Reform Bill, and they intended to use the Conciliation Bill as a "safety valve," should the amendment scheme fail. Full of confidence, the NUWSS analyzed its prospects for the coming year and foresaw only two possible impediments to its desired victory: the revival of militancy on a large scale, and the massive

---

[95]Councils of the National Union of Women's Suffrage Societies, "Memo on Special Council Meeting, Friday, December 8, 1911," Fawcett Library, London.

[96]C. C., November 16, 1911; FLAC, vol. 2, Circular from the ILP, December 1911, Fawcett Library, London; Labour Leader, January 12, 1912.

[97]C. C., December 21, 1911; The Times, December 15, 1911.

[98]Papers of Millicent Garrett Fawcett, Sir Edward Grey to Millicent Garrett Fawcett, December 14, 1911; Millicent Garrett Fawcett to Sir Edward Grey, copy, December 16, 1911, Fawcett Library, London; FLAC, vol. 1, Ji, Sir Edward Grey to Millicent Garrett Fawcett, December 20, 1911, Fawcett Library, London; Archives, Manchester Public Library, M/50, Box 9, Notes by Millicent Garrett Fawcett on a meeting held with Sir Edward Grey, December 9, 1911.

defection of Conservatives from the suffragist camp. The NUWSS predicted that either of these developments would play havoc with the suffrage issue.[99]

Unfortunately, the WSPU's reactions to Asquith's proposed Reform Bill were very different from those of the NUWSS: the militants were "livid with rage and deaf to reason."[100] On November 9, the day after Asquith's announcement, The Times reported that the WSPU had ended its truce and intended to revive militancy and its anti-Government election policy as a protest against the exclusion of women from the Reform Bill. The suffragettes' analysis of the prospects for next session directly contradicted that of the NUWSS: the Pankhursts were positive that the House of Commons would not attach a women's suffrage amendment to the Reform Bill.[101] The WSPU thought that Asquith's chief motivation for introducing a Reform measure at this juncture was a desire to destroy the Conciliation Bill, and, despite Brailsford's reassurances, the Pankhursts persisted in regarding the Prime Minister's announcement as treacherous. As one chronicler of the WSPU has written, "with regard to the probity of male politicians, the WSPU was now in the incipient stage of what was to become a most Manichean outlook."[102]

For all the near-hysteria of the WSPU's reaction to the news of the Reform Bill, there are indications that the WSPU was tiring of the truce and of the Conciliation Bill even before the news of November 7 and that Asquith's announcement may have been merely a much needed excuse for the resumption of militancy.[103] In addition, the idea of Lloyd George as the champion of the suffrage forces undoubtedly increased the ire of the militants. The WSPU thoroughly distrusted and disliked the Chancellor of the Exchequer; according to Brailsford, Christabel Pankhurst conceived of the whole suffrage battle as a duel

---

[99]Correspondence of the National Union of Women's Suffrage Societies, 1911; Circular regarding deputation to Conservative MPs, December 7, 1911; Statement issued by the executive committee condemning militancy, November 30, 1911, Fawcett Library, London. The NUWSS had, in conjunction with the Conservative and Unionist Women's Franchise Association, begun to lobby for the Norwegian amendment within the Conservatitve Party. See C. C., December 14, 1911; NUWSS, Ex. com. mins., December 7, 1911, Fawcett Library, London.

[100]Bodleian Library, Nevinson Journals, e616, November 8, 1911.

[101]Manchester Guardian, December 12, 1911.

[102]Rosen, p. 155.

[103]Bodleian Library, Nevinson Journals, e616, October 31, 1911.

between herself and Lloyd George.[104] The interview with Asquith on November 17 did nothing to alleviate the anger of the militants. The WSPU demanded nothing less than a promise that the Government would introduce a women's suffrage bill; when the Prime Minister refused, the WSPU retaliated with a vengeance. On November 21 it staged a demonstration in Parliament Square which culminated in the arrest of 220 women.[105] Three days later the suffragettes heckled Lloyd George while he was addressing the National Liberal Federation. A shouting match ensued and Lloyd George, angered beyond reason, boasted—to the dismay of Brailsford and the delight of the WSPU—that the announcement of the Reform Bill had once and for all "torpedoed the Conciliation Bill."[106] Shortly after this the WSPU prevented the Prime Minister from delivering a speech at the City Temple.[107]

The suffragettes' actions, particularly their treatment of Asquith, outraged even those members of the House of Commons and the Cabinet who sympathized with the militants' goals. Members of all parties vehemently criticized the WSPU's behavior; the reaction of suffragists in the Cabinet was particularly strong.[108] Grey informed Lytton that it would be "repugnant" to him and to his fellow suffragists in the Cabinet to give active support to the women's suffrage movement if militancy persisted.[109] Lloyd George complained to Fawcett that the continuation of militancy would prove fatal to the prospects of women's suffrage:

> The action of the militants is alienating sympathy from the women's cause in every quarter. . . . If next year's chances of carrying either a women's amendment or a Bill are not to be totally ruined some emphatic action must be taken at once. You can hardly realise what the feeling is even among Members of Parliament who have hitherto been steadfast in support of Women's Suffrage. I feel confident that if these attacks are persisted in our hopes of being able to secure the confirmtion of a Women's Suffrage amendment in next year's Bill will be of

---

[104]Scott diary, November 16, 1911.

[105]Manchester Guardian, November 22, 1911.

[106]The Times, November 25, 1911. According to Swanwick, Lloyd George had gone over the speech with her before the meeting, and she had persuaded him to delete his remarks about "torpedoing." The militants, however, so angered him that he reinstated the phrase. Swanwick, pp. 216-17.

[107]Manchester Guardian, November 29, 1911.

[108]The Times, November 30 and December 6, 1911.

[109]Manchester Guardian, December 1, 1911.

the slightest. I have consulted Sir Edward Grey and other friends of the movement and they take an equally serious view of the situation. What do you suggest? Anti-Suffragists are of course exuberant and I feel confident that the effect of our agitations will be neutralised by the antics of the militants.[110]

Both the NUWSS and Brailsford were worried that Lloyd George's predictions were presciently accurate. The suffragists feared that the continuation of militancy would lose them the support both of sincere suffragists who wanted to teach the lesson that violence does not pay, and of "token" suffragists who were only waiting for an excuse not to support women's suffrage. Brailsford was angry with Lloyd George for striking "the strident party note" by jubilantly declaring that he had "torpedoed" the supposedly Tory-inspired Conciliation Bill, but he was quite as angry with the militants for using methods that were both futile and bankrupt, since "no degree of force which the women can use will avail to coerce the Government."[111] The NUWSS was just as furious, and Fawcett lamented that "revolutionary violence" would destroy their chances for next session.[112] Hoping to placate the politicians and public opinion, the NUWSS issued a manifesto denouncing the actions of the militants.[113] Fawcett also wrote Lloyd George a long letter which sharply condemned the WSPU and exhorted him not to withdraw support from the cause because of the behavior of the suffragettes:

---

[110]Beaverbrook Library, London, Papers of Earl Lloyd George of Dwyfor, C 8/1/1, David Lloyd George to Millicent Garrett Fawcett, copy, November 30, 1911 (hereafter cited as Lloyd George Papers). This letter is also in the Papers of Millicent Garrett Fawcett, Fawcett Library, London. Lloyd George had also told C. P. Scott that the actions of the militants were damaging the suffrage movement. See Lloyd George Papers, C 8/1/1, David Lloyd George to C. P. Scott, copy, November 30, 1911; Scott diary, December 2, 1911.

[111]Archives, Manchester Public Library, M/50, Box 10, H. N. Brailsford to Millicent Garrett Fawcett, November 26, [1911]. The Conciliation Bill had, of course, been drafted by a committee composed of members of all parties. In revising the bill in 1911, Brailsford had taken great pains to accommodate Liberal criticisms of the 1910 proposal. In no sense was it a "Tory-inspired" proposal. See also Manchester Guardian, December 4, 1911.

[112]Papers of Millicent Garrett, Millicent Garrett Fawcett to Louisa Garrett Anderson, December 3, 1911, Fawcett Library, London. Anderson concurred with her aunt and resigned from the WSPU in protest of the militants' actions. Ibid., Louisa Garrett Anderson to Millicent Garrett Fawcett, December 4, 1911.

[113]NUWSS, Ex. com. mins., November 30, 1911, Fawcet Library, London; The Times, December 1, 1911.

I regret and deplore, condemn also, if the word must be used,
the disgusting scenes of November 21 and 29 as much as you do.
The disorders of which the events of November 21st and
November 29th are specimens are symptoms of a social and
political disease. You may punish the offenders, but mere
punishment does not affect the causes of the disease. Force
is no remedy. You must seek the causes and endeavor to remove
them. . . . As your desire to secure the enfranchisement of
women before the next general election becomes clear, the
supporters and perpetrators of violence will be more and more
isolated.[114]

Fawcett did not relish public denunciations and recriminations, but she
and her colleagues in the NUWSS were convinced that this was the only
way to stem the tide of desertions from the suffrage camp. The WSPU
was deaf to reason and would not heed direct appeals from the NUWSS.[115]
Fawcett was distressed by this rift in the suffrage movement, but to
avert disaster in the House of Commons, the NUWSS must disown and
disassociate itself from the militants. If the suffragettes escalated
their efforts, the NUWSS doubted that it could continue to mollify
either the outraged politicians or the public. Fortunately, the WSPU,
exhausted by its November outburst of energy, did not persist in its
violent exploits; by the end of 1911, the threat militancy posed to the
suffrage cause appeared to be dormant.

If the militants imperiled the passage of some measure of
women's suffrage in 1912, the Conservatives' response to Asquith's
proposed Reform Bill also augured that difficult times lay ahead for
the proponents of women's suffrage. Conservative MP's had supported
the Conciliation Bill precisely because it was a moderate measure which
enfranchised only a very small number of women. Moreover, it was a
nonpartisan measure: in drafting the proposal the Conciliation
Committee had taken great care to frame a bill that was not biased
toward any one party. Asquith's announcement of a Reform Bill which
could be amended to give votes to women frightened Conservatives for
several reasons. First of all, it seemed to make women's suffrage a
party issue. The Liberal Government had seized the initiative, and if
women were included in the bill, the Government would be responsible
for piloting the bill through both houses of Parliament. In addition,
many Conservatives believed that the Government had designed its
amendment proposal with the intention of "torpedoing" the Conciliation
Bill and ensuring that women's suffrage would be granted only on terms
that would benefit the Liberal Party. As one Conservative complained,

---

[114]Papers of Millicent Garrett Fawcett, Millicent Garrett
Fawcett to David Lloyd George, copy, December 2, 1911, Fawcett Library,
London.

[115]Ibid.

"Asquith is nothing but a ponderous and self-righteous posing trickster over this women's suffrage business."[116]

Many Conservatives interpreted Asquith's proposal as an indication that there would not be moderate reform, along the lines of the Conciliation Bill, but a very comprehensive installment of women's suffrage. Bonar Law, the new leader of the Conservative Party and a proponent of women's suffrage, mirrored the attitude of many Conservative suffragists when he wrote that he opposed any large extension of the franchise:

> I have felt, and feel strongly, that women should not be deprived of votes on account of their sex; but, on the other hand, the suffrage is already sufficiently extended, for it is a most dangerous thing that absolute power should rest with any one class, and it is still more dangerous if there is a great extension of that power while there is in the country a distinct danger of a revolutionary movement. I have always felt, therefore, that the argument that it would not do to allow women who are in actual majority to control power has nothing in it, because women are not a class; yet, on the other hand, if the franchise is radically lowered, then, of course, the women in every class will vote as the men of that class and that would mean, in my belief, a most alarming extension of power in a direction which at present at least is dangerous. . . . On the other hand, I should presumably have been delighted to see the Conciliation Bill passed, for it might have settled the question for a long time, and without any of the evil effects which I dread.[117]

The Conservatives were also very suspicious of Lloyd George's unexpected conversion to women's suffrage. The Earl of Selborne, a staunch Conservative suffragist, wrote his wife: "I cannot stand Mrs. Fawcett's 'My dear Mr. Lloyd George' and I think she is quite wrong in her estimate both of the situation and of Mr. Lloyd George."[118]

The net effect of Asquith's November proclamation was to make the Conservatives wary of the whole subject of women's suffrage. If the Liberals intended to use the Conciliation Bill as a lever to secure

---

[116]Bodleian Library, Papers of William Waldegrave Palmer, 2nd Earl of Selborne, Ms. 102, the Earl of Selborne to the Countess of Selborne, November 19, 1911 (hereafter cited as Selborne Papers).

[117]Beaverbrook Library, Papers of Andrew Bonar Law, 33/3/17, Andrew Bonar Law to Lady Betty Balfour, copy [November 11, 1911] (hereafter cited as Law Papers).

[118]Selborne Papers, Ms. 102, the Earl of Selborne to the Countess of Selborne, December 6, 1911.

a wider measure of women's suffrage, it might not be safe to support any women's suffrage proposal. The Conservatives indicated their growing aversion to the women's suffrage question at the conference of the National Conservative Union; whereas previous conferences had passed resolutions in support of women's suffrage, the 1911 conference decided no further action should be taken on extending the franchise until the matter had been referred to the country.[119]

The NUWSS hoped it could convince the Conservative suffragists to continue their support for the Conciliation Bill and, more important, to attract their support for the "Norwegian" amendment to the Reform Bill. According to Brailsford's calculations, the votes of at least nine Conservative suffragists were necessary if the amendment was to be successful;[120] and so, throughout the winter of 1912, the NUWSS courted the Conservatives.

The chief argument used was that the Norwegian amendment added stability and moderation to the electorate and was framed in both the spirit and the interest of Conservatism.[121] Seeking Conservative support for this amendment, Eleanor Rathbone wrote: "I believe that a good many Conservative MPs alarmed at the influx into the electorate of a crowd of irresponsible young men will welcome the married woman householder as a mature and moderating influence."[122] The NUWSS collaborated with the Conservative and Unionist Women's Franchise Association, and with Conservative suffragists such as Lord Robert Cecil and the Earl of Selborne.[123] In her cultivation of the Conservatives, Fawcett purposely minimized the role of the Chancellor of the Exchequer in the campaign and maximized the role of Sir Edward Grey; Grey's standing in Conservative circles was high, and for that reason she had persuaded him to move the Norwegian amendment. Fawcett correctly gauged Conservative's reactions. Lady Cecil, describing her husband's response to the Norwegian amendment, wrote: "He attaches great importance to the amendment being moved by Sir Edward Grey as he thinks it would be impossible to get members on our side to follow

---

[119]Manchester Guardian, November 18, 1911.

[120]See C. C., December 14, 1911.

[121]Correspondence of the National Union of Women's Suffrage Societies, 1911, Account of deputation to John Harmwood-Banner (Cons., Liverpool), December 7, 1911; Correspondence of the National Union of Women's Suffrage Societies, 1912, Circular from Edith Palliser, January 10, 1912; Fawcett Library, London.

[122]C. C., December 14, 1911.

[123]NUWSS, Ex. com. mins., December 7, 1911, Fawcett Library, London.

Lloyd George."[124] At the same time, however, the NUWSS did not forget the Conciliation Bill, since it realized that this was the suffrage measure that most appealed to Conservatives.

Indeed, the Conservatives were very disinclined to support any women's suffrage measure that was more extensive than the Conciliation Bill. Although Lytton told the NUWSS that he had been successful in persuading Conservatives to support the Norwegian amendment,[125] Lord Robert Cecil was far more pessimistic about the Conservatives' attitude to the amendment; in fact, he was convinced that a franchise bill amended to include women would never become law:

> What chance then will this measure have of becoming law with the Prime Minister and some of his principal colleagues so opposed to one of its chief provisions as to regard its enactment as a national disaster? I confess it does not seem to me a very good one. Such a Bill must inevitably be rejected by the House of Lords. Will the present tottering Government have authority to override the opposition of the Second Chamber supported as all will know by the profound convictions of the Prime Minister? Any attempt to do so would reduce the provisions of the Parliament Act to the merest force. Nor for other reasons is it by any means certain that the life of the Government will be long enough to enable it to fulfill the conditions imposed by that measure.[126]

Cecil's advice, which other Conservative suffragists echoed, was to concentrate on the Conciliation Bill, which he felt might prove acceptable to the Lords.[127] In view of the Liberals' attitude to the Conciliation Bill, the NUWSS could not afford to follow Cecil's counsel, and as the new year began, the main worry to the NUWSS was not the Conservatives at all, but the Liberals.

---

[124]Archives, Manchester Public Library, M/50, Box 9, Lady Eleanor Cecil to Millicent Garrett Fawcett, December 24, 1911.

[125]NUWSS, Ex. com. mins., December 7, 1911, Fawcett Library, London.

[126]British Museum, Papers of Viscount Cecil of Chelwood, Add. Mss. 51160, Lord Robert Cecil to Miss Theilman, copy, January 2, 1912 (hereafter cited as Cecil Papers).

[127]Archives, Manchester Public Library, M/50, Box 9, Lady Eleanor Cecil to Millicent Garrett Fawcett, December 24, 1911. See also British Museum, Arncliffe-Sennett Collection, vol. 16, Lord Robert Cecil to Maud Arncliffe-Sennett, January 19, 1912; The Times, December 14, 1911, and January 4, 1912.

By the beginning of 1912 it was well known that the Cabinet was up in arms over the suffrage question.[128]   Austen Chamberlain, a leading antisuffragist and an astute parliamentary observer, wrote:

It is reported that they have had some stormy meetings of the Cabinet on the suffrage question. . . . the suffragists in the Cabinet are very angry with those of their colleagues who are to take part in the Albert Hall meeting, but I hear that Asquith turned fiercely on Lloyd George and told him that it was all his fault for trying to commit the Government and the Party at the Bath meeting.[129]

Margot Asquith complained that women's suffrage had "split us into smithereens" and reproached her husband for his reluctance to impose Cabinet unity on this question: "Henry's present position is hopeless and even ridiculous--he alone never saw the importance of enjoining silence on Grey and L. George, and this fearful mistake will break us to a certainty. What a subject to smash over!"[130] Asquith was himself concerned about the Cabinet schism and wrote gloomily, "we open 1912 with a lack of cohesion and driving part in the forces behind us."[131]

In mid-December, to heal the breach in the Cabinet, but also with the thought of quashing women's suffrage once and for all, Churchill had begun lobbying for a referendum on the women's suffrage question.   He thought that if the Cabinet ministers compromised over the suffrage problem by agreeing to abide by the country's decision on the question, the schism in the Liberal Party could be healed-- particularly if he could win over Grey and Lloyd George, the two most ardent suffragists in the Cabinet.[132] Employing both threats and

---

[128]Pall Mall Gazette, January 5, 1912, gave the following analysis of the Cabinet split. For women's suffrage--Grey, Lloyd George, Morley, Haldane, Churchill, Carrington, Earl Beauchamp, Birrell, Burns, Buxton, Pease, Runciman. Against--Asquith, Loreburn, Harcourt, McKenna, Samuels, Lord Pentland (doubtful), Crewe. The contention that Burns, Churchill, and Pease were suffragists is unfounded.

[129]Austen Chamberlain, Politics from Inside (New Haven, 1937), pp. 413-14.

[130]Margot Asquith to the Master of Elibank, January 14 and 28, 1912, as quoted in Morgan, pp. 89-90.

[131]H. H. Asquith to Winston S. Churchill, December 23, 1911, as quoted in Winston S. Churchill, Companion vol. 2, part 3, p. 1477.

[132]Winston S. Churchill to the Master of Elibank, December 18, 1911, as quoted in Ibid., vol. 2, pp. 388-89.

entreaties, Churchill begged Lloyd George to abandon his advocacy of women's suffrage:

> I cannot help feeling anxious about the women. If you and Grey go working yourself into a mawkish frenzy on the "are they not our flesh and blood" cry, all sorts of difficulties of a personal character will be added to the [word illegible] wh. on this topic loom before us; and this strong Government on wh. our life's work depends may easily come to grief. . . . if you were to get yourself into the sort of state where the enfranchisement of 6,000,000 without a fresh appeal to the country became the most important political object in your mind, I cd. not find any good foothold for common action.[133]

Churchill proposed to Lloyd George and Grey that he would agree to work for a women's suffrage amendment to the Reform Bill, provided they would promise to submit the amendment--if it were carried in the House--to a referendum. Although no definite agreement was reached, Churchill reported that "unity on these lines was not impossible."[134]

Both Brailsford and the NUWSS were concerned about these machinations for a referendum on women's suffrage. The NUWSS opposed any suggestion of a referendum on the suffrage issue because it was convinced that its cause would lose. Jane, Lady Strachey, a member of the NUWSS executive, expressed this feeling when she predicted "the result of such an experiment would be the ruin of our cause for an incalculable period of time."[135] Unfortunately, however, the referendum scheme appealed to a large segment of both the Conservative and Liberal Parties. By removing the thorny question from the hands of the politicians and leaving it to the electorate to decide the women's fate, a referendum would absolve Members of the House of Commons of all responsibility for the women's suffrage question. Many Conservatives felt that any major constitutional change, such as the Parliament Act or a women's suffrage measure, should receive the approval of the country.[136] Lady Selborne, head of the Conservative and Unionist Women's Franchise Association, and her brother, Lord Robert Cecil, both

---

[133]Lloyd George Papers, C 3/15/12, Winston S. Churchill to David Lloyd George, December 16, 1911. Churchill wrote a similar letter to Grey. See Winston S. Churchill, vol. 2, p. 390.

[134]Winston S. Churchill to H. H. Asquith, December 21, 1911, as quoted in Winston S. Churchill, vol. 2, pp. 391-92.

[135]Papers of Jane, Lady Strachey, Lady Strachey to the Countess of Selborne, January 23, 1912, Fawcett Library, London.

[136]The Times, February 8, 1912.

supported the referendum scheme.[137] Many Liberals favored a referendum because, like Churchill, they felt that this would heal the growing rift in the party over the suffrage question.

By the end of January 1912, the NUWSS was concerned that a referendum would, in fact, be held on the women's suffrage question.[138] Both Grey and Lloyd George were showing signs of succumbing to Churchill's blandishments. Grey, in a widely publicized statement, had announced that the Government would not oppose the referendum scheme but would leave the question to a free vote of the House of Commons; and Lloyd George, for the sake of Cabinet unity, appeared willing to attach a referendum proviso to the women's suffrage amendment to the Reform Bill.[139]

Working in close collaboration with C. P. Scott and Brailsford, the NUWSS tried to smash the referendum scheme. Fawcett, Courtney, and Swanwick discussed the referendum proposal at length with Scott and urged him to intercede with Lloyd George on their behalf.[140] An NUWSS deputation to Lloyd George only succeeded in irritating him because it refused even to consider his referendum plan, but Scott was more successful. He convinced Lloyd George to abandon the idea, and Lloyd George promised to do everything possible to prevent a referendum and even suggested forming a committee of Conservative and Liberal suffragists to work against the proposal.[141]

Although the suffragists had succeeded in dissuading Lloyd George from agreeing to Churchill's referendum proposal, the whole controversy had given the NUWSS a severe jolt and sapped its confidence in the certainty of victory for the women. Now even the Liberals, whose support for the amendment scheme had appeared assured, seemed

---

[137]Law Papers, 24/4/91, the Countess of Selborne to Andrew Bonar Law, November 29, [1913].

[138]NUWSS, Ex. com. mins., February 1, 1912, Fawcett Library, London; Millicent Garrett Fawcett, "Women's Suffrage and the Referendum," Englishwoman, 13, no. 38 (February 1912): 127.

[139]C. C., January 25, 1912; Archives, Manchester Public Library, M/50, Box 10, H. N. Brailsford to Millicent Garrett Fawcett, January 22, [1912]; M/50, Box 9, Kathleen Courtney to Millicent Garrett Fawcett, January 22, 1912.

[140]J. L. Hammond, C. P. Scott of the Manchester Guardian (New York, 1934), p. 110.

[141]Scott diary, January 24, 1912. Brailsford had tried to persuade Lloyd George to resign if the Government acceded to the referendum proposal, but Lloyd George was unwilling to do this.

inclined to throw the women over. Churchill's intrigues had lent credence to the gossip about Cabinet disunity, and in February and March of 1912 the NUWSS received further reports of dissension within the Cabinet over the suffrage issue. Lady Frances Balfour confided to Fawcett that both Loreburn and Lloyd George had threatened to resign over women's suffrage, and that Asquith was so angry about Lloyd George's advocacy of women's suffrage that "he would not speak to him for some days."[142] Divisions within the Cabinet over the suffrage question had grown so intense that ,according to Lady Constance Lytton, the Government was "beginning to fear the situation they have created for themselves on this question."[143] The NUWSS was very concerned that many Liberals, alarmed by the public disagreements and possible resignation of ministers, might withdraw their support from the women's cause in order to end the controversy and thereby strengthen the divided Government.[144]

The already dim prospects grew dimmer the first week in February when the Government announced that it was postponing the Reform Bill. This meant that the Conciliation Bill would precede the Government's franchise measure.[145] The suffragists had counted on the Conciliation Bill as a measure to fall back on should the more comprehensive bill fail; with good reason, they feared that if the Conciliation Bill came up before the Reform Bill, it would be difficult to generate much enthusiasm among the Liberals, who had set their sights on a more extensive measure.[146] The opportunity to vote for a wider installment of women's suffrage might influence Liberals to vote against the supposedly "anti-Liberal" Conciliation Bill. Fawcett, sizing up the situation, wrote Lady Frances Balfour: "I am very full of fear about our prospects and believe we shall probably be tricked

---

[142]FLAC, vol. 1, Jii, Lady Frances Balfour to Millicent Garrett Fawcett, February 10 and March 7, 1912, Fawcett Library, London. According to Austen Chamberlain, Loreburn threatened to join a committee in the House of Lords to put down obstructive amendments to the Government Franchise Bill if it contained a women's suffrage amendment. Chamberlain, p. 424.

[143]FLAC, vol. 21, Lady Constance Lytton to Millicent Garrett Fawcett, February 6, 1912, Fawcett Library, London; Archives, Manchester Public Library, M/50, Box 9, Lady Constance Lytton to Millicent Garrett Fawcett, February 6, 1912.

[144]National Union of Women's Suffrage Societies, Annual Report, 1912, p. 13.

[145]C. C., February 8, 1912; Hammond, p. 110.

[146]Bodleian Library, Nevinson Journals, e616, November 8, 1911.

again though anything more plain and positive than the pledge Asquith gave us on November 17 cannot be imagined."[147]

Bad news was just around the corner. On March 1 the WSPU for the first time attacked private property, smashing store windows in the West End, and three days later the suffragettes went on rampages in Knightsbridge and Kensington.[148] These outrages horrified political circles and touched off rumors of worse deeds to come. According to Lady Frances Balfour, Asquith told Haldane and Grey that "the police believed there was a plot to assasinate Lloyd George."[149]

As had so often been the case in the past, violence only stiffened the spines of the politicians and made them determined not to bow to the militants' demands. Despite appeals from the NUWSS not to punish law-abiding suffragists because of the actions of a "small and decreasing minority," many MP's responded to the militancy by withdrawing their support from the Conciliation Bill.[150] The Times jubilantly declared that "the window-smashing outrages have given such a setback to the cause of womens suffrage as none of its opponents could have hoped for under normal conditions"; many politicians confirmed these predictions by announcing they would vote against the Conciliation Bill to show disapproval of militant methods.[151] Members of Parliament complained to the NUWSS about the WSPU's actions and testified to the adverse effects of militancy. One member, Alan Burgoyne (Cons., Kensington, N.), wrote:

> I know well that none of your body is in sympathy with those unsexed harridans but the odium of association attaches to the whole of those who hold the principle of their views. . . . In the House of Commons the matter was for days the subject of comment and a resolve entered the minds of a growing number of those who formerly supported the Conciliation Bill to withdraw their support during the present Parliament.
> I can only tell you that my attitude is shared by over four score of the former supporters of this measure and the

---

[147]FLAC, vol. 1, Jii, Millicent Garett Fawcett to Lady Frances Balfour, February 11, 1912, Fawcett Library, London.

[148]F. W. Pethick-Lawrence, p. 88; The Times, March 2 and 5, 1912.

[149]FLAC, vol. 1, Jii, Lady Frances Balfour to Millicent Garrett Fawcett, March 7, 1912, Fawcett Library, London.

[150]See Correspondence of the National Union of Women's Suffrage Societies, 1912, Circular from the NUWSS to Members of Parliament, March 8, 1912; Manchester Guardian, March 8, 1912.

[151]The Times, March 7, 11, 18, 22, and 25, 1912.

damage done to the movement will be seen in the Division which will eventuate on March 22nd.[152]

Even the Women's Freedom League, once a practitioner of militancy, criticized the WSPU's actions: "When everything depends on the good will of the average member of Parliament and his electors, suffragists have to be doubly careful that the favourable majority built up over the years of hard work done by the National Union should not be turned into an adverse one."[153]

In the opinion of the NUWSS, the militants could not have chosen a more inopportune time to conduct their raids. The antisuffragists, led by F. E. Smith (Cons., Liverpool, Walton), Harcourt, and Loreburn, had already begun to mount a campaign against the Conciliation Bill. They devoted special attention to the Nationalists and played upon their fears that Loreburn, whom the Irish regarded as their staunchest supporter in the Cabinet, might resign over the women's suffrage question; they also hinted that the time necessary for consideration of the subsequent stages of the Conciliation Bill might jeopardize the prospects of Home Rule.[154] Militancy gave the antisuffragists a second string for _their_ bow. They could now make the effective appeal that it would be both cowardly and dishonorable to give in to violence by voting for women's suffrage and could urge fellow MP's to voice their disapproval of militant methods by voting against the Conciliation Bill.[155] Austen Chamberlain claimed that the WSPU's actions had left the antisuffragist camp ebullient: ". . . there is a growing feeling that it may be possible to defeat the Bill on the Second Reading. If a few more windows were smashed the Bill would be smashed at the same time, but I expect we shall hear nothing more of the militants till after the vote has been taken."[156]

---

[152]Correspondence of the London Society for Women's Suffrage with the North Kensington Society for Women's Suffrage, Alan Burgoyne to Miss Chadwick, March 15, 1912, Fawcett Library, London.

[153]Manchester Guardian, March 6, 1912.

[154]Chamberlain, p. 447; Correspondence of the London Society for Women's Suffrage with the East St. Pancras Society for Women's Suffrage, Augusta Harrington to Philippa Strachey, March 6, 1912, Fawcett Library, London; Manchester Guardian, March 13, 1912.

[155]The Times, March 12, 1912; Manchester Guardian, March 11, 1912.

[156]Chamberlain, p. 447. Harrison, Separate Spheres, pp. 175–76, indicates that in the winter of 1912, the National League for Opposing Woman Suffrage was having both organization and financial problems; thus, the exploits of the militants in March 1912 came as an especially "welcome diversion" to the NLOWS and injected vitality into the flagging organization.

Among the leaders of the NUWSS, it was generally understood that the Conciliation Bill, which had received such a successful reading ten months earlier, was probably going down to defeat. Lady Frances Balfour wrote to Fawcett, "I don't believe we could be worse off than we are just now. There is a regular stampede."[157]

For two years the NUWSS had worked to build up a favorable majority for the Conciliation Bill. It had written letters, organized deputations, courted politicians, collaborated with political associations, and devised countless other lobbying strategies; since Asquith's November announcement these efforts had, if anything, increased.[158] The LSWS, for example, had held 199 meetings in three months and had twice sent deputations to each of the 71 MP's in its bailiwick; other federations had engaged in similar propaganda efforts.[159] The NUWSS had sponsored a meeting in the Albert Hall which the Manchester Guardian termed "probably the most impressive held in London"; £7,000 had been collected.[160] After the March outbreak of militancy, the NUWSS frantically tried to stop the flow of desertions in the House of Commons by sending letters and deputations to those who had announced their intentions of withdrawing support from the bill. Fawcett and Courtney had also seen Lloyd George and tried to persuade him to use his influence to counteract the effects of militancy and to secure the Irish vote.[161] In the end, all these efforts proved futile. On March 28 the House of Commons killed the

----

[157]FLAC, vol. 1, Jii, Lady Frances Balfour to Millicent Garrett Fawcett, March 7, 1912, Fawcett Library, London.

[158]For examples of this work see: Correspondence of the National Union of Women's Suffrage Societies, 1912, Circular from Edith Palliser, February 16 and 28, 1912, Fawcett Library, London; Marshall Papers, Correspondence of Eleanor Acland and Catherine Marshall, February 1912, passim.

[159]Correspondence of the London Society for Women's Suffrage, "Report of Meetings, 1911," Fawcett Library, London; Correspondence concerning the Conciliation Bill, 1912, "Report on work in the London area," Fawcett Library, London; East Midland Federation, Annual Report, 1911-1912 (n.p., n.d.), passim; West Midland Federation, Annual Report, 1911-1912, passim.

[160]Manchester Guardian, February 24, 1912.

[161]Correspondence of the National Union of Women's Suffrage Societies, 1912, Circular from Edith Palliser, March 9 and 22, 1912; NUWSS, Ex. com. mins., March 21, 1912; Fawcett Library, London.

Conciliation Bill by a vote of 222 to 208.[162] Analyzing her reaction to
the news of the defeat, Fawcett wrote, "I felt that what I had been
working for for 40 years had been destroyed at a blow."[163]

The differences between the vote on the Conciliation Bill in
1912 and the vote in 1911 are interesting (see Table 2). The 1912 vote
had far fewer abstentions than the 1911 vote, and most of the
abstentions—particularly among the Conservatives—became negative
votes in the second voting. In 1912, of those MP's who either voted or
paired for the 1911 bill, 70 abstained from either voting or pairing,
and 34 voted or paired against the measure.[164] The number of switches
from neutral or favoring to opposition was particularly large in the
Nationalist Party: all the Nationalists who voted for the bill in 1911
withdrew their support, and 11 of these MP's, joined by 19 Nationalists
who abstained in 1911 (including John Redmond), voted against the
bill.[165] The Labour Party vote in 1912 is also interesting because in
January 1912 the annual Labour Party Conference had formally committed
itself to women's suffrage; yet the number of Labour MP's who voted for
the 1912 Conciliation Bill decreased since 1911, and the number of
abstentions rose.[166]

The reversal in March 1912 of the vote of some ten and a half
months earlier cannot be explained by one single cause. A number of
influences were at work, some stronger than others. Unquestionably,
the Nationalist's Party opposition to the bill had much to do with its
defeat. According to Brailsford, Redmond had ordered his followers not
to give any support to the bill.[167] Antisuffragists had encouraged the
Nationalists to fear that the Liberal Government, upon whom their hopes
for Home Rule depended, would break up over the women's suffrage issue.
The Irish also believed that if further facilities were given to the
Conciliation Bill, there might not be enough parliamentary time left

----

[162]The Times, March 29, 1912. The bill was scheduled to be
read on March 22 but the Government took the day to consider emergency
legislation on the Coal Miners' strike and the second reading was
postponed until March 28.

[163]Millicent Garrett Fawcett, What I Remember, pp. 205-6.

[164]An Analysis of Voting on Women's Suffrage Bills in the
House of Commons since 1908, NUWSS pamphlet (n.p., n.d.), p. 3.

[165]Peter Rowland, The Last Liberal Governments: Unfinished
Business, 1911-1914 (London, 1971), pp. 137-38.

[166]C. C., February 1, 1912.

[167]Manchester Guardian, March 30 and April 5, 1912.

Table 2[a]

Comparison of the Vote on the Conciliation Bill, May 5, 1911,
with the Vote on March 28, 1912

	For			Against			Abstain
	Voted	Paired	Total	Voted	Paired	Total	
Conciliation Bill, 1911, passed second reading May 5, 1911, by 167							
Liberals	145	25	170	36	12	48	51
Conservatives	53	25	78	43	43	86	108
Nationalists	31	—	31	9	—	9	44
Labour	26	5	31	—	—	—	11
TOTAL	255	55	310	88	55	143	214
Conciliation Bill, 1912, defeated on second reading, March 28, 1912, by 14							
Liberals	117	18	135	73	8	81	48
Conservatives	63	13	76	114	24	138	61
Nationalists	3	—	3	35	1	36	45
Labour	25	2	27	—	—	—	15
TOTAL	208	33	241	222	33	255	169

[a]Information contained in this table is compiled from An Analysis of Voting on
Women's Suffrage Bills in the House of Commons Since 1908, NUWSS pamphlet (n.p., n.d.)

for consideration of the Home Rule Bill;[168] the WSPU's continued attacks on Liberal proponents of Home Rule, such as Churchill, may also have influenced the Nationalists' attitude to the Conciliation Bill.[169] In any case the Nationalist Party's assessment of the relationship between Home Rule and women's suffrage was disastrous for the Conciliation Bill.

The Labour Party's vote was also critical in determining the fate of the bill. This vote, too, was influenced by an outside issue, in this case a coal miners' strike. Because of the strike, the miners' representatives were not in London on March 28; this accounts for the large number of Labour abstentions.[170] In view of the January conference resolution, it is probable that these absent members of the Labour Party would have voted for the bill; had they done so, the bill would have passed by one vote. As in the case of Home Rule, the competition of an outside issue was detrimental to the suffragist cause.

In apportioning the blame for the defeat of the Conciliation Bill, it is important to emphasize that the rampages of the militants had disastrous repercussions upon the suffrage bill. Although members of the WSPU denied that their actions were responsible for the bill's extinction, the evidence speaks otherwise.[171] Within both the Liberal and, more important, the Conservative Party, the effect of militancy was very pronounced. Twenty-six MP's (16 Lib., 10 Cons.) who were pledged to support the bill voted against it because of militancy;[172] even more serious was the change from abstainer to opponent (19 Lib.,

----

[168]Millicent Garrett Fawcett, The Women's Victory and After: Personal Reminiscences, 1911-1918 (London, 1920), pp. 21-22; Manchester Society for Women's Suffrage, Annual Report, 1913 (n.p., n.d.), p. 13.

[169]C. C., April 4, 1912.

[170]Manchester Guardian, March 30, 1912; The Times, March 30, 1912.

[171]Rosen, p. 162, downplays the impact of militancy on the 1912 vote on the Conciliation Bill, but his analysis does not explain why Liberals who were pledged to support the bill subsequently broke their pledges, or why such a large number of Conservatives who either supported or remained neutral to the bill in 1911 voted against it in 1912.

[172]Correspondence of the National Union of Women's Suffrage Societies, 1912, Circular from Edith Palliser and Kathleen Courtney, March 30, 1912, Fawcett Library, London.

47 Cons.) and from supporter to abstainer (17 Lib., 23 Cons.)[173] Even with the loss of the Irish vote, these votes would have secured the passage of the Conciliation Bill.

In analyzing the shift in votes between 1911 and 1912, Brailsford, Fawcett, prominent members of the parties, and political correspondents all underscored the actions of the militants. The WSPU's outrages provided unenthusiastic supporters of the suffrage cause with an excuse to withdraw support from the Conciliation Bill. Both Fawcett and Brailsford publicly blamed the militants for bringing about a change in public opinion. Fawcett said in an interview in the Manchester Guardian: ". . . the doings of the militants had undermined our position so far as public opinion was concerned, and had alienated public sympathy from the movement. We have to bear the odium created by the most recent militant outbreaks. The members who wanted to 'rat' were provided with an excuse, and they had not their own people in the constituencies which would have been behind them if the militants had remained quiet."[174] Brailsford, in the same newspaper, emphasized the political consequences of the suffragettes' actions: "The disastrous effect of the recent militancy was that it scandalised public opinion. The pressure which had hitherto kept unsteady members true to their pledges was temporarily relaxed and an atmosphere created in which these men supposed that they might safely face their constituents with a dishonourable vote on their records."[175] Within the Conservative Party leading suffragists bemoaned the effects of militancy: Selborne complained about "the foolish militants," and Cecil termed their actions "ruinous," "a godsend" for the antisuffragist forces.[176] And Sir Edward Grey, writing to Fawcett about the Liberal defections from the suffragist ranks, likewise placed the blame for the bill's defeat squarely on the militants: "What really upset the Conciliation Bill was the resentment caused by the senseless window breaking. But for that the Irish vote would not have been effective. If there are no more outrages there will soon be a reaction favourable to the suffrage."[177]

---

[173]Rowland, pp. 137-38; Correspondence concerning the Conciliation Bill, 1912, "Memorandum on the Voting of London MPs on March 28, 1912, compared with the voting on May 5, 1911," Fawcett Library, London; Manchester Guardian, March 30, 1912.

[174]Manchester Guardian, March 30, 1912.

[175]Ibid., April 5, 1912.

[176]Law Papers, 25/3/26, the Earl of Selborne to Andrew Bonar Law, March 13, 1912; Lord Robert Cecil, "The Suffrage Crisis," Englishwoman, 14, no. 40 (April 1912): 3-5.

[177]Papers of Millicent Garrett Fawcett, Sir Edward Grey to Millicent Garrett Fawcett, April 5, 1912, Fawcett Library, London.

The testimonies of leading politicians and the statements of MP's as well as the evidence of the broken pledges and the shift in voting patterns between 1911 and 1912 indicate that militancy was the single most important factor in securing the defeat of the Conciliation Bill.[178] Proponents of the WSPU and apologists for the militants have tried to defend the suffragettes by arguing that the vote on the Conciliation Bill was not important. According to this reasoning, the Conciliation Bill would never have come through the House of Commons intact; adult suffragists and antisuffragists would have amended the bill so drastically that the House of Commons would finally have rejected it.[179] This argument, founded on second-guessing, completely overlooks the psychological importance of the vote of March 28. Possibly the House of Commons might not have passed the Conciliation Bill through all stages, but that possibility in no way diminishes the importance of the vote on the bill's second reading.

Both the leaders of the NUWSS and prominent suffragists in the House of Commons placed great weight on this vote. They felt, with good reason, that it was essential for the House of Commons to show that it supported the principle of votes for women by giving the Conciliation Bill a favorable second reading. Without this sort of pressure, neither the incumbent Liberal Government, nor subsequent Governments were under any obligation to pursue the suffrage issue. Fawcett and Brailsford had other reasons for continuing to keep the Conciliation Bill alive: it was a nonparty measure, acceptable to members of all parties, which offered the chance, as the Government Reform Bill might not, of a nonpartisan solution to the suffrage question. Moreover, the Conciliation Bill was useful as a spur to Liberals and Labourites to devise a more comprehensive solution to the suffrage problem; it was, after all, the prospect of the Conciliation Bill which had driven Lloyd George into the arms of the suffragists. With the demise of the Conciliation Bill, the suffragists lost a very useful weapon for cudgeling the Liberals.

The defeat of the Conciliation Bill made a tremendous impact on the course of the suffrage movement: it destroyed the chance of a nonparty solution to the suffrage question and it led to the breakup of the Conciliation Committee, which had served not only as a lobby for women's suffrage but also as a meeting ground where members of different parties could discuss their differences on the suffrage question.[180] The NUWSS had looked on the Conciliation Bill both as a

---

[178]See, for example, The Times, March 30, 1912; West Midland Federation, Annual Report, 1911-1912, pp. 15-16, 36, 39.

[179]Rosen, p. 162.

[180]Leventhal, p. 153.

bargaining chip and as something to fall back on in the event that the amendment scheme to the Reform Bill failed; these possibilities no longer existed.

The vote of March 28 had a great influence on the NUWSS. For more than two years the suffragist organization had made the Conciliation Bill the focal point of all its activities. In cooperation with Brailsford and the Conciliation Committee, and with other suffrage organizations and political associations, the NUWSS had worked for the success of this compromise solution to the complex problem of women's suffrage. Owing to the chicanery of politicians, divisions within the suffrage movement, the complication of party considerations, and the competition of other political issues, the task had assumed an almost Sisyphean character. Yet the NUWSS had managed to function as an effective parliamentary lobby; even a rival organization, the WFL, which disagreed with the NUWSS over the question of tactics, credited the NUWSS with building up parliamentary support for the Conciliation Bill.[181] The NUWSS naturally reacted with both anguish and ire at seeing its efforts of two years undone in one day; but it rebounded with a characteristic, almost reflex, action. Two days after the fateful vote the executive committee directed the societies to begin working on building up support for the women's suffrage amendments to the Reform Bill.[182] The leaders cautioned that the passage of a suffrage amendment depended on the suffragists' ability to neutralize the impact of militancy and to convince the Nationalists that their opposition to women's suffrage might damage the prospects of Home Rule.

For the moment, it was to be business as usual; but the vote on March 28 prompted a reevaluation of old allegiances and political strategy by the NUWSS. Though the NUWSS had since its founding in 1897 steadfastly maintained a position of political neutrality, its sympathies--based on family traditions, a conception of women's suffrage as an integral component of liberalism, and an analysis of voting support for women's suffrage in the House of Commons--had always lain with the Liberals. To some extent the confidence in the Liberals had been shaken by the struggles with the Asquith government, particularly the debacle of the 1910 Conciliation Bill. But the confidence had been largely restored by Asquith's promise that his Government would accept a women's suffrage amendment to the Reform Bill, by the friendship of Cabinet ministers such as Grey and Lloyd George, and by the Liberals' enthusiastic response to the amendment scheme. At the same time, the failure of the Conservative Party to

---

[181]The Times, March 6, 1912.

[182]Correspondence of the National Union of Women's Suffrage Societies, 1912, Circular from Kathleen Courtney and Edith Palliser, March 30, 1912, Fawcett Library, London.

demonstrate any real enthusiasm served to strengthen the NUWSS Liberal inclinations.[183]

The vote on March 28 exploded the myth of the Liberal Party as the friend of the women's suffrage movement and left the NUWSS thoroughly disillusioned with the Liberals. The NUWSS had counted on the Liberals, and their betrayal seemed to imply a great deal about the present state of liberalism. The NUWSS was particularly angry at those Liberals who had allowed militancy to color their views and who had in consequence broken their pledges to support the bill. It also blamed the Liberal leadership for the Nationalists' opposition to the bill: the NUWSS was convinced that if Liberal suffragists had tried to assuage Irish fears about the impact of the Conciliation Bill upon Home Rule, the vote on March 28 might have gone differently. Expressing her dissatisfaction with the Liberals and, in particular, with Lloyd George, Kathleen Courtney wrote: "I can't help thinking that if Lloyd George had exerted himself a little the defeat might have been saved. Brailsford says he (L. G.) didn't do one single thing he said he would do in connection with the second reading."[184]

Disillusioned with the Liberals, unoptimistic about the Conservatives, the NUWSS looked for comfort in a new quarter: the Labour Party. Early in April 1912, Fawcett gave an indication of the direction in which her thoughts were moving:

It must not be overlooked that although 13 or 14 members were absent on account of the impending ballot on the continuance of the coal strike, every Labour member in the House gave us his support, and that this course had been sanctioned by an official resolution previously adopted by the party. It may well be a subject for careful thought and discussion at our next Council meeting whether under these circumstances we should not modify our existing election policy and support Labour candidates.[185]

---

[183]The Conservatives' response to women's suffrage discouraged even the most steadfast party supporters. In February 1912, Lady Betty Balfour wrote to Bonar Law: "The sad thing is that so many of our Conservative Suffragists are like you--wildly in favor of woman suffrage, but quite unwilling to help to bring it about, whereas in the Conservative Antisuffragists there is a vein of real fervor and enthusiasm and they are quite willing to bring active pressure on their party to prevent its being brought about." Law Papers, 25/2/31, Lady Betty Balfour to Andrew Bonar Law, February 17, 1912.

[184]Archives, Manchester Public Library, M/50, Box 9, Kathleen Courtney to Millicent Garrett Fawcett, April 8, 1912.

[185]C. C., April 4, 1912.

The undoing of two years of hard work in a single night caused the NUWSS to redefine its whole relationship with the political parties. In a way, the formation of the alliance with the Labour Party is the epilogue to the story of the NUWSS fight for the Conciliation Bill.

CHAPTER V

THE ELECTION FIGHTING FUND AND THE FRANCHISE BILL

With the defeat of the Conciliation Bill, the NUWSS rested its hopes on the women's suffrage amendments to the Franchise and Registration Bill; yet, the suffragists' prospects were negligible if the same conditions that had extinguished the Conciliation Bill prevailed. If the vote on the women's suffrage amendments were to be successful, the NUWSS would, in some way, have to prevent the coalescing of forces that had occurred on March 28. The NUWSS and its supporters in Parliament believed that the cessation of militancy would undercut the antisuffragist campaign against the amendments; the Pankhursts chose to turn a deaf ear to this argument and the suffragists unhappily acknowledged that they could not persuade the WSPU to abandon militancy. With the House of Commons, the NUWSS still thought it had some influence. The vote on the second reading indicated that the Liberals and the Irish held the keys to victory on the vote on the Franchise Bill; the NUWSS did not dismiss the Conservatives, but it felt, quite correctly, that its cause was more popular with the rank and file of the Liberal Party than with the Tories.[1] Therefore if the suffragist forces within the Liberal Party could be strengthened, and those who had abstained on March 28 could be persuaded to support the amendments, there was a good chance that the House of Commons would incorporate women's suffrage in the Franchise Bill. About the Irish Nationalists, whose fortunes were so intertwined with the Liberal Party, there was less reason to be sanguine. Fawcett, complaining to Sir Edward Grey about the Nationalists' vote on the Conciliation Bill, predicted that there would be little chance of carrying a women's suffrage amendment if the Irish persisted in their opposition to the cause: "The fact that not one of Mr. Redmond's followers voted for the Bill, though 31 voted for it last year, is very ominous for the future unless something can be done to win them back to

---

[1]This belief is substantiated by the fact that in only 7 out of the 21 divisions held on women's suffrage before 1917 did support for women's suffrage among Conservatives outweigh opposition; on two of these seven occasions (June 1884 and November 1912) the Conservatives' vote on women's suffrage was determined by a desire to "dish" the Liberals. Conversely, in every division on women's suffrage except June 1884 and November 1912, the Liberals and Radicals contributed a higher percentage of votes for women's suffrage than did the Conservatives. Brian Harrison, Separate Spheres, pp. 27, 39. See also Chapter 1, note 82.

a more reasonable attitude.[2] If a repetition of March 28 were to be averted, the NUWSS would have to secure, at the least, the neutrality of the Irish. The Liberals' attitude to women's suffrage would exert a great influence on the behavior of the Nationalists.

Between April 1912 and January 1913, the NUWSS turned its energies to the job of building up a parliamentary majority for the women's suffrage amendments to the Franchise and Registration Bill. The main objects of the pressure were the Liberals and the Irish, who had to be drawn back to solid support. As in the past, the lobbying took the form of letters, memorials, meetings, and deputations. Some mention was also made of the women's suffrage amendment to the Home Rule Bill, the "Snowden amendment." The Irish were much opposed to this amendment, and the NUWSS thought it would be possible to use it as a way of showing the Nationalists that the suffragists could place obstacles in the path of Home Rule and perhaps coerce the Irish into remaining neutral on, if not supporting, the women's suffrage amendments to the Franchise Bill.[3] Lastly, the NUWSS adopted a new by-election policy: the Election Fighting Fund. This marked an important new departure in its political strategy.

The failure of the Conciliation Bill had severely shaken the NUWSS confidence in the Liberal Party, particularly in the party's leadership, and had simultaneously demonstrated that the Labour Party was committed to women's suffrage. By their official support of the Conciliation Bill, the Parliamentary Labour Party (PLP) had given substance to the women's suffrage resolution adopted at the January party conference.[4] The NUWSS thought it was justified in showing the erring Liberals that they could not continue to toy with the suffragists, and at the same time rewarding the Labour Party for its steadfast support for women's suffrage. The Election Fighting Fund (EFF) was worked out as a means of combining these several political motivations into a single strategy. If successful, the strategy would not only punish the Liberals but even entice them with the carrot being offered to the Labourites.

The EFF scheme, as first outlined in May 1912, was quite simple: the NUWSS agreed to form a special committee—the EFF—which would raise "a sum of money for the specific object of supporting

[2]Papers of Millicent Garrett Fawcett, Draft of a letter from Millicent Garrett Fawcett to Sir Edward Grey, April 1, 1912, Fawcett Library, London.

[3]C. C., April 18, 1912; Archives, Manchester Public Library, M/50, Box 9, Kathleen Courtney to Millicent Garrett Fawcett, April 8, 1912.

[4]C. C., May 2, 1912.

individual candidates standing in the interests of Labour in any constituency where the N. U. thinks it advisable to oppose a Liberal Antisuffragist" and offered to "support such candidates by the organization of a vigorous campaign on their behalf."[5] The new policy was not anti-Government in the same sense as the WSPU's election policy: it did not challenge all Liberals, only the antisuffrage ones. Moreover, unlike the militants' policy, there was a positive content to the EFF: it would work to build up the forces of the prosuffrage Labour Party in the House of Commons. The NUWSS did not regard the EFF as an abandonment of its former "best friend of women's suffrage" by-election policy. Rather, its support for Labour was simply a recognition that "a suffragist who belonged to a suffrage party was a better friend than a suffragist who belonged to a party which was Anti-Suffrage or neutral."[6] As Fawcett admitted, the defeat of the Conciliation Bill had administered a "fatal shock" to the old by-election policy of the NUWSS: forty-two "best friends" had voted against the bill and ninety-one had abstained. The EFF would add a new and more solid dimension to the interpretation of "best friend": in deciding whether or not to support a candidate, the NUWSS would take into account not only the individual's views but also the views of his party.[7]

In short-range terms the NUWSS adopted the EFF to rid the House of Commons of antisuffragists and to augment the suffragist forces, thereby increasing the chance of a successful vote on the women's suffrage amendments to the Franchise Bill.[8] The EFF was not aimed indiscriminately at all antisuffragists, however--only at Liberal antisuffragists--and its main purpose was to coerce members of the

---

[5]NUWSS, Ex. com. mins., April 18, 1912; Correspondence of the National Union of Women's Suffrage Societies, 1912, Circular from Kathleen Courtney, May 2, 1912; Fawcett Library, London.

[6]Millicent Garrett Fawcett, What I Remember, p. 206.

[7]Millicent Garrett Fawcett, The Women's Victory and After, p. 29. There were to be a few exceptions to this rule. "Tried friends," that is, those who placed women's suffrage above party, were to be supported regardless of their party's attitude to women's suffrage. The number of MP's who fell into this category was exceedingly small and included such stalwart suffragists as Walter McLaren and Lord Robert Cecil.

[8]David Morgan, Suffragists and Liberals, p. 106, contends that the NUWSS had abandoned the hope of amending the Reform Bill. He maintains that the NUWSS did not design the EFF to have an immediate impact on the Liberals but only to give Labour more opportunity at the next General Election. His interpretation of the evidence he cites to support this belief is very questionable, and it is contradicted by most of the evidence in the NUWSS archives.

Liberal Party into supporting the women's suffrage amendments to the Reform Bill.[9] Brailsford's analysis of the causes of the Liberals' antipathy to the Conciliation Bill agreed with that of the NUWSS in finding that many party members were afraid of the disruptive influence of women's suffrage on the Cabinet and feared the electoral effects of the bill: "There was a general sense in the House that women's suffrage was dangerous. It is fear which defeated us, and a calculation of party advantage. The belief which confronts us is that it may be dangerous to Liberalism to carry women's suffrage. It lies with us to arrange that it will be much more dangerous to delay it."[10]

In adopting the EFF, the NUWSS attempted to make such an arrangement. It intended to show the Liberal Party managers that "in consequence of the defeat of the Conciliation Bill and the uncertainty about the Government Reform Bill an increased number of three-cornered contests would take place."[11] Since the Liberals' control over the House of Commons was no more than tenuous, three-way contests which would divide the progressive vote could well prove disastrous for the Liberals and put the Conservatives back in power. The NUWSS realized that the Liberal Party machine resisted women's suffrage because of its electoral implications; it designed the EFF to persuade the Liberals that it would be more damaging to delay than to conclude a settlement of the women's suffrage question. In assessing the prospect of an increased number of three-cornered by-elections, the Liberal Party managers might decide to press for the passage of women's suffrage amendments to the Reform Bill, rather than risk the loss of Liberal seats.[12] Through the EFF the NUWSS also intended to influence, indirectly, the behavior of the Nationalists: the Irish, disturbed by the possible loss of Liberal seats at a time when Home Rule hung in the balance, might reverse their attitude to women's suffrage.[13]

The new policy also had a subtler, long-range rationale. The NUWSS intended, should the women's suffrage amendments to the Reform Bill fail, to continue the EFF policy with an eye to the next General Election: the object would be to increase the number of seats which Labour would contest at the election and to eliminate the

---

[9]The New Development in the Policy of the N.U.W.S.S., NUWSS pamphlet (n.p., n.d.).

[10]H. N. Brailsford, "The Reform Bill and the Labour Party," Englishwoman, 14, no. 41 (May 1912): 124-54.

[11]C. C, May 23, 1913.

[12]Correspondence of the National Union of Women's Suffrage Societies, 1912, Circular from Kathleen Courtney, May 2, 1912, Fawcett Library, London.

[13]C. C., September 26, 1912.

antisuffragist element in the Liberal Party, particularly in the Cabinet. Brailsford, who was still the NUWSS parliamentary watchdog, had assured the suffragists that "Two changes in the present disposition of forces in the House would ensure our success; the elimination of the present antisuffragist element in the Liberal ranks and any considerable increase in the Labour strength."[14] A contest between Liberals and Labourites for the same seats might result in an electoral victory for the Conservatives, but that was a risk the NUWSS was willing to take. At this point, the suffragists were inclined to feel that their position could be no worse under a Conservative Government, particularly as the leadership of the party included a distinguished suffragist component; and besides, they were convinced that the Liberals would agree to a women's suffrage measure if they believed that the suffrage issue would prove a handicap to them at the General Election.[15]

The negotiations that led to the formation of the EFF reveal much about the Labour Party and the NUWSS as political organizations. As had so often been the case in the past, Brailsford, himself a Liberal, played a guiding role in shaping the NUWSS policy, and he was responsible for the suffragists' decision to formulate an alliance with Labour.

Brailsford had for some time been critical of the NUWSS by-election policy and had questioned its effectiveness in influencing the behavior of Members of the House of Commons. However, he also criticized the anti-Government by-election policy of the militants as being too sophisticated and too demanding for the average voter; in addition, until the defeat of the Conciliation Bill, he preferred to give the Liberals the benefit of the doubt on the question of women's suffrage because he thought an anti-Government policy might be self-defeating.[16] The demise of the bill convinced Brailsford that it was time to jettison the Liberals and "to show the Government that we can make ourselves very objectionable"; but this would have to be done in a way which would "rally the votes of some large section of the electors, without demanding from them the heroic sacrifice of most of their opinions."[17] Accordingly, he suggested to Kathleen Courtney that the NUWSS form an alliance with the Labour Party; as Brailsford envisaged

---

[14]Brailsford, "The Reform Bill and the Labour Party," p. 128.

[15]C. C., June 20, 1912.

[16]Brailsford, "The Reform Bill and the Labour Party," p. 126.

[17]Archives, Manchester Public Library, M/50, Box 9, Kathleen Courtney to Millicent Garrett Fawcett, April 8, 1912; Brailsford, "The Reform Bill and the Labour Party," p. 126.

it, this new coalition would not indiscriminately challenge all Liberals, but only antisuffrage Liberals.[18]

The ground was ready for such a suggestion. There are indications that Fawcett and other members of the NUWSS executive had been dissatisfied with the NUWSS by-election policy for some months; the House of Commons vote on March 28 only intensified this feeling.[19] On April 4, in an article published in Common Cause, Fawcett hinted that the NUWSS was prepared to redefine its by-election policy. Soon afterward she received a letter from Courtney which relayed Brailsford's suggestion and assured her that opinion within the NUWSS was in favor of such a move: "A good many letters have come to the office urging us to do something and it is evident that there is any amount of keenness in the country. So I do think the question arises as to whether the psychological moment has come for us to enter into provisional arrangements with the Labour Party and then lay a proper scheme before a meeting of the General Council."[20] Ten days later, on April 18, the executive committee voted to summon a council on May 14 to consider changing the by-election policy.[21] Brailsford and Courtney had given Fawcett the final push. As Fawcett admitted, Brailsford had convinced her that the only way to gain the respect of the Liberal "whips and wirepullers, was to prove, by by-election work, that the suffragists could transfer seats from one side of the House of Commons to the other."[22]

The next step was for the NUWSS to approach the Labour Party and negotiate a "scheme of cooperation." After much correspondence with Arthur Henderson, the Labour Party secretary, the officers of the NUWSS met with him on April 30 to discuss the proposed plan; Henderson, in turn, sought out Hardie's and MacDonald's reaction to the NUWSS proposal.[23] Two weeks later, Fawcett and Courtney conferred with

---

[18]Archives, Manchester Public Library, M/50, Box 9, Kathleen Courtney to Millicent Garrett Fawcett, April 8, 1912.

[19]Ibid.

[20]Ibid.

[21]NUWSS, Ex. com. mins., April 18, 1912, Fawcett Library, London.

[22]Fawcett, The Women's Victory and After, p. 37.

[23]Archives of the Labour Party, Transport House, London, LP/wom/12/1, Kathleen Courtney to Arthur Henderson, April 19, 1912; LP/wom/12/2, Arthur Henderson to Kathleen Courtney, copy, April 20, 1912; LP/wom/12/3, Kathleen Courtney to Arthur Henderson, April 23,

MacDonald, as chairman of the Parliamentary Labour Party (PLP), in an effort to come to some agreement with Labour.[24]

The officials of the Labour Party were hardly enthusiastic about the NUWSS proposal. The NUWSS wanted to make it explicit that, as a reward for Labour's support for women's suffrage, it intended to establish a fund to help Labour candidates fight Liberal antisuffragists, and it wanted to make a public statement that the sole purpose of the fund was to support "individual candidates standing in the interests of Labour in any constituency where the N. U. thinks it advisable to oppose a Liberal Antisuffragist."[25] The Labour Party, although not averse to accepting the suffragists' financial assistance, wanted to obfuscate the issue and to delete from the resolution the phrase "the interests of Labour." The party's representatives were not eager to advertise that the party was a willing partner to an agreement that would pit Labour against its supposed ally the Liberal Party. MacDonald also feared that if the NUWSS announced that it intended to raise a fund to help Labour, this would "expose his party to the charge of being bought for an object" and would "weaken in the eyes of the public the independence of his party."[26]

Henderson's and MacDonald's skepticism was partly based on the complicated attitude of the Labour Party toward the whole question of women's suffrage. Notwithstanding the party resolution on the subject, there were three, if not four, different opinions within the party, ranging from that of George Lansbury (MP from Bow and Bromley), the most radical, to that of MacDonald. Lansbury thought women's suffrage should take precedence over every other issue and he wanted the party

---

1912; LP/wom/12/4, Kathleen Courtney to Arthur Henderson, April 23, 1912; LP/wom/12/5, Arthur Henderson to Kathleen Courtney, copy, April 25, 1912; LP/wom/12/6, Kathleen Courtney to Arthur Henderson, April 26, 1912; LP/wom/12/7, Arthur Henderson to Kathleen Courtney, copy, April 26, 1912 (hereafter cited as Labour Party Archives); NUWSS, Ex. com. mins., May 2, 1912, Fawcett Library, London.

[24]Papers of Millicent Garrett Fawcett, Copy of notes on an interview held by Millicent Garrett Fawcett and Kathleen Courtney with J. Ramsay MacDonald, May 13, 1912, Fawcett Library, London.

[25]NUWSS, Ex. com. mins., May 2, 1912, Fawcett Library, London.

[26]Labour Party Archives, LP/wom/12/11, Arthur Henderson to Edith Palliser, copy, May 3, 1912; Papers of Millicent Garrett Fawcett, Copy of notes on an interview held by Millicent Garrett Fawcett and Kathleen Courtney with J. Ramsay MacDonald, May 13, 1912, Fawcett Library, London.

to vote against every Government-sponsored measure as a protest against the Liberals' attitude toward the women's cause. Snowden and Hardie opposed any further electoral reform if women were excluded but were unwilling to put women's suffrage ahead of all other issues.[27] MacDonald, who as unquestionably the most powerful man in the Labour Party had many supporters, more or less favored women's suffrage but was prepared to sacrifice women in order to secure universal male suffrage.[28] At best, MacDonald was a tepid suffragist and the behavior of the militants had dampened whatever enthusiasm he may formerly have had for the cause.[29] MacDonald could not bear the militants' unwomanly behavior, and complained somewhat paradoxically that their actions demonstrated "those petti-fogging qualities which, insultingly to women, used to be known under the generic title of 'feminine'" and made him question whether women should vote.[30] Henderson's position on women's suffrage was somewhere between those of Snowden and MacDonald: emotionally he sympathized with Snowden and Hardie, but from a political point of view he sided with MacDonald.[31] In any case, the women's suffrage problem was, as MacDonald's biographer has written, as "potent a source of disunity in the Labour movement as industrial unrest."[32] The Labour Party officials apparently feared—no doubt with good reason—that an agreement with the NUWSS, even an informal one, might well bring these tensions to the surface and only exacerbate discord within the party.[33]

If the new agreement with the NUWSS threatened to inflame disagreements over women's suffrage within the party, it also challenged Labour's whole relationship with the Liberal Party. In 1903 MacDonald, then Secretary of the Labour Representation Committee (LRC),

---

[27]Colin Cross, Philip Snowden (London, 1966), pp. 113-14.

[28]A. Fenner Brockway, Inside the Left: Thirty Years of Platform, Press, Prison, and Parliament (London, 1942), p.34.

[29]FLAC, vol. 19, J. Ramsay MacDonald to Mrs. Cavendish Bentinck, March 15, 1911; J. Ramsay MacDonald to Mrs. Cavendish Bentinck [1912], Fawcett Library, London.

[30]David Marquand, Ramsay MacDonald (London, 1977), pp. 148-49; C. C., July 4, 1912.

[31]Labour Party Archives, LP/wom/12/16, Arthur Henderson to Kathleen Courtney, copy, May 15, 1912.

[32]Marquand, p. 147.

[33]For a discussion of some of the other issues over which the party was divided see Marquand, pp. 138-40, 144, passim.

and Herbert Gladstone, acting as Chief Whip of the Liberal Party, had worked out an informal entente: the Liberal Party promised not to oppose LRC candidates in thirty-five specified seats, and MacDonald, in return, promised that the LRC would avoid sponsoring candidatures which might split the anti-Conservative or progressive vote.[34] The Liberals had promoted such an agreement because they realized that a Labour candidate drew votes away from a Liberal; the Gladstone-MacDonald pact was a cornerstone of the relationship of the Liberal and Labour parties and, moreover, one which had benefited both parties.[35]

Labour took this entente seriously and, at least in one instance, threatened to withdraw from the House of Commons for a fortnight in protest against the Liberal Party's contesting what it regarded as Labour's seat.[36] In General Elections the Labour Party had lived up to the agreement and, on the whole, had avoided three-cornered contests; this certainly helped the Liberals in 1906 and, in the opinion of one historian, Robert Blake, may have cost the Conservatives the election in January 1910.[37] Although at by-elections three-cornered contents were more frequent, the NUWSS proposal promised that the electoral struggles between the Liberals and Labour would increase. Given the precariousness of the Government's parliamentary majority, by-elections very much mattered to the Liberals, particularly three-cornered contests which split the progressive vote. MacDonald continued to champion the political partnership between the two parties, and to those, such as Hardie, who criticized the partnership, he always pointed out that the enemies of the Liberals were the enemies of Labour. He had no desire to be party to any scheme that might jeopardize Labour's relations with the Liberals or further reduce the Government's already slim majority.[38]

Besides these considerations of possible party disunity and the matter of the entente with the Liberals, the Labour Party also had to consider how the NUWSS proposal might affect both its financial and its political independence. Since the Osborne judgment of 1909, the Labour Party had been very short of funds; but it had no wish to risk being

---

[34]Robert Blake, The Conservative Party from Peel to Churchill (New York, 1970), p. 175.

[35]P. F. C. Clarke, Lancashire and the New Liberalism (Cambridge, 1971), pp. 311-39.

[36]Manchester Guardian, July 3, 1912.

[37]Blake, p. 175.

[38]Marquand, p. 137.

charged with bribery.[39] As MacDonald told Fawcett, the EFF would certainly provoke accusations that Labour was "being bought."[40] MacDonald frankly admitted that he feared the suffragists might feel that they should have a say in the party's political decisions in return for their financial support; he was particularly apprehensive that the NUWSS might try to dictate which seats Labour should contest, and would insist on the Labour Party's opposing the Reform Bill should it exclude women.[41] In fact, the Labour Party constitution specifically debarred the party from forming an "alliance" with any organization; though the NUWSS proposal was not a formal alliance as such, it seemed to threaten the independence that the Labour Party was so determined to preserve.

MacDonald was right to suspect that the suffragists were "using" the Labour Party. Fawcett wanted the best of both worlds: she intended to preserve the "nonparty attitude" of the NUWSS while at the same time supporting Labour candidates.[42] She viewed an agreement with Labour as a "temporary accident," an alliance which was, for the moment, both convenient and politically useful to the suffragists. Once the EFF had brought the Liberals to heel, the suffragists would sever their connections with Labour.[43] But there were many members of the NUWSS who found the idea of even a temporary relationship with Labour repugnant. They identified the Labour Party with socialism and had no desire to be connected with this creed.

In persuading the NUWSS to establish the EFF, Fawcett emphasized that the NUWSS had not abandoned its traditional "nonparty attitude" and argued that the adoption of the EFF involved an extension of, rather than a fundamental change in, the NUWSS old policy of supporting those candidates who had shown themselves to be the best friends of women's suffrage; in the future, however, in judging between candidates, the NUWSS would take into account not only the individual

---

[39]In 1909 the House of Lords upheld an injunction against the Railway Servants which restrained the union from using its funds for political purposes. This decision, which was known as the Osborne judgment, had a serious impact on Labour finances. Cross, p. 115.

[40]Papers of Millicent Garrett Fawcett, Copy of notes on an interview held by Kathleen Courtney and Millicent Garrett Fawcett with J. Ramsay MacDonald, May 13, 1912, Fawcett Library, London.

[41]Ibid.; Fred Leventhal, "The Conciliation Committee," p. 154.

[42]Archives, Manchester Public Library, M/50, Box 9, Draft of letter by Millicent Garrett Fawcett [April 1912].

[43]Correspondence of the London Society for Women's Suffrage, Millicent Garrett Fawcet to Miss Benecke, March 11, 1913, Fawcett Library, London.

opinion of candidates but also their parties' attitude to women's suffrage. In order to minimize the radical implications of the suffrage—Labour entente and to sell her more timid colleagues on the idea of the EFF, Fawcett emphasized that the NUWSS was prepared to give its support to members of the Conservative and Liberal parties as soon as these parties took a strong stand on women's suffrage.[44] "I cannot join the Labour Party because I am not a socialist," she declared, but the support of Labour candidates should not be misconstrued as support for the Labour program.[45] In Fawcett's view, it was no more than passing political convenience that linked suffragists to the Labour Party; the alliance was in no sense intended as permanent, nor did it imply any loss of the NUWSS independence of action.[46]

To preserve the notion that the NUWSS intended to retain its nonparty status, and to satisfy those in the organization who did not favor the EFF, the NUWSS executive purposely set the EFF somewhat apart from the parent organization. The EFF was placed under the aegis of the NUWSS executive, but its finances were completely separate and it had it own staff and its own executive, which included men and women who did not belong to the NUWSS.[47] Fawcett and her colleagues on the executive realized that in matters other than women's suffrage, the members of the NUWSS were inclined to be conservative, and might not welcome any alliance with Labour, which was, after all, the party of the working class. Fawcett anticipated that if those conservative-minded women were compelled to make what they saw as a choice between loyalty to their class and loyalty to their cause, they would abandon their feminist inclinations in favor of class interests. The evident separation of the EFF from the NUWSS organization was supposed to make any choice of that sort unnecessary. Always, the NUWSS took pains to stress the limited nature of the partnership with Labour: "We are suffragists first," Fawcett delcared; "We belong to all parties, and to none."[48]

---

[44]C. C., May 23, 1912; Fawcett, The Women's Victory and After, p. 33.

[45]Christian Commonwealth, June 26, 1912.

[46]Millicent Garrett Fawcett, "The Election Policy of the National Union," Englishwoman, 14, no. 42 (June 1912): 2414–45.

[47]Correspondence of the National Union of Women's Suffrage Societies, 1912, Memorandum from Kathleen Courtney, May 2, 1912, Fawcett Library, London.

[48]Christian Commonwealth, June 26, 1912. A few months later, as a way of illustrating her attitude to political parties, Fawcett

Nonetheless, a good many members of the NUWSS remained unhappy with the EFF, and some eventually left.[49] The EFF was criticized as being a break with the NUWSS past policy, and a threat to old party loyalties. Some suffragists disliked any connection, however tenuous, with the Labour Party and carped that the NUWSS was "casting in its lot with socialism."[50] Still others felt that it was politically unwise to adopt the EFF because it would only irritate the Liberals. John Galsworthy, representing this last point of view, complained to Fawcett that the EFF would so exasperate the Liberals that it would destroy any hope of passing the women's suffrage amendments to the Reform Bill.[51] To some extent, these criticisms were undeniable: the EFF did involve a fundamental change in the "nonparty" policy of the NUWSS. No matter how much Fawcett and her friends wished to deceive themselves or the rest of the organization, the EFF was bound to alter the NUWSS relationship with both the Liberal and the Labour parties. Even if the entente with Labour was temporary and conditional, its purpose would be solely to help Labour candidates fight Liberals. How could such a proposal not prejudice the nonparty status of the NUWSS?

---

quoted a young lady's remark about her fiancé: "I do not love him. I do not hate him. He is to me as that footstool." Correspondence of the London Society for Women's Suffrage, 1912, Account of Fawcett's speech at a reception held at the Westminster Palace, October 15, [1912], Fawcett Library, London.

[49]In 1914 some prominent members of the NUWSS, including Eleanor Rathbone and Margery Corbett-Ashby, left the NUWSS because they disliked the EFF and felt that it would be a mistake to work for the return of Labour candidates at the General Election. They feared that this would split the progressive vote and result in the return of the Conservative Party, which, they said, would never introduce any legislation on women's suffrage. This disagreement over the EFF caused much rancor and unhappiness within the NUWSS. Correspondence of the NUWSS regarding the "secret committee," Circular from Eleanor Rathbone and Olivia Japp, February 7, 1914; Statement by S. Cross, Eleanor Rathbone, and Winifred Haverfield on the activities of the "secret Committee," [1914]; Mr. Armstrong to Millicent Garrett Fawcett, April 17, 1914; Millicent Garrett Fawcett to Mr. Armstrong, April 20, 1914, Fawcett Library, London; Marshall Papers, Eleanor Rathbone to Catherine Marshall, November 14, 1914. See also note 52 below.

[50]Correspondence of the London Society for Women's Suffrage, Philippa Strachey to Helena Swanwick, May 20, 1912, Fawcett Library, London; Labour Party Archives, LP/wom/12/14, H. N. Brailsford to Arthur Henderson, May 6, [1912].

[51]FLAC, vol. 1, Jii, John Galsworthy to Millicent Garrett Fawcett, August 18, 1912, Fawcett Library, London.

Although a vocal minority at the May council of the NUWSS opposed the new scheme, Fawcett and her supporters succeeded in persuading the delegates to adopt the EFF proposal.[52] At the same time the council voted to inaugurate a program known as "the Friends of Women's Suffrage" (FWS): this program, consciously modeled on the American Carrie Chapman Catt's Woman Suffrage Party, enabled those who sympathized with the NUWSS but could not afford to join, to enroll as "Friends" of the organization by signing a simple statement of approval of the principle of women's suffrage.[53] The scheme was aimed at attracting the support of members of the working class in order to rid the NUWSS of its middle class image,[54] and its appearance gave substance to the predictions of those suffragists who had divined that the EFF would draw the NUWSS closer to the working class. From the executive's point of view, the FWS, working as an adjunct of the EFF, would compensate for any falling off in membership which might result from the adoption of the EFF, and it would provide a valuable nucleus of information and organization within the constituencies for any political party allied with the NUWSS.[55]

The Labour Party did not officially accept the NUWSS proposal until the first week in July. Brailsford, always the mediator, was probably responsible for prevailing upon the party to put aside its objections to the EFF plan. Even before the NUWSS had actually adopted the EFF, Brailsford wrote Henderson a long letter in which he reproached the Labour Party leadership for its reluctance to sanction the proposal and asked him to reconsider his position:

The suppression of any reference to Labour candidates in the formal definition of the scheme is to all our minds totally

---

[52]Correspondence of the National Union of Women's Suffrage Societies, 1912, Resolutions Passed at the Council Meeting—May 14th and 15th, 1912, Fawcett Library, London. The opposing minority included some very influential members of the NUWSS, among them Emily Davies, Eleanor Rathbone, and Margery Corbett-Ashby.

[53]C. C., May 9, 1912. The Central and East of England Society had adopted a similar scheme as early as 1897.

[54]Correspondence of the National Union of Women's Suffrage Societies, 1912, Memo on the FWS by Maude Royden and Ida B. O'Malley, April 24, 1912, Fawcett Library, London.

[55]Councils of the National Union of Women's Suffrage Societies, Proceedings of the Special Council held May 14 and 15, 1912, Fawcett Library, London; Hitchin, Stevenage, and District Society for Women's Suffrage, Annual Report, 1912-1913 (Welwyn, n.d.), p. 6.

impossible. If you must insist on that, the whole plan falls
to the ground. A vague resolution telling of support for
"individual candidates" would mean nothing or anything, and
would bring in no money. It would be generally interpreted to
mean the pursuit of the hopeless old plan of suffrage
candidatures--which everyone knows to be a futility. . . . To
get money one must have an intelligible, hopeful scheme, which
the resolution as amended by you would not be. You will not
be surprised to hear that there is a good deal of doubt and
opposition to the scheme inside the National Union. . . . I
leave you to guess the effect on these critics of the news
that the Labour Party, while apparently quite glad to take the
women's money, refuses to accept their support publicly. . . .
all who have been urging that the Labour Party should be
trusted and helped are made to look ridiculous. . . .

I hardly think you have realized the potentialities of
this scheme. . . . I believe that in the course of a fighting
alliance most of them [suffragists] would end by becoming
decided and permanent adherents of the Labour Party. But that
certainly will not happen if at this crucial juncture women
realize that you do not care to avow any cooperation with
them, and in effect reject a plan which involves from most of
them sacrifices of party ties.[56]

Brailsford's criticisms must have made some impression on the leaders
of the Labour Party; moreover, the tempting prospect of new recruits as
well as additional funds may have helped overcome their objections to
the alliance. Although the Labour Party Executive did not meet
officially to consider the proposal until early July, by the end of May
the Labour Party had begun to cooperate with the NUWSS.[57] On July 2
the Executive adopted a resolution offered by MacDonald, which called
for acceptance of money and support from the NUWSS for candidates
contesting seats where Liberal antisuffragists might be easily opposed.
The partnership between the suffragists and Labour had formally
begun.[58]

---

[56]Labour Party Archives, LP/wom/12/14, H. N. Brailsford to
Arthur Henderson, May 6, [1912].

[57]Labour Party Archives, LP/wom/12/20, Edith Palliser to Arthur
Henderson, May 21, 1912; LP/wom/12/21, Assistant Secretary [no name
given] to Edith Palliser, copy, May 22, 1912. The Holmfirth election
was fought before the Labour Party officially accepted the scheme.

[58]Labour Party Archives, LP/wom/12/27, Catherine Marshall to
Arthur Henderson, July 2, 1912; Leventhal, p. 156. The Labour Party
executive did not meet between May and July. See Labour Party
Archives, LP/wom/12/11, Arthur Henderson to Edith Palliser, copy, May
3, 1912.

The NUWSS purposely chose members for the first EFF committee from a broad spectrum, in order to attract funds from as wide a variety of sources as possible and establish a broad base of support. The new committee included men such as the writers Israel Zangwill and Laurence Houseman, who had close ties to the WSPU; staunch Liberals, such as Muriel, Countess de la Warr; supporters of Labour, such as Margaret McMillan; and prominent suffragists such as Brailsford and Lytton.[59] The driving force behind the new committee was its secretary, Catherine Marshall.[60] Marshall, the daughter of a suffragist family with close ties to the Liberal Party, had worked her way up through the ranks of the NUWSS, beginning as secretary of the Keswick Women's Suffrage Society, and had eventually achieved a place on the NUWSS executive. As acting parliamentary secretary to the NUWSS, she had learned the art of pressure—group politics and had become familiar with the politics of suffrage within the House of Commons. Marshall was a zealot where suffrage was concerned, yet she managed to temper her determination with charm and humor. She was both perspicacious and persuasive and was an indefatigable worker; above all, she was a born organizer.[61]

Under Marshall's direction the EFF committee quickly recruited a staff of organizers, led by the very capable Margaret Robertson; in two months the EFF executive also succeeded in raising £4,130-6-3.[62] Almost before the committee had set the wheels of the new organization in motion, it was faced with the prospect of fighting four by-elections. The Labour Party, which had never contested more than one by-election at a time, was as overwhelmed by this task as the suffragists were.[63] But even in this first venture, the EFF organization and the local Labour committees worked well together. Wisely, the EFF executive, whenever possible, recruited suffragists

---

[59]Minutes of the Executive Committee of the Election Fighting Fund, June 14, 1912, Fawcett Library, London (hereafter cited as EFF mins.).

[60]Jo Newberry of Lucy Cavendish College, Cambridge University, is writing a biography of Marshall.

[61]During World War I she put her considerable abilities to use as political secretary of the No—Conscription Fellowship. Brockway, p. 68; Keith Robbins, The Abolition of War: The Peace Movement in Britain During the First World War (Cardiff, 1976), pp. 7, 82-86.

[62]EFF mins., July 5, 1912; NUWSS, Ex. com. mins., August 1, 1912; Fawcett Library, London.

[63]Manchester Guardian, July 3, 1912.

with Labour sympathies to serve both as organizers and as volunteer workers at these by-elections.[64]

The EFF staff went to great efforts to emphasize to the electors the links between the suffrage cause and the Labour Party. It opened committee rooms, canvassed for the Labour candidates, held joint meetings with Labour, and even supplied motor cars to take Labour voters to the polls.[65] The perseverance of the suffragists impressed the Labour Party. Arthur Peters, chief agent of the party, declared that there were "no more enthusiastic supporters and workers than the members of the National Union of Women's Suffrage Societies."[66] The Labour Leader called the suffragists "among the most effective regiments in the army of Labour."[67]

Besides the by-election work, the EFF during the period between June 1912 and January 1913, was also busy making preparations for the next General Election and agitating to strengthen the Labour Party's commitment to women's suffrage. After consulting with officials of the Labour Party, the EFF started laying the groundwork for contesting seats held by prominent antisuffragist Liberals—particularly those of the Cabinet ministers who opposed women's suffrage: Accrington (Harold Baker), E. Bristol (Charles Hobhouse), N. Monmouth (Reginald McKenna), Rossendale (Lewis Harcourt), and Rotherham (J. A. Pease).[68] The EFF also began organizing work in certain Labour constituencies which the suffragists feared might come under attack at the next election: Blackburn (Philip Snowden), Gorton (J. Hodge), E. Leeds (J. O'Grady),

---

[64]Fawcett, The Women's Victory and After, p. 38; EFF mins., July 21 and 25, 1912, Fawcett Library, London. Margaret Robertson, chief organizer for the EFF, was a member of the ILP. Brockway, pp. 33, 42.

[65]C. C., July 4 and 11, 1912; The Times, June 18, 1912; West Riding Federation, Annual Report, 1913 (n.p., n.d.), p. 6; Edinburgh Federation, Annual Report, 1913 (Edinburgh, 1912), p. 7; EFF mins., August 2, 1912, Fawcett Library, London.

[66]Labour Party Archives, LP/wom/12/28, Catherine Marshall to Arthur Henderson, July 2, 1912; LP/wom/12/32, Asst. Secretary to Catherine Marshall, copy, July 29, 1912; EFF mins., August 2, 1912, Fawcett Library, London.

[67]Labour Leader, June 27, 1912, and January 9, 1913.

[68]EFF mins., October 18, December 6, and December 20, 1912, Fawcett Library, London; C. C., October 24, 1912, and January 17, 1913.

and W. Bradford (F. W. Jowett).[69] The object of all of these preparations was twofold—to defend the seats held by Labour MP's who had "taken a strong line on the Women's Suffrage question" and to attack the seats of Liberal antisuffragists.[70] The EFF intended to build up strong local organizations in the constituencies that could be used effectively at the General Election to secure the return of Labour-suffrage candidates. According to Marshall, the Labour Party had said it was prepared to contest any constituency in the northeastern area and would attack several seats held by the Liberals, provided it had the support of the EFF; with this end in mind, the EFF began to organize in Gateshead, North Leeds, East Bradford, and Bishop Auckland.[71]

At this time the EFF organizers also began to propagandize for women's suffrage among the trade unions. The miners, who had consistently opposed women's suffrage resolutions at the annual conferences of the Labour Party, were singled out as the main target. The EFF committee reasoned that if the unions put pressure on the Parliamentary Labour Party, it might officially resolve to oppose the third reading of the Reform Bill if women were excluded. At the very least, these propaganda efforts would make the rank and file of the party more aware of, and presumably more enthusiastic about, the suffragigsts' demands.[72]

Although the executive of the EFF, in consultation with the NUWSS executive, was responsible for formulating all these plans and creating the organization to carry them out, many of the federations of the NUWSS began to establish regional EFF committees in order to make

---

[69]NUWSS, Ex. com. mins., October 17, 1912, Fawcett Library, London; Marshall Papers, Catherine Marshall to Arthur Henderson, copy, October 14, 1912; C. C., October 24, 1912; EFF mins., October 4, 1912, Fawcett Library, London.

[70]Marshall Papers, Catherine Marshall to Arthur Henderson, copy, October 14, 1912.

[71]EFF mins., August 2, October 4, and October 18, 1912, Fawcett Library, London. These seats were held respectively, by H. L. Elverston, R. H. Barron, Sir W. E. B. Priestley, and Sir H. Havelock Allan.

[72]EFF mins., November 22 and December 6, 1912, and NUWSS, Ex. com. mins., January 17, 1913, Fawcett Library, London; Manchester and District Federation, Annual Report, 1913 (Manchester, n.d.), p. 12.

the implementation of the EFF more effective.[73] Also, many federations which did not form local EFF committees did undertake the Friends of Women's Suffrage scheme, and that proved very successful.

The affiliates seem to have recognized that the reservoirs of working class support for women's suffrage were largely untapped. The EFF established a visible and demonstrable link between Labour and women's suffrage, and the NUWSS could use this Labour-suffrage partnership to attract workers' support for the suffrage cause. The FWS provided the local affiliataes with a new means of reaching the working class by enabling workers, male or female, to become adherents of the suffrage organization without making any financial contribution. The NUWSS branches sent volunteers into working class neighborhoods to canvass for women's suffrage and to register those who were sympathetic as "friends"; these "friends" then met periodically to discuss women's suffrage. By the end of 1912, over one hundred branches of the NUWSS had inaugurated the FWS program.[74] NUWSS headquarters anticipated that these new footholds among the working class would be very valuable to the suffragists at the General Election, particularly in the voter-registration drive. The potential for both the organization and registration of workers which the FWS offered would be especially appealing to the Labour Party; the NUWSS intended to dangle this prospect before Labour in order to secure its commitment to the cause of women's suffrage.[75]

The effectiveness of the EFF can be measured in part by the results of the four by-elections in which the EFF participated, since the EFF was established with by-elections in mind and the major portion of its financial and organizational resources was devoted to that activity.[76] At first glance (see Table 3), the EFF work in these elections may seem to have come to naught; but one must remember that the EFF had four interrelated goals in mind for these by-elections: to increase the number of Labour MP's in the House of Commons; to decrease the number of Liberal MP's in order to make the Labour Party more important in the House relative to the Liberal Party; to rid the House

---

[73]National Union of Women's Suffrage Societies, Annual Report, 1912, p. 28; Manchester and District Federation, Annual Report, 1913, p. 11; C. C., February 14 and 21, 1913.

[74]National Union of Women's Suffrage Societies, Annual Report, 1912, p. 31.

[75]The Friend of Women's Suffrage, no. 1, July 1913.

[76]The EFF spent £1,254-85-4 at these four by-elections. This figure does not include the loans which the EFF made to the Labour Party. National Union of Women's Suffrage Societies, Annual Report, 1912, p. 45.

Table 3

By-Elections at Which the Election Fighting Fund Was Used, 1912

Holmfirth—June 1912 [a]		January 1910 election results [b]	
S. Arnold, Lib.	4,749	H. J. Wilson, Lib.	6,339
G. Ellis, Cons.	3,379	R. G. Ellis, Cons.	3,043
W. Lunn, Lab.	3,195	W. Pickles, Lab.	1,643
Liberal majority	1,370	Liberal majority	3,296
Hanley—July 1912 [c]		December 1910 election results	
R. L. Outhwaite, Lib.	6,647	E. Edwards, Lab.	8,343
G. H. Rittner, Cons.	5,993	G. Rittner, Cons.	4,658
S. Finney, Lab.	1,694	Labour majority	3,685
Liberal majority	654		
Crewe—July 1912 [d]		December 1910 election results	
E. Craig, Cons.	6,260	W. S. B. McLaren, Lib.	7,629
H. Murphy, Lib.	5,294	E. Y. Craig, Cons.	5,925
J. Holmes, Lab.	2,485	Liberal majority	1,704
Conservative majority	966		
Midlothian—September 1912 [e]		December 1910 election Results	
Major J. A. Hope, Cons.	6,021	Master of Elibank, Lib.	8,837
Hon. A. Shaw, Lib.	5,989	Major J. A. Hope, Cons.	5,680
R. Brown, Lab.	2,413	Liberal majority	3,157
Conservative majority	32		

[a] Common Cause, June 27, 1912; The Times, June 19, 1912; Dod's Parliamentary Companion, 1912 (Londnon, 1912), p. 217.

[b] At the December 1910 election, the Liberal candidate, Wilson, ran unopposed.

[c] Common Cause, July 4, 1912; Dod's Parliamentary Companion, 1912, p. 194.

[d] Common Cause, August 1, 1912; Dod's Parliamentary Companion, 1912, p. 184.

[e] Common Cause, September 19, 1912; Dod's Parliamentary Companion, 1912, p. 190.

of Liberal antisuffragists; and to secure enough votes for the Labour candidate to demonstrate Labour's importance in the constituency.[77]

In terms of these goals, only one by-election (Hanley) was a total failure for the EFF; two (Crewe and Midlothian) were extremely successful, and one (Holmfirth) was a qualified success. At Holmfirth, the first test of the EFF, although the Labour candidate was not victorious, the intervention of Labour did substantially reduce the Liberal majority, and the election undoubtedly left Labour richer in terms of an organizational base in the constituency. Hanley, which followed on the heels of Holmfirth, was a huge disappointment. Not only did Labour lose a seat to the Liberals, but the poll of the Labour candidate was much below that of both the Liberal and the Conservative candidates. The suffragists, with justification, blamed the defeat on the fact that the local Labour organization was in the hands of the Liberals (who had not run a candidate in December 1910).[78] At Crewe, also in July, Labour's contesting the election cost the Liberals a seat. The NUWSS regarded the Liberal's loss, by 32 votes, of the seat at Midlothian, Gladstone's old constituency, which the Liberals had held since 1880, as a real vindication of the EFF policy.[79]

Although other issues besides women's suffrage, notably industrial grievances, played some part in the Liberals' defeat at Crewe and Midlothian, Labour's presence at these by-elections, which was encouraged, financed, and organized by the EFF, did determine the outcome of the contests.[80] Snowden may have overstated the case when he declared that the Liberals' loss of Crewe and Midlothian was due solely to the suffragists; however, Arthur Peters, chief agent of the Labour Party, substantiated this contention when he told members of the EFF that the Liberals' defeat was in no small degree due to their organization.[81] As one historian has written, the EFF coincided with an "upsurge in Labour candidatures in Liberal held constituencies," and it "did a lot to make the new candidatures effective and almost certainly extended the range of practicable candidatures into hitherto

---

[77]The Election Fighting Fund: What It Has Achieved, NUWSS pamphlet (n.p., n.d.), Fawcett Library, London.

[78]C. C., July 4 and 11, 1912; Martin Pugh, Electoral Reform in War and Peace, p. 9.

[79]Fawcett, The Women's Victory and After, p. 36.

[80]At Crewe, for example, the Liberals had aroused great resentment by bringing in the military during the railway strike. C. C., August 1, 1912.

[81]Philip Snowden, "The By-Elections and Woman Suffrage," Englishwoman, 14, no. 46 (October 1912): 4; C. C., September 26, 1917.

hopeless seats."[82]   So far as women's suffrage was concerned, these by-elections were undoubtedly successful to the extent of creating interest in constituencies that had formerly been untouched.   Both the NUWSS and the Labour Party gained an organizational base in these constituencies that was bound to be of help to Labour in the next General Election.[83]

Not much evidence is available by which to measure the Liberals' response to the EFF, but there are indication that the Liberals connected the loss of Crewe and Midlothian with the suffragists.   John W. Gulland (Lib., Dumfries Burghs), a Liberal Whip, told Marshall that the EFF's by-election activities had caused great consternation in the Liberal Party.[84]   The Manchester Guardian on September 22, 1912, assessing the results of the Midlothian by-election, sternly warned the Government: ". . . if the forces at work in Midlothian (including those of the suffragists) were all to continue to move with their present direction and velocity for the next three years, their normal result would be at the end of that time the return of a small conservative majority at a General Election."

In the case of the Labour Party, the impact of the EFF was much more profound and direct.   The EFF gave the women's suffrage issue a new and more elevated status in the Labour Party: it erased much of the bitterness caused by the militants and brought the Labour Party and the suffragists closer together.   The Labour Party, as a whole, was extremely impressed by the EFF.[85]   The Labour Leader paid tribute to the "tact, insight, and ability" of the suffragists, and even MacDonald, who had held so many reservations about the EFF, admitted that he could not "praise too highly the hard, unpleasant work done by the Representatives of the National Union of Women's Suffrage Societies.[86]   As a result of the EFF, Labour began to cooperate more closely with the suffragists, and the constituency organizations of the Labour Party and the local societies of the NUWSS even began to hold joint meetings.[87]

The link between the NUWSS and the ILP became particularly close.   Local branches of the ILP collaborated with affiliates of the

---

[82]Pugh, p. 23.

[83]C. C., August 1, 1912.

[84]EFF mins., November 8, 1912, Fawcett Library, London.

[85]Labour Party Archives, LP/wom/12/35, Asst. Secretary to Catherine Marhsall, copy, August 30, 1912.

[86]Labour Leader, January 9, 1913, and August 1, 1912.

[87]See, for example, NUWSS, Ex. com. mins., July 4, 1912, Fawcett Library, London; East Midland Federation, Annual Report, 1912-1913 (Nottingham, n.d.), p. 17; Manchester Guardian, November 18, 1912.

NUWSS to lobby for Liberal and Labour support for the women's suffrage amendments to the Reform Bill.[88] Representatives of the EFF frequently consulted with W. C. Anderson, chairman of the ILP: among other matters they discussed how the suffragists could influence the selection of Labour candidates and the possibility of the EFF's paying the salary of an ILP organizer who could represent the interests of both Labour and women's suffrage.[89] The ILP's contact with the EFF deepened its commitment to the women's cause; in December 1912, the chief agent of the ILP informed Isabella Ford, a member of the EFF executive and a former member of the executive of the ILP, that the representatives of the ILP in the House of Commons would vote against the third reading of the Reform Bill if women were excluded.[90]

Although the Labour Party as a whole was not so fervently dedicated to the women's cause as the ILP was, the EFF did influence it to take a stronger stand on women's suffrage.[91] In August 1912, Henderson told Marshall that there was a growing feeling within the PLP that Labour should vote against the third reading of the Reform Bill if it did not include women.[92] Shortly after this, at the request of the EFF committee, officials of the Labour Party began to put pressure on Redmond to allow a free vote on the women's suffrage amendments to the Reform Bill.[93] Finally, and most dramatically, the Labour Party Conference in January 1913, took a much stronger stand on women's suffrage than had the 1912 conference, calling "upon the Party in Parliament to oppose any Franchise Bill in which women are not included."[94] Altogether, the actions and declarations of members of

---

[88]NUWSS, Ex. com. mins., September 9 and October 17, 1912, Fawcett Library, London; National Union of Women's Suffrage Societies, Annual Report, 1912, p. 29.

[89]EFF mins., June 14, October 4, November 22 and December 20, 1912, Fawcett Library, London.

[90]EFF mins., December 20, 1912.

[91]The NUWSS wanted the PLP to promise to oppose the third reading of the Reform Bill if it did not contain any measure of women's suffrage. The PLP, probably because of MacDonald, was unwilling to make such a promise.

[92]EFF mins., August 2, 1912.

[93]EFF mins., November 8, 1912; NUWSS, Ex. com. mins., October 17, 1912; Fawcett Library, London.

[94]C. C., February 7, 1913; The Election Fighting Fund: What It Has Achieved, NUWSS pamphlet (n.p., n.d.). The resolution passed by a vote of 870,000 to 437,000. The miners, who had opposed a women's

the Labour Party and representatives of Labour organizations indicate that women's suffrage was fast becoming a more popular issue within the Labour Party. Much of the evidence seems more than coincidental: the party became more enthusiastic about women's suffrage after the initiation of the EFF, and suffragist sentiment within the party became more pronounced the longer the EFF-Labour entente operated.[95]

The entente was not without its rough spots. On at least three occasions in the first half-year of working together Labour and the NUWSS were quite in disagreement. In June 1912 the EFF's offer of £500 to the local Labour organization at Ilkeston, without having first consulted the Labour Party executive, infuriated the executive and lent credence to MacDonald's predictions that the suffragists intended to interfere in the internal politics of the party.[96] Fortunately, Henderson and Marshall were able to smooth over the differences and agree that such a circumvention of authority would not recur.[97] In October, the WSPU's decision to make war on the Labour Party unless it promised to vote against the Government on every question again threatened to dampen the party's enthusiasm for women's suffrage.[98] The NUWSS managed to prove to the party that its attitude was not the same as that of the militants, and it soothed Labour MP's with reminders of the EFF's support for Labour at the recent by-elections.[99]

---

suffrage resolution in 1912, remained neutral in 1913. The EFF work with the miners probably helped encourage the miners to take a slightly more favorable position.

[95]EFF mins., September 20, 1912, Fawcett Library, London.

[96]EFF mins., June 14, 1912; The Times, June 17 and 25, 1912; Manchester Guardian, June 18, 1912.

[97]Labour Party Archives, LP/wom/12/24, Catherine Marshall to Arthur Henderson, June 20, 1912; LP/wom/12/25, Arthur Henderson to Catherine Marshall, copy, June 20, 1912; LP/wom/12/26, Arthur Henderson to Catherine Marshall, copy, June 26, 1912; Correspondence of the National Union of Women's Suffrage Societies, Circular from Catherine Marshall, July 23, 1912; NUWSS, Ex. com. mins., July 18, 1912, Fawcett Library, London.

[98]Andrew Rosen Rise Up, Women! p. 197; C. C., October 31, 1912.

[99]Correspondence of the National Union of Women's Suffrage Societies, 1912, Circular from Kathleen Courtney, October 15, 1912; Philippa Strachey to Miss Cooke, October 18, 1912, Fawcett Library, London.

A month later the NUWSS decision to support George Lansbury, who had resigned his Labour seat and was contesting Bow and Bromley as an independent, again brought the suffragists into conflict with Labour.[100] Lansbury had made himself a thorn in the Labour Party executives' side over the question of women's suffrage, and the executive was extremely annoyed when the NUWSS, instead of going along with the party, actively campaigned for Lansbury.[101] Lansbury lost, and a month after the election, probably owing to the diplomatic efforts of Marshall and Henderson, the NUWSS and Labour were once more in working agreement.[102]

It was, indeed, the EFF that kept the entente working so well. Even though the EFF had not yet succeeded in winning a seat for Labour, the suffragists' hard work in the constituencies and their cooperation with Labour Party organizations and officials had won them the respect of the party and made Labour more responsive to women's suffrage. Much of the suspicion and mistrust which officials of the party had harbored toward the suffragists evaporated under the influence of the EFF.

The NUWSS as an organization was, in turn, influenced by the activities of the EFF and the contact with the Labour Party which accompanied it. Encouraged by the loss of Liberal seats at Crewe and Midlothian, and pleased by the Labour Party's response to the suffragists, the NUWSS Council voted to expand the EFF as a sign of its increased commitment to Labour: the EFF would now be used not only to oppose antisuffrage Liberals but also to defend the seats of Labour MP's and carry out organization work for Labour in the constituencies in preparation for the General Election.[103]

Through the EFF, the NUWSS had strengthened its ties with the Labour Party, and it now looked as though the suffragists might soon have an ally that would represent their cause in the House of Commons—the women's suffrage resolution passed at the Labour Party Conference in 1913 indicated that this was not an unrealistic proposition. Although the Labour Party was decidedly the minor party in the House of

---

[100]NUWSS, Ex. com., mins., November 14, 1912, Fawcett Library, London; C. C., November 22, 1912.

[101]The Times, October 17, 1912; Manchester Guardian, November 27, 1912.

[102]The results of the election were: Reginald Blair, Cons., 4,042; George Lansbury, Ind., 3,291. See also EFF mins., December 6 and 20, 1912, Fawcett Library, London.

[103]Labour Party Archives, LP/wom/12/39, Catherine Marshall to Arthur Henderson, October 5, 1912; LP/wom/12/42, Catherine Marshall to Arthur Henderson, October 14, 1912.

Commons, it had a potential for influencing political developments that was much greater than its numbers. Labour had brought "new strength to the Edwardian Liberal revival."[104] As a member of the coalition, its position was not altogether unlike that of the Irish in 1885. Neither the Nationalists, eager for Home Rule, nor the Liberals, eager to stay in power, could afford to neglect the desires of the Labour Party. If the Labour Party made women's suffrage a top priority, the other members of the coalition would have to give serious consideration to this demand.

One of the aims behind the adoption of the EFF by the NUWSS was to put pressure on the Liberals and the Irish Nationalists to support the women's suffrage amendments to the Reform Bill. In the spring of 1912, the NUWSS also began to lobby for an amendment—commonly known as the Snowden amendment—to clause 9 of the Home Rule Bill as another means of persuading the Irish to look more favorably on women's suffrage. Under this amendment, which was borrowed verbatim from Birrell's Irish Council Bill of 1907, the municipal register would be used to determine who would vote for the Irish Parliament. The municipal register included approximately 150,000 women who would, therefore, automatically qualify as electors for the proposed Parliament.[105] The idea of such an amendment originated with Brailsford (who had thought of the EFF), and he hoped to use it against the Irish as a way of keeping them from voting on the women's suffrage amendments to the Reform Bill as they had voted on the Conciliation Bill in March 1912. As Courtney wrote Fawcett:

Mr. Brailsford's proposition was that no amendment to the Reform Bill could be carried if the Irish Party voted on it as they voted on the Second Reading of the Conciliation Bill. I think he is right here, for on a wide amendment we could not hope to get as many Unionists as for the Conciliation Bill, and on a narrow amendment we should lose a certain number of Liberals, so that we could not cover our defeat by 14 votes. It therefore becomes essential . . . to win the support of the Irish. Mr. Brailsford is, I understand, writing to the Irish Societies telling them to ask the Conciliation Committee to organize the moving of a women's suffrage amendment to the Home Rule Bill; it appears the Irish really dislike this plan.[106]

---

[104]Clarke, p. 339.

[105]The Times, August 2, 1912; Correspondence of the National Union of Women's Suffrage Societies, 1912, Mrs. Haslam to the NUWSS, November 4, 1912, Fawcett Library, London.

[106]Archives, Manchester Public Library, M/50, Box 9, Kathleen D. Courtney to Millicent Garrett Fawcett, April 8, 1912.

Brailsford hoped the Irish would "barter enfranchisement in England for the exclusion of women voters at home."[107]   At his urging, the Conciliation Committee adopted the scheme and Snowden agreed to move the amendment on behalf of the Committee.

The NUWSS executive—for reasons that were partly vindictive, partly sensible—enthusiastically endorsed Brailsford's proposal. The Irish vote of March 28 was fresh in the suffragists' minds, and any scheme that placed obstacles in the path of Home Rule had a certain emotional appeal for these normally fair-minded women. Tactically, the idea was even more appealing. Brailsford was sure that, if the Irish repeated their March performance, no women's suffrage amendments would be included in the Reform Bill. The NUWSS thought it could use the Snowden amendment as a bargaining tool with the Irish. The Nationalists would dislike the Snowden amendment not only because it would infringe upon the authority of the Irish to decide who should vote for the Irish Parliament but also because, if successful, it would introduce a new and emotionally charged issue into the already explosive Home Rule proposal. If Redmond, the Nationalist leader, would agree at least to remain neutral to the women's suffrage amendments to the Reform Bill—if not to support them—the Snowden amendment would be withdrawn. Fawcett was prepared to use any lure to win over the intractable Irish and even hinted—though she had no basis for such a claim—that the WSPU might agree to suspend militancy if Redmond were to strike a bargain with the suffragists.[108]

The first problem was, of course, to convince the Irish that the Snowden amendment had a good chance of being included in the Home Rule Bill; from April to November, the suffragists sought to do just this, lobbying for support for the proposed amendment. The branch societies of the NUWSS wrote letters to MP's, contacted party agents, held meetings in support of the amendment, and even sent deputations to discuss the amendment with their MP's.[109] In addition, Marshall and Courtney, representing the Parliamentary Committee of the NUWSS, held interviews with leaders of the Liberal, Labour, and Nationalist parties

---

[107]Leventhal, p. 157.

[108]C. C., August 1, 1912; The Times, July 25, 1912.

[109]Correspondence of the National Union of Women's Suffrage Societies, 1912, Circular from Edith Palliser, May 3, 1912; Circular from Catherine Marshall, October 21, 1912; Correspondence of the London Society for Women's Suffrage regarding the Snowden Amendment, passim; Correspondence of the London Society for Women's Suffrage, Circular from Philippa Strachey, June 19, 1912; NUWSS, Ex. com. mins., July 4, 1912; all in the Fawcett Library, London.

about the amendment; at the NUWSS instigation, a number of suffragist MP's also lobbied actively for the amendment.[110]

Naturally, the appeals varied according to the bias of the party being courted. To Conservatives the NUWSS emphasized that both Bonar Law and Carson supported the amendment and it ingeniously argued that a vote for the amendment did not signify either a commitment to Home Rule or to women's suffrage. To Liberal antisuffragists, the NUWSS emphasized that the proposed Irish Parliament would only deal with matters of local government and that so prominent a Liberal as Churchill was in favor of giving women votes for governmental bodies which dealt with local and domestic, as opposed to Imperial, questions.[111] Of course, the greatest effort was made with the Nationalists, and to that end the NUWSS sent a special organizer to Ireland to coordinate the NUWSS campaign with that of the Irish Women's Committee for Securing Votes Under the Home Rule Bill.[112]

All the strategy failed. Redmond was not concerned enough about the Snowden proposal to strike the bargain hoped for by the suffragists. Although the NUWSS had publicly denied that the Snowden amendment "was in the nature of a tactical move," the suffragists did not really want the proposal to come before the House for debate and division.[113] Nevertheless, on November 5 the House of Commons voted on

------

[110]NUWSS, Ex. com. mins., October 17 and November 7, 1912, Fawcett Library, London.

[111]Correspondence of the National Union of Women's Suffrage Societies, 1912, Circular from M. Mackenzie, October 23, 1912, Fawcett Library, London.

[112]Correspondence of the National Union of Women's Suffrage Societies, 1912, Mrs. Duncan to Miss Cooke, June 11, 1912; Correspondence of the London Society for Women's Suffrage, Aileen Connor Smith and Geraldine Lennox to Philippa Strachey, October 23, 1912; Fawcett Library, London.

[113]The private correspondence of the NUWSS does not support the denial. In addition, Helena Swanwick admitted in October, at a meeting of the London Society for Women's Suffrage, that the NUWSS was lobbying for the Snowden amendment in hopes of persuading the Irish to adopt a more favorable attitude to the women's suffrage amendments to the Reform Bill. See also the Manchester Guardian, October 23 and November 2, 1912. Tactically, too, withdrawal of the amendment would have indicated that Redmond had promised not to oppose the women's suffrage amendments to the Reform Bill.

and defeated the amendment by a majority of 173.[114] Fearful that passage of the amendment might damage the prospects of Home Rule, the Government sealed the fate of the measure by putting its whips on against the amendment.

In spite of the defeat, the proceedings of November 5 were interesting in two respects: MacDonald made his maiden speech on the women's suffrage question, sharply criticizing the Government, and twenty-nine Liberals disobeyed the Government whip by voting for the amendment, while another fifty-six Liberals abstained.[115] Although the Labour Party did not give its official support to the amendment, the NUWSS was, on the whole, pleased by the show of support for the amendment from the Liberal and Labour camps and, in particular, by MacDonald's speech. Speaking for the suffragist camp, Common Cause noted:

> The debate . . . has well served our turn. It has given our friends of the Labour Party an opportunity for advancing our cause at the cost of detaching themselves from the coalition. It has subjected the Irish Party to an afternoon of heckling which their betrayal of last March richly deserved. It has shown Mr. Redmond that there are Liberals who care enough for women's suffrage to vote against the Government. And finally it has exhibited the Ministry in a frankly antisuffrage attitude which justifies to the full our adoption of a Fighting Fund.[116]

The number of Liberal and Labour votes for the amendment was small, but the NUWSS had hopes that it might be enough to influence Redmond to adopt a more favorable attitude to the women's suffrage amendments. In the debate Redmond, echoed by other leaders of the Irish party, had promised that his followers would be free to vote as they chose on the women's suffrage amendments.[117] Snowden, encouraged by this development, wrote Fawcett: "I am more hopeful today than I have been for a long time. The debate yesterday did enormous good. It put the Irish in a position which prevents them from repeating their policy on the Conciliation Bill." And he added, "It has left many Liberals

---

[114]The Times, November 6, 1912; Manchester Guardian, November 6, 1912. The vote was as follows: For the amendment--Lab., 27; Lib., 29; Cons., 80; Ind. Nat., 5. Against the amendment--Lab., 5; Lib., 173; Cons., 64; Nat., 72. Abstain--Lab., 8; Lib., 56; Cons., 136; Nat. 4.

[115]C. C., November 14, 1912.

[116]Ibid., November 8, 1912.

[117]Christian Commonwealth, November 13, 1912.

anxious for an early opportunity to remove the reproach of their vote last night."[118]

The NUWSS was not so wholeheartedly optimistic as Snowden. It fully realized that no matter how encouraging the debate or division may have been, the strategy behind the amendment had failed; Redmond had not come to a firm agreement with the suffragists, and the NUWSS, which neither liked nor trusted the Irish leader, did not have much confidence in his pledge of November 5. The suffragists recognized that supporters of women's suffrage and, in particular, members of the Liberal and Labour parties would have to make the Irish the prime object of their attention if the Reform Bill were to include women's suffrage.[119] Unfortunately the Nationalists, egged on by the antisuffragists who were "incomparably better organized" than ever before, remained convinced that women's suffrage—whether in the form of the Snowden amendment or in the form of a women's suffrage amendment to the Reform Bill—posed a threat to Home Rule.[120] The suffragists would have to convince the Irish that it would be more hazardous to their cause to oppose women's suffrage than to support it; the NUWSS recognized that this would not be an easy task.

Both the Snowden amendment and the EFF were stepping-stones to a larger goal: the inclusion of women's suffrage in the Franchise and Registration Bill. With the demise of the Conciliation Bill, the women's suffrage amendments offered the only remaining opportunity for the enactment of women's suffrage; if one of these was not included in the Reform Bill, the suffragists had little hope that anything could be done before the next General Election to enfranchise women. From April 1912 to January 1913, therefore, the NUWSS' most immediate and important objective was to secure support for the women's suffrage amendments to the Franchise Bill.[121] Asquith had announced in November 1911 that the Liberal Government intended to introduce in the next session of Parliament a franchise bill which could be amended to include women. The Liberals had designed the bill to abolish the practice of plural voting and to shorten the residency qualification; the party managers felt that in these two respects, the existing

---

[118]Papers of Millicent Garrett Fawcett, Philip Snowden to Millicent Garrett Fawcett, November 6, 1912, Fawcett Library, London.

[119]NUWSS Ex. com. mins., November 21 and December 5, 1912, Fawcett Library, London; Labour Party Archives, LP/wom/12/42, Catherine Marshall to Arthur Henderson, October 14, 1912.

[120]C. C., November 14, 1912.

[121]Morgan, p. 166, asserts that the NUWSS had, by the summer of 1912, abandoned all hope of amending the Reform Bill. All the evidence contradicts this contention.

franchise laws greatly benefited the Tories.[122] The proposed Franchise Bill, and the Home Rule Bill were the two major pieces of legislation which the Government wanted to enact in the 1912-13 session.

The Franchise Bill was read for the first time on June 17 and passed its second reading on July 12.[123] The suffragists' "best opportunity," the opportunity to obtain the inclusion of women in a Government-sponsored Reform Bill, had arrived.[124] In its original draft, the Franchise Bill had not contained any mention of women's suffrage, but by July 1912, the women's suffrage amendments which the House would consider on the bill's third reading had been formulated and placed on the order papers.[125] The women's suffrage amendments dealt with two sections of the Franchise Bill: Clause 1, section (1), the formal, prefatory enfranchising section which stipulated that "every male person" who was qualified in terms of the act could register and vote; and Clause 1, section (2), which defined the qualifications that had to be met in order to vote. (See Table 4). To win the vote, the suffragists had to amend both sections of Clause 1. As Brailsford noted: "It follows from the structure of the bill that suffragists have two trenches to carry. Women must first be made eligible for the Parliamentary franchise, and when that is done some positive qualification must be conferred upon them."[126]

Four amendments appeared on the order paper in July: the Grey amendment, the Henderson amendment, the Dickinson amendment, and the

---

[122]CAB 37/108/148, November 8, 1911; CAB 37/108/181, December 1911; CAB 37/111/88, July 4, 1912; Lloyd George Papers, C3/15/18, Winston Churchill to David Lloyd George, January 1913.

[123]The Times, June 18, 1912; Manchester Guardian, July 13, 1912. Asquith, in supporting the Franchise Bill, had expressed his conviction that the House of Commons would not be so ill-considered as to amend the bill on behalf of the women: "I dismiss as altogether improbable the hypothesis that the House of Commons is likely to stultify itself by reversing in the same session the considered judgment at which it has arrived." Fawcett acerbically commented, "Considering the means which had been taken to defeat the Conciliation Bill . . . this almost surpassed in arrogance and effrontery what one had become accustomed to expect from the Liberal Prime Minister." Fawcett, What I Remember, p. 204.

[124]Morgan, p. 101.

[125]C. C., July 18, 1912.

[126]Manchester Guardian, July 17, 1912.

Table 4<u>a</u>

The Franchise and Registration Bill and the
Proposed Women's Suffrage Amendments

===

FRANCHISE AND REGISTRATION BILL

Clause 1

(1) Subject to the provisions of this Act, every male person
shall be entitled to be registered as a Parliamentary elector for a
constituency, if that person is qualified in accordance with this Act
to be registered in that constituency, and while so registered shall be
entitled to vote at an election of a member to serve in Parliament for
that constituency; but a person shall not be registered or vote for
more than one constituency.

(2) For the purposes of this Act a person shall be qualified
to be registered in a constituency as a Parliamentary elector if that
person resides, or is an occupier of land or premises, in that
constitutency, and has so resided, or been an occupier, for a
continuous period of at least six months last past, or during such a
period has so resided for part of the period, and so been an occupier
for the remainder of the period.

GREY AMENDMENT

This amendment would delete the word "male" from the phrase
"every male person" in clause 1, section (1). This amendment was a
preliminary step to the other three amendments: if it was not carried,
and the word "male" was retained, it would not be possible to confer a
qualificatiton on women in clause 1, section (2). If it was
successful, the House of Commons would still have to decide which women
should be qualified, and how they should qualify (clause 1,
section [2]).

HENDERSON AMENDMENT
(Also called the Adult Suffrage Amendment)

This amendment would add to the phrase "every person" in
clause 1, section (1), the words "of either sex"; it would also
incorporate this phrase in clause 1, section (2). Thus, all women who
met the six months' residency qualification stipulated in clause 1,
section (2) would receive the vote. It would enfranchise approximately
10 million women.

Table 4—continued

DICKINSON AMENDMENT
(Also called the Norwegian Amendment)

This amendment, which would be inserted in clause 1, section (2), would qualify a woman to register "if she is over 25 years of age and is the inhabitant occupier, as owner or tenant, or the wife of such an inhabitant occupier, of a dwelling-house in that constituency, and has resided therein for a period of at least six months past. Provided that except herein enacted no women shall be registered as joint occupiers in respect of the same dwelling." In effect, the amendment gave the vote to all women householders and wives of householders and thereby would enfranchise approximately 6 million women.

CONCILLIATION AMENDMENT
(Also called the Lyttelton Amendment)

This amendment, which would be included in clause 1, section (2), stipulated that "a person being a female shall be qualified to be registered in a constituency as a Parliamentary elector if she is a local government elector for the purpose of all local government elections in that constituency." This meant, essentially, that only women householders could qualify to register; the amendment would enfranchise approximately 1½ million women.

---

[a]The information contained in this table has been compiled from the following sources: C. C., June 27, 1912; Henry Brailsford, Women and the Reform Bill, NUWSS pamphlet (n.p., n.d.); Correspondence of the National Union of Women's Suffrage Societies, 1912, Circular from Edith Palliser [July 1912], Fawcett Library, London; Correspondence of the London Society for Women's Suffrage, Circular from Philippa Strachey [July 1912], Fawcett Library, London.

Conciliation amendment.[127] Even before the amendments had appeared on the order paper, the NUWSS had begun to evaluate the Liberal and Conservative parties' attitudes to the amendments in order to decide how it could most effectively lobby for the inclusion of women's suffrage in the Reform Bill. The suffragists assumed, correctly, that the Labour Party would support all the women's suffrage amendments, and they felt, with reason, that the Nationalists were less concerned with the particulars of the amendments than they were with the effect that women's suffrage as an issue would exert on the Liberal Party. It was obvious to the NUWSS that it would have to work to build up a majority for the Grey amendment: if this amendment failed, there would be no possibility of enfranchising women under the Reform Bill. But which of the remaining amendments should it concentrate upon?

There seemed to be no chance at all that the House of Commons would approve the Henderson amendment—its provisions were too comprehensive for either the Liberals or the Conservatives—and this amendment was ruled out long before July. The Dickinson amendment seemed to have the best chance of success. The suffrage wing of the Liberal Party liked this amendment, which was felt to be beneficial to the electoral interests of the Liberals, and both Grey and Lloyd George had given it their support; Liberals who had criticized the Conciliation Bill on the grounds that it was too narrow were prepared to back the Dickinson amendment. Passage of this amendment would, however, depend upon the support of some twenty to thirty Tories.[128] Although Lord Robert Cecil felt that the Dickinson amendment would

---

[127]Sir Edward Grey, Lord Robert Cecil, the Hon. Alfred Lyttelton (Cons., St. George's, Hanover Square) and Philip Snowden had agreed to speak for the Grey amendment. Arthur Henderson, Philip Snowden, and J. H. Thomas (Lab., Derby) had agreed to speak for the Henderson amendment. W. H. Dickinson, F. D. Acland (Lib., Canborne, N.W.), Sir John Rolleston (Cons., Hartfordshire, E.), and E. A. Goulding (Cons., Worcester) had agreed to speak for the Dickinson amendment. The Hon. Alfred Lyttelton, C. S. Goldman (Cons., Penryn and Falmouth), Murray MacDonald (Lib., Falkirk Burghs), and G. J. Bentham (Lib., Lincolnshire, West Lindsey) had agreed to speak for the Conciliation amendment.

[128]Correspondence of the National Union of Women's Suffrage Societies, 1912, Circular from Edith Palliser [July 1912], Fawcett Library, London. Brailsford had originally estimated that only nine Conservative votes were necessary to secure passage of the Dickinson amendment (see Chapter 4, p. 126). The vote on the Conciliation Bill in March 1912 must have caused him to revise his estimate. The vote on March 28 made it clear that he could not count on support from the Irish. In addition it showed that as long as militancy persisted, some MP's, although they were in favor of granting votes to women, would not vote for any women's suffrage measure in protest against militancy.

enfranchise too many women, he had agreed to give it his support, and he admitted that a number of Conservatives might support the proposal because they felt "married women are responsible people who would add an element of stability and moderation to the electorate."[129] The Conservative and Unionist Women's Franchise Association had also given its support to the Dickinson plan, noting that the Conservative Party would benefit from the enfranchisement of wives since the family was "the foundation of Conservatism."[130] These rumblings from the Conservative Party convinced the NUWSS that there was a real possibility of convincing Conservative suffragists to vote for the Dickinson amendment, provided the Tories could be persuaded that the amendment would benefit their electoral interests: the NUWSS might succeed in promoting the idea that the addition of six and a half million women to the electorate would compensate for the elimination of the plural vote and the enactment of a shorter residency qualification.

The NUWSS, however, decided that it should not gamble all its resources on one amendment. The experience of the Conciliation Bill had shown the NUWSS and its suffragist colleagues in the House that the Conciliation amendment was too narrow to appeal to the Liberals, but they hoped that if the Dickinson amendment came up first (and suffragists in the House had made sure that this would be the case) and failed to pass, they might be able to persuade the Liberals to vote for this less desirable proposal if the choice were between enfranchising one and a half million women or not enfranchising any women at all.[131] The NUWSS was probably overoptimistic in this calculation, but it was not depending on the goodwill of the Liberals alone. It intended to barter with the Liberals: the NUWSS would agree to work for the Dickinson amendment if the Liberals agreed to support the Conciliation amendment as a second choice. As an additional enticement to the Liberals, the NUWSS also promoted the idea that if the Liberals wanted to extend the provisions of the Conciliation amendment after it had passed, they could bring in a bill to alter the municipal franchise on which it was based.

---

[129]Cecil Papers, Add. mss. 51075, vol. I, Memo on the Number of Women Who Would Be Enfranchised by the Amendments to the Reform Bill, July 8, 1912; NUWSS, Ex. com. mins., July 14, 1912, Fawcett Library, London. Cecil favored a complicated plan that would give a vote to all widows and unmarried women over twenty-five, and half a vote to all married women. This plan was never translated into an amendment.

[130]The Conservative and Unionist Women's Franchise Review [1912], p. 258.

[131]Cecil Papers, Add. mss. 51075, vol. I, Memo on the Number of Women Who Would Be Enfranchised by Amendments to the Reform Bill, July 8, 1912; Manchester Guardian, July 3, 1912.

By the summer of 1912 the NUWSS had decided to focus its energies on the Dickinson and Conciliation amendments and, specifically, to try and win Conservative support for the former and Liberal support for the latter.[132] From July to January it mounted a massive propaganda effort on behalf of the women's suffrage amendments to the Reform Bill, concentrating, in particular, on the Dickinson and Conciliation amendments. As in the past, the NUWSS kept in close touch with the suffrage groups in the House of Commons which MP's had formed to promote each of the amendments.[133] It was also very active in the Joint Campaign Committee for Women's Suffrage, an organization which representatives of the principal women's suffrage societies and suffragist MP's had organized to lobby for women's suffrage both in the constituencies and in the House of Commons.[134] In its dealings with all of these bodies, the NUWSS stressed the need to coordinate the activities of the suffrage forces.[135]

The NUWSS campaign in support of the women's suffrage amendments was, by any standard, impressive. Fawcett told Maud Arncliffe-Sennett, a stalwart suffragist, that she intended to devote all her energies to lobbying for the women's suffrage amendments, and her attitude was reflected in the entire NUWSS organization.[136] Between July and January the NUWSS sponsored a wide variety of demonstrations and meetings, from a huge public gathering in the Albert Hall at which £5,394-14-3 was collected, to drawing room meetings in country villages; in one week in October, 137 meetings were held.[137] NUWSS headquarters organized postcard campaigns to MP's from their constituents and the branch societies sent memorials to MP's which were signed by prominent persons in the constituencies, including town councillors and members of political associations. For three months, a

---

[132]Correspondence of the National Union of Women's Suffrage Societies, 1912, Circular from Edith Palliser [July 1912], Fawcett Library, London.

[133]In addition to these groups, suffragists in the House of Commons had also formed party groups to lobby for women's suffrage within each party. Fawcett, The Women's Victory and After, pp. 44-45.

[134]National Union of Women's Suffrage Societies, Annual Report, 1912, p. 14.

[135]NUWSS, Ex. com. mins., July 18, 1912; Correspondence of the National Union of Women's Suffrage Societies, 1912, Circular from Edith Palliser [July 1912]; Fawcett Library, London.

[136]British Museum, Arncliffe-Sennett Collection, vol. 19, Millicent Garrett Fawcett to Maud Arncliffe-Sennett, September 25, 1912.

[137]C. C., October 17 and November 8, 1912; London Society for Women's Suffrage, Annual Report, 1912, p. 12.

hired van toured the countryside drumming up support for the women's suffrage amendments.[138] The local branches, which were in constant contact with headquarters throughout this period, sent deputations to their local MP's to secure support for the amendments; the Parliamentary Committee of the NUWSS tried to follow up these deputations by interviewing every MP.[139] Various women's political organizations, such as the Women's Liberal Federation and the Conservative and Unionist Women's Franchise Association, were enlisted to help lobby, and the NUWSS also cooperated with and, to a large extent, coordinated its activities with those of the other constitutional suffrage societies.[140] Throughout this period the NUWSS was in close contact with its leading supporters in Parliament, in particular, Arthur Henderson, Lord Robert Cecil, and Sir Edward Grey. The Parliamentary Committee constantly tested the House of Commons' mood on the women's suffrage amendments; Marshall, as acting secretary of the committee, frequently held interviews with prominent suffragists in the various parties in order to keep abreast of the parties' attitudes to the amendments. The suffragists felt that if they were well informed about developments in Parliament, they would be in a position to apply pressure where it was most needed.[141]

Despite these massive campaigning efforts, the forces that had destroyed the Conciliation Bill--the militants and the Irish--

---

[138]Correspondence of the National Union of Women's Suffrage Societies, 1912, Millicent Garrett Fawcett to Edith Palliser, September 18, 1912, Fawcett Library, London; Surrey, Sussex, and Hants Federation, Annual Report, 1912-1913, p. 7; West Lancashire, West Cheshire, and North Wales Federation, Annual Report, 1913 (Liverpool, 1913) p. 7; West Midland Federation, Annual Report, 1912-1913 (n.p., n.d.), p. 8.

[139]Eastern Counties Federation, Annual Report, 1913 (n.p., n.d.), p. 10; Surrey, Sussex, and Hants Federation, Annual Report, 1912-1913, p. 7; Kentish Federation, Annual Report, 1913 (Tunbridge Wells, n.d.), p. 28; Marshall Papers, Memorandum on the activities of the Parliamentary Committee of the National Union of Women's Suffrage Societies (n.d.).

[140]West Lancashire, West Cheshire, and North Wales Federation, Annual Report, 1912 (Liverpool, 1912), p. 7; C. C. Osler, The Vital Claim: An Appeal from Liberal Women to Women Liberals, NUWSS pamphlet (n.p., n.d.); Correspondence of the London Society for Women's Suffrage, Memorandum on a meeting of the constitutional suffrage societies, October 16, 1912, Fawcett Library, London.

[141]NUWSS, Ex. com. mins., July 14, July 18, October 17, November 7, December 5, December 19, 1912; January 2 and January 17, 1913; Fawcett Library, London.

threatened to coalesce once again to defeat the women's suffrage amendment. In July 1912, at the very time the NUWSS inaugurated its campaign for the amendments, the militants began a campaign of a very different sort—arson.[142] Simultaneously, they increased the severity of their attacks upon supporters of the Government. On July 18, Redmond and Asquith narrowly escaped injury when a suffragette threw a hatchet into the carriage in which they were riding.[143] An angry Times on July 20 commented, "there has been no more cowardly outrage in the history of the movement."

Both the NUWSS and its supporters in the House of Commons spoke out against what they described as the "provocative and bellicose" actions of the WSPU.[144] Fawcett publicly criticized the militants for "the criminal violence even more detestable than any in which they have previously indulged"; the militants were, she said, "the most powerful allies the antisuffragists have."[145] Privately, she pleaded with the WSPU to call a temporary halt to militancy until after the House of Commons had acted on the women's suffrage amendments, but her appeals got nowhere. Annie Kenney, in reply, noted with rather questionable logic that the King held his throne because of a revolution and cited other historical examples to show, as she contended, that only violent means could achieve political ends.[146]

Some three months after these events, in October 1912, the Pethick-Lawrences, who quite disagreed with Christabel Pankhurst about the escalation of violence, were forced out of the WSPU. With their departure, reason and restraint no longer had any voice in the counsels of the militants, and arson, window breaking, and other forms of violence became the hallmark of the suffragettes.[147]

---

[142]E. Sylvia Pankhurst, The Suffragette Movement, p. 401. On July 13 two members of the WSPU were arrested near Nuneham House, the country residence of Lewis Harcourt. It was obvious, from the contents of their bags, that they intended to burn it. Five days later, on July 18, two suffragetes tried to set fire to the Theatre Royal in Dublin. Rosen, pp. 169-70.

[143]Earl of Oxford and Asquith, Memories and Reflections (London, 1928), vol. 1, pp. 261-62.

[144]The Times, July 23, 1912.

[145]C. C., July 25, 1912.

[146]Correspondence of the National Union of Women's Suffrage Societies, 1912, Millicent Garrett Fawcett to the Hon. Sec. of the Women's Social and Political Union, July 19, 1912, Fawcett Library, London; C. C., July 25, 1912.

[147]Rosen, pp. 173-74.

As Pethick-Lawrence later wrote in his memoirs, the Pankhursts refused "to be deflected by criticism or appeal one hair's breadth from the course which they had determined to pursue."[148]

As before, the militant campaign had long-lasting reverberations in the House of Commons. The suffragettes' actions "made most politicians feel that their only moral obligation was to resist any surrender to violence," and, rightly or wrongly, many MP's regarded voting for the women's suffrage amendments as just such a surrender.[149] By January 1913 many of the suffrage movement's staunchest advocates in the House were seriously concerned about the adverse effect militancy would have on the voting on the amendments. Lord Robert Cecil wrote Balfour, "I am consumed by anxiety to prevent the militant women from committing more outrages"; in his opinion, the militants were "more attached to their own methods than to the good of the cause."[150] The Pankhursts, it seemed, no longer cared about the reaction of the audience for whom the spectacle was being staged: the tactics had become more important than the cause of women's suffrage.

On the eve of the scheduled vote on the amendments to the Franchise Bill, the WSPU finally agreed to call a truce and suspend militancy until after the House had divided on the amendments.[151] Once again, however, the truce had come too late. As in March 1912, militancy, particularly militancy which encouraged the burning of property and the maiming of Cabinet ministers, provided lukewarm supporters of women's suffrage with an excuse to vote against the amendments and gave the opponents of women's suffrage a powerful argument to use in their efforts to dissuade MP's from supporting women's suffrage. It is impossible to tabulate exactly the impact of militancy, but there is no doubt that militancy adversely affected the House of Commons' attitude to women's suffrage.[152] At the very time when suffragists both inside and outside the House of Commons were doing everything possible to secure the inclusion of women in the Franchise Bill, the militants, whatever their intentions, were

---

[148]F. W. Pethick-Lawrence, Fate Has Been Kind, p. 100.

[149]Leventhal, p. 157.

[150]Balfour Papers, Add. mss. 49737, Lord Robert Cecil to Arthur Balfour, January 22, 1913.

[151]NUWSS, Ex. com. mins., January 17, 1913, Fawcett Library, London; Rosen, p. 186. Evelyn Sharp, a former member of the WSPU, persuaded Emmeline Pankhurst to declare the truce.

[152]See, for example, W. H. Dickinson, "The Franchise Bill and Women's Suffrage," Englishwoman, 15, no. 45 (September 1912): 255; Christian Commonwealth, September 9, 1912; The Times, December 4 and 11, 1912.

undermining all their efforts, and they refused to desist until it was too late. LLoyd George went so far as to prophesy that, had the House divided on the women's suffrage amendments, militancy would have been responsible for securing their defeat.[153]

Aside from the militants, the NUWSS' main concern was the attitude of the Irish Nationalists. If the Irish voted in January as they had in March, none of the women's suffrage amendments would pass the House of Commons. The NUWSS seems to have felt that it had a better chance of persuading the Nationalists to change their attitude to women's suffrage than it did of convincing the WSPU to suspend militancy. The Irish, unlike the militants, might be brought round by reason and political leverage. Had militancy itself not been an issue in the House of Commons, the Irish would probably not have had the power to determine the fate of the suffrage question; as it was, the added issue of militancy in effect gave the Irish the powers of life and death over the suffrage measures. In January 1913, there were 84 Nationalists in the House of Commons. According to the NUWSS calculations, 43 of them supported women's suffrage, 16 opposed it, and 25 were neutral. If Redmond left the members of his party free to vote according to their convictions, there was a good chance the House of Commons might enact some measure of women's suffrage; if he did not, there was almost no chance the Franchise Bill would include women.[154]

The raison d'être of the Irish party, and the only issue which mattered to the Nationalists, was Home Rule. They looked at all issues through the prism of Home Rule, voting not on the intrinsic merits of a measure but rather on how it affected Home Rule. By the summer of 1912, the struggle for Home Rule had become increasingly bitter. To some it looked as if civil war might break out; others thought the stresses and strains of Home Rule might split the Liberal Party.[155] The more bitter the struggle became and the closer Home Rule came to actuality, the more protective, almost paranoic, was the attitude the Irish adopted toward their cause.

The Nationalists believed, quite correctly, that the fate of Home Rule was indissolubly linked with that of the Asquith Government. Anything that in any way threatened the stability of this Government indirectly imperiled Home Rule. Urged on by the antisuffragists, the

---

[153]Scott diary, February 3, 1913.

[154]C. C., December 20, 1912 and January 24, 1913; Labour Leader, January 2, 1913.

[155]In October Lady Frances Balfour wrote to Fawcett, "Salisbury is here full of great scenes in Ulster, and the feeling is that the Government must give it up, or their party divide in the face of it." FLAC, vol. 1, Jii, Lady Frances Balfour to Millicent Garrett Fawcett, October 1, 1912, Fawcett Library, London.

Irish took the position that the passage of women's suffrage would cause the breakup of the Liberal Government. In the spring of 1912, a member of the Irish Party, anticipating the debate over the women's suffrage amendments to the Reform Bill, had dismally forecast: ". . . day after day they will be advertising their own dissensions, and when the week is over there will be nothing left of the Government's prestige. I question whether there will be anything left of the Government."[156] From June 1912 to January 1913 this attitude seems, if anything, to have deepened along with their concern for Home Rule. The militants' activities in Dublin in July 1912, and, in particular, their attack upon Redmond and Asquith, reinforced the worries of the Irish; but Asquith's political prestige probably mattered quite as much to the Irish as his physical well-being. They did not want to support any measure which in any way seemed to weaken his authority, and they believed it would be very embarrassing for the Prime Minister, whose antisuffragist opinions were well known, to accept the inclusion of women's suffrage in a Government measure.[157] They even suggested that Asquith might resign rather than take responsibility for a Franchise Bill which gave votes to women. Convulsions at the Cabinet level would, they believed, doom Home Rule.[158]

The antisuffragist forces in the House of Commons did everything possible to encourage the Nationalist Party's fears that the Government might break up over the women's cause.[159] The rumor spread that not only Asquith but also Harcourt and Churchill might resign if women's suffrage were included in the Franchise Bill.[160] Supporters of

---

[156]As quoted in Brailsford, "The Reform Bill and the Labour Party," p. 122.

[157]See, for example, C. P. Scott's account of his interview with John Dillon (Nat., Mayo, East) and Joseph Devlin (Nat., Belfast, West). Scott diary, January 15 and 16, 1913.

[158]See, for example, T. P. O'Connor's (Nat., Liverpool, Scotland) interview with the Chicago Tribune as quoted in C. C., February 28, 1913. See also C. P. Scott's account of his interview with John Redmond; Scott diary, January 20, 1913.

[159]Hammond, p. 112; National Union of Women's Suffrage Societies, Annual Report, 1912, p. 15; Fawcett, The Women's Victory and After, p. 47.

[160]Manchester Guardian, January 8, 1913; Christian Commonwealth, January 15, 1913. Common Cause commented sarcastically on Harcourt's threatened resignation: "The Front Bench has always been a more congenial seat to Mr. Harcourt than the sacrificial altar." Nor would Churchill ever resign office because of loyalty to a conviction:

women's suffrage in the House of Commons, including Sir Edward Grey, tried to quash these rumors, but with little effect; Asquith's public utterances were so ambiguous that they did little to allay the Nationalists' fears.[161]

The NUWSS had tried every means, from persuasion to coercion, to try and convince the Irish that women's suffrage was not a threat to Home Rule and would not be an impediment to the Nationalists' goals unless the Irish party, by its hostility to women's suffrage, alienated the support of suffragists in the House of Commons. The NUWSS had designed the EFF, in part, to put pressure on the Irish; it had backed the Snowden amendment in order to obtain Redmond's promise that he would not order his party to oppose the women's suffrage amendments.[162] Marshall had held several interviews with the Irish leaders in an effort to persuade them to take a more favorable attitude to the amendments, and the NUWSS had made financial grants to the Irish Women's Suffrage Federation and had sent an organizer to Ireland for the purpose of bringing pressure to bear on Redmond et al. from the Irish constituencies.[163]

The NUWSS had also prevailed upon suffragists in the Liberal and Labour parties to reason with the Irish. Staunch advocates of Home Rule, including Snowden and Scott, had argued that Irish hostility to women's suffrage might prove damaging to Home Rule.[164] Scott had warned Redmond that it would be very difficult for Home Rulers, such as himself, to choose between loyalty to Home Rule and loyalty to women's suffrage; yet, if the Irish voted against the women's suffrage

---

"In all his brief public career all his opinions have been subject to modification, save only his belief in the desirability of office." C. C., January 10, 1913.

[161]C. C., December 13, 1912; Manchester Guardian, December 10, 1912; The Times, December 17, 1912; NUWSS, Ex. com. mins., December 5, 1912, Fawcett Library, London.

[162]Labour Party Archives, LP/wom/12/26, Catherine Marshall to Arthur Henderson, July 2, 1912.

[163]NUWSS, Ex. com. mins., November 7, November 21, and December 5, 1912, and January 2, 1913; Correspondence of the National Union of Women's Suffrage Societies, 1912, Mrs. Duncan to Miss Cooke, June 11, 1912; Fawcett Library, London.

[164]NUWSS, Ex. com. mins., October 17, 1912, Fawcett Library, London; Labour Leader, November 7, 1912; Christian Commonwealth, January 15, 1913.

amendments, he would feel "there had been a betrayal by the Home Rule party of the very principle of Home Rule and that the emancipation of Irishmen had been purchased at the cost of its refusal for Englishwomen."[165] In a moment of panic, the NUWSS and its supporters in the House of Commons had even toyed with the idea of "buying off" the Irish by promising to exclude Ireland from the Dickinson amendment.[166] Since it was concern for Home Rule rather than opposition to women's suffrage itself that shaped the Nationalists' attitude to the amendments, it is doubtful that the proposed exclusion of Ireland would have mitigated Irish hostility to the amendments.

Despite all the NUWSS efforts to bring the Irish round, the suffragists, by January, doubted that the Irish would remain neutral to, much less support, the women's suffrage amendments: the NUWSS did not believe Redmond would honor his promise of November 5 that his followers would be free to vote as they chose. Some observers of Parliament felt that the Grey amendment might prove the exception to the Rule, but this alone would not enfranchise any women. The Nationalists remained obdurate in their conviction that women's suffrage would be a millstone for the Government, and therefore a millstone for Home Rule. It could, in fact, be argued that as 1912 progressed, the chances of carrying a women's suffrage amendment to the Franchise Bill declined. During the summer and autumn of 1912, the Irish became increasingly concerned about Home Rule, and the suffragettes became increasingly violent. The combination of these two forces imperiled the passage of any women's suffrage amendment.

How the House of Commons would have voted on the suffrage amendments can only be a matter of speculation because the opportunity never came. The evaluations of the prospects of the amendments by the NUWSS and its supporters in Parliament were carefully considered and might have proved sound. The NUWSS seemed to assume that the House of Commons would pass the Grey amendment, and political correspondents concurred with this view.[167] The chances for passage of the Dickinson and Conciliation amendments were much less certain. In December Cecil told the NUWSS that he had obtained sixteen definite promises from

---

[165]Scott diary, January 20, 1913.

[166]NUWSS, Ex. com. mins., January 17, 1913, Fawcett Library, London; Manchester Guardian, January 21, 1913. Lloyd George designed this plan. Scott diary, January 16, 1913.

[167]Daily Citizen, January 22, 1913; Manchester Guardian, January 22, 1913. Lloyd George told C. P. Scott that he thought the Grey amendment would not have passed the House, but he may well have made this statement in order to minimize the impact of the Speaker's ruling upon the cause of women's suffrage. Scott diary, February 3, 1913.

Conservatives to vote for the Dickinson amendment; a month later he
indicated to the NUWSS executive that the amendment might draw even
more support from the Conservative benches.[168]   But the NUWSS
calculated that even if thirty Conservatives at most supported the
amendment, it would still fail on account of the anger aroused by
militancy and the opposition of the Irish.   In mid-January Marshall
learned from John Dillon that the Irish attitude to the suffrage
amendments was hostile.   Since the Irish vote was somewhat less
essential to the passage of the Conciliation amendment than it was to
the Dickinson, by January it was the Conciliation amendment that the
NUWSS felt had the best chance of passing.[169] Conservative suffragists
who did not like the Dickinson amendment would support this moderate
proposal; in addition, Labour MP's, and, to a surprising degree,
Liberal MP's, were friendly to the Conciliation amendment.   Out of
forty MP's in the Lancashire region, all the Labour and Liberal MP's
who favored the principle of women's suffrage had agreed to support
this amendment.[170] The Labour Party had offered to put out a special
whip for the Conciliation amendment if the Dickinson amendment failed,
and the WLF had promised to throw its support behind the amendment.
Thus, on the eve of the debate the NUWSS pinned its hopes on the
Conciliation amendment.   At the same time it was acutely aware that
this amendment had only a slim chance of success if Redmond threw the
weight of the Irish party against it, and it knew there was a strong
likelihood that this would happen.[171]

On January 20 the newspapers published the probable timetable
for the women's suffrage amendments to the Franchise Bill; the House of

---

[168]NUWSS, Ex. com. mins., December 5, 1912, and January 17,
1913, Fawcett Library, London.   Cecil was very pleased about the
Conservatives' response to the amendments and thought Bonar Law's
promise to speak for the Grey amendment had boosted the fortunes of
women's suffrage within the party.   Correspondence of the London
Society for Women's Suffrage, Philippa Strachey to Emily Davies,
January 1, 1913, Fawcett Library, London.

[169]NUWSS, Ex. com. mins., January 17, 1913, Fawcett Library,
London; C. C., January 10, 1913.

[170]Archives, Manchester Public Library, M/50, Box 3, Memorandum
of the Manchester and District Federation headed "Information re
Members of Parliament on Women's Suffrage Amendments to the Franchise
Bill" [1913].   Out of the 40 MP's in the district, 25 were in favor of
women's suffrage, 7 opposed it, and 8 were undecided.

[171]NUWSS, Ex. com. mins., January 17, 1913, Fawcett Library,
London; C. C., January 17, 1913.

Commons was to begin debate on the amendments on Friday, January 24.[172] On January 23, the Speaker of the House, the Right Hon. James Lowther (Cons., Cumberland, Penrith), indicated, although he did not make a definite ruling, that if the women's suffrage amendments were inserted in the Franchise Bill, this would so change the measure that the Government would have to withdraw it and re-introduce it in another form.[173] Asquith wrote the King:

This is a totally new view of the matter which appears to have occurred for the first time to the Speaker himself only two or three days ago, and is a flat contradiction of the assumption upon which all parties in the House have hitherto treated the Bill.

In Mr. Asquith's opinion which is shared by some of the best authorities on procedure, the Speaker's judgment is entirely wrong with what took place in the case of the previous Franchise Bills in 1867 or 1884. . . . In these circumstances it is felt, not without reason, by the supporters of woman suffrage that they cannot be afforded under the present Bill the opportunity for a "free" discussion and division on their cause which was promised by the Government. . . . The general feeling of the Cabinet was that the Bill should be withdrawn, but so much depends on the nature of the statement to be made that further consideration of the matter is adjourned till Monday morning.[174]

On January 27 the Speaker ruled that the amendments, if included, would force withdrawal of the bill. The Cabinet met the same day and decided to withdraw the bill. As a gesture of condolence to the suffragists, it promised to give facilities for a private member's suffrage bill next session; members of the Government would be free to vote as they pleased, but the Government would not assume any responsibility for the measure.[175] The saga of women's suffrage and the Reform Bill had come to an unexpected end.

---

[172]Manchester Guardian, January 20, 1913.

[173]National Union of Women's Suffrage Societies, Annual Report, 1912, p. 16. Lowther made his final decision over the weekend of January 25-26. James W. Lowther, A Speaker's Commentaries, vol. 2 (London, 1925), p. 137.

[174]CAB 41/34/4, January 25, 1913. Women's suffrage amendments had been moved for inclusion in the Reform Bills of 1867 and 1884. There was no suggestion that such amendments were out of order. J. Arthur Price, "The Speaker's Ruling," Englishwoman, 17, no. 51 (March 1913): 257-64.

[175]CAB 41/34/5, January 28, 1913.

The Speaker's ruling and the subsequent action of the Cabinet caused an uproar both inside and outside the House of Commons. Asquith was genuinely surprised by the ruling and later pronounced the decision "not only unpalatable but unexpected."[176] Despite Asquith's innocence, many MP's, including members of the Government, believed that the Government had betrayed the women; Lloyd George and Haldane had even threatened to resign if the Government did not honor its promises.[177] Snowden exulted in the Government's embarrassment: "To have forced women suffrage into the position it has today as the overthrower of Cabinet unity and constitutional procedure is almost as great success as winning it [the vote]. No question since 1886 has dominated politics as women suffrage does today. It is surely the very eve of victory."[178]

Snowden was optimistic, but the Labour Party, at its Annual Conference, January 30, did protest against the Government's action by passing a resolution which dictated that the PLP must oppose any franchise measure that did not include women.[179] Snowden assured Fawcett that the Conference's action precluded the Liberals from reintroducing any Franchise Bill which dealt only with male suffrage: "The importance of this vote is tremendous. It has killed any Franchise Bill which might have been intended. I was talking to two members of the Cabinet yesterday (George was one) and they quite fully confirmed that it had just put the idea of reintroducing a man Franchise Bill into the region of the impossible."[180]

The extinction of the women's suffrage amendment was also, no doubt, a defeat for the Government: the Liberal Government would not obtain the franchise reform which they so much desired, and which had been designed with an eye to the next General Election.[181] Unwittingly, the suffragists had driven a nail in the coffin of the Liberal Party. As one historian has written: "Paradoxically, the new Liberalism's failure was not over social democracy but political democracy. A fourth Reform Act was needed, yet the only terms on which

---

[176]Earl of Oxford and Asquith, vol. 1, p. 221. See also Roy Jenkins, Asquith: Portrait of a Man and an Era, p. 250; Pugh, p. 41.

[177]Morgan, p. 117; Austen Chamberlain, Politics from Inside, p. 519.

[178]Papers of Millicent Garrett Fawcett, Philip Snowden to Millicent Garrett Fawcett, January 26, 1913, Fawcett Library, London.

[179]C. C., February 7, 1913.

[180]Papers of Millicent Garrett Fawcett, Philip Snowden to Millicent Garrett Fawcett, January 31, 1913, Fawcett Library, London.

[181]Pugh, pp. 42-43.

it could come were by including woman suffrage. Asquith's failure to see either the necessity or the urgency of this is the most serious criticism that can be made of his leadership."[182]

The wailing and gnashing of teeth, offers of sympathy and condolence, and the satisfaction derived from having blocked further franchise reform did not help the cause of women's suffrage, however. No matter how important the Labour Party's resolution was for the future, it did not revive the opportunity which the Speaker's ruling had snatched away. The whole episode had lowered the prestige of the Government, but more important, it had extinguished the suffragists' "best opportunity" for obtaining votes: no private bill could compensate for the loss of protection by the Parliament Act and the immunity from the danger of wrecking amendments which inclusion in a Government Franchise Bill would have guaranteed to the women.[183] Moreover, the withdrawal of the Franchise Bill meant that it would be impossible to include women on the electoral register before the next General Election. The NUWSS did not believe that Asquith had connived with the Speaker, but it did feel that the Government had been negligent and sloppy in its handling of the matter; in addition, the NUWSS apparently believed, erroneously, that the Government had known of the Speaker's intention some weeks before the ruling and had done nothing to avert it.[184] The NUWSS did not accept the offer of time for a private member's bill as a substitute for the potential inclusion of women's suffrage in a Government measure: the experience of the Conciliation Bill had taught the suffragists that no private member's bill could pass the House of Commons. Fawcett and Courtney had seen Acland and Grey, both of whom had tried to persuade them to accept the Government's offer. Common Cause wryly commented: "We have not forgotten all the emphatic statements by Mr. Lloyd George, Sir Edward Grey, and the Master of Elibank designed to persuade us how hopeless it was to attempt to carry a Private Member's Bill, and how safe was the opportunity of the Reform Bill. Today the pleading is reversed. We lack the agility to share in these political gyrations."[185]

---

[182]Clarke, p. 399.

[183]Cecil Papers, Add. mss. 51075, Press release by the National Union of Women's Suffrage Societies, January 25, [1913]; C. C., February 7, 1913.

[184]Morgan, p. 118, asserts that the suffragists believed that Asquith had collaborated with the Speaker to secure the ruling. The evidence does not support this contention. See, for example, West Lancashire, West Cheshire, and North Wales Federation, Annual Report, 1913, p. 6. See also Scott diary, February 3, 1913.

[185]NUWSS, Ex. com. mins., February 6, 1913, Fawcett Library, London; C. C., January 31, 1913.

Fawcett, hardened by the experience of the Conciliation Bill, was now convinced that a women's suffrage measure needed the protection of the Government in order to be enacted into law. The obstacles in the path of a private measure were insurmountable: the Conservatives might not support any women's suffrage measure if it involved invoking the Parliament Act, the Irish would oppose any women's suffrage measure, and the antisuffragists would introduce "wrecking amendments" in Committee in order to diminish support for the measure.[186] With these considerations in mind, Fawcett firmly rejected the Government's offer of facilities for a private bill and demanded a Government measure for women's suffrage:

> The chances of obstruction and cross-voting in Committee, the difficulty of combining suffragists of all parties in a valid majority, the hazardous position of any Bill introdudced next session under the Parliament Act, and above all, the certainty that Irish Members and ultra-official Liberals would again cast a tactical vote to relieve the Prime Minister from embarrassment, these considerations convince the National Union that in pronouncing this offer inadequate it is prejudicing no real chance for women's suffrage.[187]

Fawcett's gloomy assessment of the situation was not an exaggeration: even members of the Cabinet who favored women's suffrage admitted that the Government's offer was a gesture to save face, and that no private member's bill could pass the House of Commons.[188]

The Government's withdrawal of the Franchise Bill brought to an end a very long chapter in the history of the women's suffrage movement. The Speaker's ruling guaranteed that women's suffrage was now a dead issue in the House of Commons and would remain so until after the next General Election. Up until January 1913, the NUWSS had been willing to accept something less than a Government bill for women's suffrage--a private member's bill, a Conciliation Bill, the possibility of including, by amendment, women's suffrage in a Government Franchise Bill. Ever since the Liberals had returned to power in 1906, the House of Commons had, each year, considered a measure which would give votes to women. During this entire period the NUWSS had focused its energies on the House of Commons, with the hopes of persuading MP's to enact women's suffrage in some form. In the years between 1910 and 1913, the NUWSS had progressively taken a more

---

[186]C. C., February 7, 1913; NUWSS, Ex. com. mins., February 6, 1913, Fawcett Library, London.

[187]Millicent Garrett Fawcett, "A Government Measure," Englishwoman, 17, no. 50 (February 1913): 121.

[188]Scott diary, February 3, 1913.

commanding role in the suffrage movement; suffragists both inside and outside Parliament had become increasingly certain that the House of Commons would enact some measure of women's suffrage before the next General Election. In the last half of 1912, the NUWSS activities had come to a crescendo; unprecedented growth accompanied this activity and the NUWSS had increased in size at the rate of a thousand members a month.[189] The NUWSS had become the driving force behind the demand for women's suffrage; the lobbying for the women's suffrage amendments, the Snowden amendment, and, in particular, the EFF were indications that the NUWSS had become more aggressive and imaginative, and less patient and trusting in its dealings with the politicians, especially with the Liberals.

In January 1913 the NUWSS finally abandoned all hope of obtaining women's suffrage by means of anything less than a Government Bill. The NUWSS, wearied and exasperated by the Liberal's dallying with the women's suffrage question, had become too politically pragmatic and too self-assured to accept gratefully whatever crumbs the Liberals chose to throw to the women. It recognized the Government's offer of a private bill for what it was--a token. Thus, in January 1913, the strategy and the activities of the NUWSS underwent a change. The House of Commons was no longer the focal point for the NUWSS, and the NUWSS took no interest in the measure for women's suffrage which came before the House in 1913.[190] The NUWSS was now only interested in a Government Bill, and it was convinced that the next General Election would determine whether such a bill would become a reality. Thus, from January 1913 to the outbreak of war in 1914, the NUWSS' main interest was the next General Election; its goal was to place more members of the Labour Party in the House of Commons and to make sure that if the Liberals did return to power, the new Liberal Government would introduce a Government bill for women's suffrage. At the same time, as a way of hedging its bets, the NUWSS negotiated with the Conservatives to obtain a commitment from them to introduce a women's suffrage measure, should they return to office. In the past the NUWSS had focused its sights on a women's suffrage measure before the House of Commons; in the future its attention would be centered on the General Election and the parliamentary constituencies--on party agents, political associations, trade unions, or any organization or individual who might prove helpful in the upcoming election. In the past, the

---

[189]Marshall Papers, The Position of the N.U.W.S.S., February 1913, NUWSS pamphlet (n.p., n.d.); C. C., August 15, 1912. For evidence of this growth at the local level see Eastern Counties Federation, Annual Report, 1913, p. 13.

[190]On May 6, 1913, the House of Commons defeated W. H. Dickinson's Representation of the People Bill by 47 votes. This bill would have given votes to women over twenty-five who were either householders or wives of householders. Constance Rover, Women's Suffrage and Party Politics in Great Britain, p. 185.

NUWSS had lobbied for any measure that would give votes to women; in the future it would support a women's suffrage measure only if it had the sponsorship of the Government. In the past the NUWSS had negotiated with the political parties to win their support for some suffrage proposal before the House of Commons; in the future it would negotiate with the party leaders to see what the parties would do for the women should they be victorious at the next General Election.

The events of January 1913 changed both the strategy of the NUWSS and the character of its activities. It is possible to criticize the NUWSS, as the militants did, for having been naïve in believing in the possibility of enacting a privately sponsored measure for women's suffrage and for having been too patient, even passive, in responding to the subterfuge, temporizing, and procrastination of the Liberal Government. Yet it can also be argued that the NUWSS was much more politically astute than its critics suggest. Up until January 1913, it was not a "given" that no privately sponsored measure of women's suffrage such as the Conciliation Bill would pass the House of Commons. Leading members of the political parties and political analysts such as Scott and Brailsford all concurred that it was possible to enact women's suffrage in this fashion. The increased activity of the antisuffragists in the period between 1908 and 1913 is, in its own way, a testimony that a real possibility existed for enacting women's suffrage without the blessing of the Government.[191] When it came to deciding how this could be done, and what tactics should be used to persuade the House of Commons to pass such a measure, opinion was once again behind the NUWSS: militancy would never win votes in the House of Commons; peaceful agitation, whether in the form of deputations or an EFF, was the most realistic way to win the support of MP's.

In a sense, the militants fulfilled their own prophecies: their actions made it difficult for any private measure for women's suffrage to pass the House of Commons and made much of the public and many politicians sympathetic to the Government's cavalier treatment of the suffrage question. It is, in fact, possible to turn the militants' criticisms around at the militants themselves and to accuse them of having been naïve, as well as idealistic and unpragmatic, in the approach to the House of Commons and the Liberal Government. The suffragettes were the most visible and most strident representatives of the women's suffrage movement, but it was the suffragists of the NUWSS who were, in the years 1910 to 1913, responsible for whatever advances women's suffrage made in the House of Commons and for building up support for women's suffrage at the constituency level. The suffragettes were the philosophers and the impresarios of the women's movement; the women of the NUWSS were political workhorses and the steadying main line in the struggle for the vote. In the early years the WSPU gave life to the women's suffrage movement in Britain, but it was the NUWSS that supported and sustained the movement and, at both the constituency and parliamentary level, kept women's suffrage alive as a political issue.

---

[191]Harrison, _Separate Spheres_, p. 121.

CHAPTER VI

1913-1914: CONVERTING THE PUBLIC AND THE PARTIES

TO THE SUFFRAGE CAUSE

After the withdrawal of the Franchise Bill in January 1913, the NUWSS, realizing that it was improbable that the present Parliament would enact any measure of women's suffrage, however limited, turned its attention from Parliament to the parliamentary constituencies and the British public. The fortunes of the suffragists now rested on the next General Election, which would be held, at the latest, in 1915.[1] If the next Government, Liberal or Conservative, were to sponsor a bill for women's suffrage, they would have to be convinced that it would be politically unwise to delay the enactment of women's suffrage any longer and that the country saw women's suffrage as a "desirable and beneficient change." According to Asquith, if this were the case, even the most antisuffragist of governments could not prevent the suffragists' success and "no Political Party would attempt to do so."[2] Thus, from February 1913 to the outbreak of war in August 1914, the NUWSS threw itself into the laborious tasks of propagandizing for women's suffrage in the constituencies, counteracting the efforts of the militants and keeping the constitutional suffrage movement before the public eye, extending its organizational network, and building up support for the suffrage cause. At the same time the NUWSS kept in close communication with prominent politicians and, alternating flattery with threats, tried to secure a commitment that the next Government elected would introduce some measure for women's suffrage.

From 1913 to 1914, the NUWSS bombarded the British public with an unprecedented amount and variety of suffragist propaganda; it strove to make women's suffrage a truly popular cause and to create a clamorous demand for women's suffrage that no Government could, with

---

[1]Correspondence of the National Union of Women's Suffrage Societies, 1913, Circular from Helena Auerbach and Millicent Garrett Fawcett [1913]; Proceedings of the Councils of the National Union of Women's Suffrage Societies, Proceedings of the Provincial Council, May 1913; Fawcett Library, London.

[2]Papers of Henry, 1st Earl of Oxford and Asquith, Bodleian Library, vol. 89 f. 47, Proceedings of the NUWSS deputation to H. H. Asquith, August 8, 1913 (hereafter cited as Asquith papers).

impunity, ignore. Its motivations for undertaking this campaign were mixed. Leading political figures such as Grey and Lloyd George constantly confronted the NUWSS with the accusation that women's suffrage was not a "popular" cause, in the broadest sense of the term.[3] Although this accusation was undoubtedly true--in 1913 the average British man and woman were apathetic to franchise reform in general and if they did have feelings on women's suffrage, were more likely to be opposed than not--it also gave the politicians a convenient excuse for not acting on the women's demand, thereby averting interparty strife over this electoral apple of discord.[4] The conversion of the public would at least remove this pretext for inaction. Equally important, the NUWSS felt that its propaganda efforts would isolate the militants and prevent the public from branding the whole suffrage movement with the tar from the suffragette brush. In February 1913, the WSPU had begun "a concerted campaign of destruction of public and private property," smashing the orchid house at Kew, setting a railroad carriage ablaze, and bombing Lloyd George's house; by 1914, the King was complaining of receiving letters from suffragettes threatening to shoot him.[5] The militants were now at war not only with the Government but also with the British public, and their actions did more to alienate public opinion than to create sympathy for the cause. The NUWSS hoped that its propaganda efforts would decimate the bad feelings engendered by militancy and show the suffrage movement in a more sober and respectable light.[6]

A great deal of the NUWSS work in this period was very much as before--meetings, teas, lectures, letters, processions, bazaars--but there was a significant change. Whereas the NUWSS had formerly based its appeal for women's suffrage on nineteenth-century liberal

---

[3]An Account of the Northern Men's Federation for Women's Suffrage Deputation to Sir Edward Grey, October 22, 1913, NUWSS pamphlet (n.p., n.d.); Lloyd George Papers, C9/5/10, Typescript account of a meeting between the NUWSS and the suffragist ministers, August 8, 1913.

[4]Martin Pugh, Electoral Reform in War and Peace, 1906-1918, p. 30, discusses popular attitudes to franchise reform in the period between 1906 and 1914.

[5]Andrew Rosen, Rise Up, Women! pp. 189-90; Selborne Papers, Ms. 79, the Earl of Selborne to the Countess of Selborne, June 14, 1914.

[6]Brian Harrison, Separate Spheres, pp. 193-95, discusses the public impact of militancy; see also Philip Snowden, The Present Position of Women's Suffrage, NUWSS pamphlet (n.p., n.d.). In 1913 the NUWSS received firsthand knowledge of the public impact of militancy during its Pilgrimage for Women's Suffrage. Fawcett, The Women's Victory and After, pp. 55-56; K. M. Harley, "The Pilgrimage," Englishwoman, 19 (September 1913): 254-62.

arguments, claiming that men and women were equally rational and capable of determining their own destinies and that this natural equality should be reflected in their political status, it now began stressing the differences between men and women.[7] Women, the NUWSS said, had interests and capabilities that were different from those of men, and it was because of these differences that they should have a voice in the body politic: women were not the equals of men, and no man could speak for them. Rather than stressing the "anti-male" aspect, however, the NUWSS took pains to make it clear that it was not encouraging a revolt against domestic life; on the contrary, it said, women had a special aptitude for and knowledge of domestic matters, and a special interest in moral reform which men did not share and which ought to be represented in government.[8]

In part, this change in emphasis came about because of the change in the audience at whom the propaganda was directed. Increasingly, the NUWSS had been broadening its base beyond the upper middle class Liberal nucleus that had formed the backbone of the suffragist movement. The affiliated societies--particularly in the Midlands in the North--had expanded the membership into other classes, and the entente with Labour in 1912 had strengthened the NUWSS ties with the working class. After 1913 the NUWSS, using the "argument from expediency"--the idea that women needed the vote to protect their interests as wives, mothers, and workers--set out to capture working class women.[9] The expediency argument was much less threatening to male workers as well in that it did not challenge men's role in the family by claiming, as the old liberal argument had done, that women were the equals of men, nor did it in any way imply that women wanted to throw off their domestic function. By implicitly disclaiming that women's suffrage would disrupt the family and by emphasizing the differences between men and women, the suffragists made the idea of

---

[7]Richard Evans, The Feminists: Women's Emancipation Movements in Europe, America and Australasia (London, 1977), passim, argues that all suffrage movements, in Europe, the United States, and Australia, changed the rationale behind their argument for the enfranchisement of women. He contends that women's suffrage was accepted only when it abandoned its liberal justification.

[8]See, for example, editorials and articles in C. C., 1914, passim; Correspondence of the National Union of Women's Suffrage Societies, 1913, Circular from NUWSS headquarters regarding obtaining resolutions on women's suffrage from trade unions [1913]; Fawcett Library, London.

[9]This term is borrowed from Aileen S. Kraditor, The Ideas of the Woman Suffrage Movement, 1890-1920, p. 45-46. See also chapter 1, note 60, and Marshall Papers, Report of the Election Fighting Fund to the Half-Yearly Council of the N.U.W.S.S., [October 1913]; Manchester Society for Women's Suffrage, Annual Report, 1914 (n.p., n.d.), p. 12; London Society for Women's Suffrage, Annual Report, 1913, p. 18.

women's suffrage much more acceptable. Paradoxically, by underscoring the unique "feminine virtues" of women and by denying the ideas of natural equality, the suffragists made women's suffrage a more popular cause.

During the 1913-14 period, the NUWSS hired organizers, such as Selina Cooper and Ada Nield Chew, who were of working class origin and had close ties to the labor movement, to propagandize for the suffrage cause in working class areas.[10] In its appeals the NUWSS claimed that the sex barrier and the class barrier were due to the same spirit of monopoly and privilege, and that women and workers were linked by a common interest in tearing down these barriers.[11] The organizers emphasized that working women were "sweated" and used to keep down the wages of men and argued that home and family were adversely affected by the long hours and low pay of workers, male and female. The implication was that if women could vote, all workers would benefit: sweating would be abolished, social welfare legislation would be enacted, and the working class home would become a healthier, happier place.[12]

Efforts were made to reach organized labor, that is, the trade unions, not only to gain their support for the suffrage movement but also as a way of exerting pressure on the Labour Party--and indirectly on the Liberal Party--to keep up to the mark on the suffrage question.[13] In May 1913, the Council of the NUWSS directed all affiliates of the NUWSS to collect resolutions from trade unions in support of women's suffrage.[14] Throughout the next fourteen months the societies gave top priority to this work, and unions of cab drivers, bakers, miners, and textile workers all became the focus of the NUWSS

---

[10]Jill Liddington, "Rediscovering Suffrage History," History Workshop 4 (1978): 196-98.

[11]C. C., April 17, 1914; Labour Leader, August 28, 1913.

[12]The Friends of Women's Suffrage, no. 1 (July 1913); Correspondence of the National Union of Women's Suffrage Societies, 1913, Circular from NUWSS headquarters regarding obtaining resolutions on women's suffrage from trade unions [1913], Fawcett Library, London.

[13]Marshall Papers, Report of the Election Fighting Fund to the Half-Yearly Council of the N.U.W.S.S. [October 1913].

[14]Proceedings of the Councils of the National Union of Women's Suffrage Societies, Proceedings of the Provincial Council, May 1913, Fawcett Library, London.

propaganda.[15] The Election Fighting Fund took charge of a large part of this work and at one time had fifteen organizers working in industrial centers in the North collecting resolutions in favor of women's suffrage.[16] This work with the trade unions did bear fruit; on September 5, the Trade Union Congress, which represented over 2,000,000 working men, passed a resolution which strongly protested the Government's handling of the women's suffrage question: ". . . this Congress protests against the Prime Minister's failure to redeem his repeated pledges to women, and calls upon the Parliamentary Committee to press for the immediate enactment of a Government Reform Bill, which must include the enfranchisement of women."[17] The NUWSS had been instrumental in securing this statement.[18]

The example of the Miners' Federation, which had traditionally been antipathetic to women's suffrage, gives another illustration of the NUWSS success in convincing organized labor to support the suffrage cause.[19] In October 1913, the NUWSS, after months of propagandizing among the mining populace of the North, staged a huge demonstration in conjunction with the annual meeting of the Miner's Federation. Robert Smillie, president of the National Federation of Miners of Great Britain and president of the Scottish Miners' Federation, John Robertson, vice-president of the Scottish Miners' Federation, and William Brace, president of the South Wales Miners' Federation, all

---

[15]Kentish Federation, Annual Report, 1913, p. 7; West Riding Federation, Annual Report, 1913 (Leeds, n.d.), pp. 15-16; West Lancashire, West Cheshire, and North Wales Federation, Annual Report, 1913, p. 7; Manchester and District Federation, Annual Report, 1913, p. 11.

[16]National Union of Women's Suffrage Societies, Annual Report, 1913 (n.p., n.d.), p. 51.

[17]NUWSS, Ex. com. mins., September 18, 1913, Fawcett Library, London; C. C., September 12, 1913.

[18]Marshall Papers, Margaret Robertson to Catherine Marshall, September 18, 1913. Robertson wrote a very amusing account of her exploits at the Congress: "Did I tell you about the agonies at the TUC? How the miners actually decided to vote against and I had to chase all around and see them individually and get them to meet again and reverse it (deadly secret of course that I had anything to do with it). That sort of thing makes the gray hairs sprout."

[19]For accounts of the NUWSS work with the miners, see the Marshall Papers, Reports of the EFF organizers' work [1913]; C. C., September 5, 1913.

made speeches in support of women's suffrage.[20] Four months later, after the NUWSS had done more work for the suffrage cause in mining areas, the Miners' Federation, at the Labour Party Conference at Glasgow, endorsed a resolution which stated that no franchise reform would be acceptable to Labour if it excluded women's suffrage; this was the first time the miners had supported such a proposal.[21]

Analyzing the results of its work with the trade unions, the NUWSS termed it "one of the most valuable pieces of propaganda ever undertaken."[22] This activity attracted new support for the suffrage movement and strengthened the ties between the Labour Party and the suffragists. Moreover, this cooperation between the forces of organized labor and the supporters of women's suffrage did not go unnoticed by the Liberal Party; Grey, Ponsonby, and Acland all told Catherine Marshall that the NUWSS work with the trade unions had made an impression upon the party.[23]

Organized labor, however, was not the only target for NUWSS propaganda during this period. To enlist the working class at-large in the suffrage movement, the NUWSS relied on the work of the Friends of Women's Suffrage (FWS), which had been initiated with this end in mind. The FWS expanded rapidly in 1913-14, and by August 1914 it numbered over 46,000 Friends.[24] In addition to this, the societies formed suffrage clubs—partly social and partly educational—for working class men and women in industrial areas such as Macclesfield and South Salford.[25] In poor urban areas, the NUWSS established suffrage committees, which included workers, to serve as centers for suffrage propaganda: the London Society, which formed seven such committees in

---

[20]C. C., October 17, 1913.

[21]NUWSS, Ex. com. mins., December 4, 1913, Fawcett Library, London; C. C., February 16, 1914. In 1912 the Miners' Federation had opposed a similar resolution and in 1913 it had remained neutral to it.

[22]West Lancashire, West Cheshire, and North Wales Federation, Annual Report, 1913, p. 7.

[23]NUWSS, Ex. com. mins., December 18, 1913, Fawcett Library, London; Marshall Papers, Notes on an interview with F. C. Acland, April 14, 1913; Notes on an interview with Arthur Ponsonby, June 20, 1913.

[24]National Union of Women's Suffrage Societies, Annual Report, 1913, pp. 17-18. This is based on the estimate that was made in January 1914. The NUWSS did not issue an annual report for 1914, probably because of the war.

[25]Manchester Society for Women's Suffrage, Annual Report, 1914 (n.p., n.d.), p. 12; Manchester and District Federation, Annual Report, 1913, pp. 12, 47.

working class districts of the South and East End and opened a suffrage shop to disseminate information about votes for women, reported that this work had been "particularly encouraging.[26] In 1913 the NUWSS also inaugurated an "educational campaign" which, although not aimed exclusively at workers, was obviously formulated to have special appeal to this segment of the populace. The campaign undertook to enlighten public opinion on the causes that lay at the heart of the women's suffrage movement, and a number of these causes, such as the position of women in industry or the disabilities of wives and mothers, were of particular interest to workers.[27] Throughout 1913 and 1914 the NUWSS societies sponsored lectures, meetings, and debates on these specially selected topics, and publicized this "educational campaign" in the local press, all in an effort to stir "the imagination and consciousness" of the public, particularly its working class segment.[28]

It is impossible to gauge how successful the NUWSS efforts were with regard to the working class, but it seems fair to say that for the first time a sustained effort had been made to make women's suffrage an issue for the working class populace throughout Britain. Sylvia Pankhurst had done some work in lower class districts in London, but now an organizational nucleus for women's suffrage had been created in many working class neighborhoods previously untouched by suffrage propaganda. Through the FWS, the NUWSS had established a permanent line of communication with workers. This activity, combined with the work with trade unions and the EFF's support for the Labour Party, had, at the very least, done much to eliminate the prejudice that the women's suffrage movement responded only to the needs of the middle and upper classes and, moreover, that it was a movement composed of a coterie of hatchet-wielding, man-hating suffragettes.

The "Pilgrimage for Women's Suffrage" was the most spectacular single piece of propaganda undertaken by the NUWSS during this period, and was probably the most impressive demonstration for women's suffrage ever staged in Britain. The Pilgrimage was not designed specifically

---

[26]FLAC, vol. 10, Philippa Strachey to Lady St. Davids, November 3, 1913, Fawcett Library, London; C. C., November 21, 1913; Correspondence of the London Society for Women's Suffrage, Report on work in the East End by Winifred Foulkes, 1913, Fawcett Library, London; London Society for Women's Suffrage, Annual Report, 1913, p. 18.

[27]Proceedings of the Councils of the National Union of Women's Suffrage Societies, Proceedings of the Provincial Council, May 1913, Fawcett Library, London; National Union of Women's Suffrage Societies, Annual Report, 1913, pp. 14-15.

[28]See Surrey, Sussex, and Hants Federation, Annual Report, 1913, pp. 17-19; Edinburgh National Society for Women's Suffrage, Annual Report, 1914 (Edinburgh, 1913), p. 11.

for the working class, but it undoubtedly reached many working men and women. The Pilgrimage was designed to demonstrate the dedication of the supporters of women's suffrage, to spread the suffrage gospel to all corners of Britain, and most important, to recapture public opinion, which the lunacies of the militants had estranged from the suffrage cause.[29] It succeeded on all three counts.

The Pilgrimage, which began on June 18, 1913, was a march of bands of members of all the NUWSS societies, from every part of Britain--Land's End to John o' Groats--to London. The pilgrims, wearing the badges of the NUWSS, converged on eight main roads and arrived in London July 25. A huge meeting of some 70,000 was then held at Hyde Park, followed by a service at St. Paul's. Along the route, as the pilgrims made their way to London, meetings were held and speeches were given. From all accounts the Pilgrimage was a tremendously successful piece of propaganda. Some £8,777 was raised during its course, the suffragist message was heard in parts of Britain that had not really heard it before, and the crowds, with very few exceptions, were warm and enthusiastic.[30] As an added bonus, the Pilgrimage convinced a number of Liberal ministers, including Asquith, to receive deputations from the NUWSS. Although nothing came of these interviews, the ministers—echoed by the Press--conceded that the Pilgrimage had helped to dissipate the ill-will left by the militants and had shown the suffrage movement in a very favorable light.[31] From the standpoint of publicity, the Pilgrimage benefited both the NUWSS and the cause of women's suffrage.

During the 1913-14 period, the NUWSS aim was to keep women's suffrage before the British public and to make women's suffrage a popular cause, but it did not lose sight of Parliament altogether. It snubbed the Dickinson Bill, the only bill to enfranchise women which the House of Commons considered in this period, but it took advantage of several opportunities to raise the women's suffrage issue in

[29]C. C., June 20, 1913.

[30]K. M. Harley, "The Pilgrimage," Englishwoman, 19 (September 1913): 254-63; Manchester and District Federation, Annual Report, 1913, pp. 10-11; Kentish Federation, Annual Report, 1913, pp. 12-13; Fawcett, The Women's Victory and After, pp. 54-59.

[31]Asquith Papers, vol. 39 f. 47, Proceedings of the NUWSS deputation to H. H. Asquith, August 8, 1913; Lloyd George Papers, C9/5/10, Typescript account of a meeting between the NUWSS and the suffragist ministers, August 8, 1913; Correspondence of the National Union of Women's Suffrage Societies, 1913, Circular from the NUWSS describing a meeting with the Rt. Hon. Reginald McKenna, July 30, 1913, Fawcett Library, London.

Parliament.[32] It did not entertain the hope that the present Parliament would do anything for the women, but still it did not want women's suffrage to become a dead issue in the parliamentary arena. At the least, some discussion of women's suffrage was valuable as publicity and propaganda for the movement.

Devolution gave the NUWSS important openings for bringing the suffragsts' claims to the attention of the House of Commons. The Irish Home Rule movement had spawned similar movements in Scotland and Wales, and in 1914 Scottish and Welsh Home Rule bills were introduced in the House of Commons.[33] The NUWSS did not expect these bills to pass, but it saw in them a golden opportunity to raise the demand for women's suffrage: even the antisuffragists argued that women should have a voice in "domestic," as opposed to "imperial" legislation, and the proposed national parliaments would deal only with this sort of domestic legislation. The NUWSS believed that the House of Commons should officially recognize "the principle that women should be admitted as electors for National domestic legislatures." This principle might someday be put into practice and this limited suffrage for local parliaments might serve as the "thin edge of the wedge" for suffrage for the Imperial Parliament.[34] Thus, the NUWSS lobbied, successfully, to secure the inclusion of women's suffrage in the Welsh and Scottish Home Rule bills, organizing meetings, writing letters, and holding deputations to MP's.[35] Although nothing came of either of

---

[32]After the debacle of the Franchise Bill, the NUWSS came to believe that no private member's bill could pass the House of Commons. Dickinson's bill was defeated on its second reading, May 6, 1913, by a vote of 268 (Con. 140, Lib. 74, Nat. 54) to 221 (Cons. 28, Lib. 146, Lab. 34, Nat. 13).

[33]The Welsh Home Rule Bill was introduced for its first reading March 11, 1914. It did not receive a second reading. E. T. John (Lib., E. Denbyshire), who introduced the bill, had worked closely with the NUWSS. NUWSS, Ex. com. mins., February 19 and March 19, 1914, Fawcett Library, London. The Scottish Home Rule Bill was read a second time May 15, 1914. Closure was refused and there was no division.

[34]Lloyd George Papers, Cll/1/14, Circular from Catherine Marshall, May 14, 1914, Fawcett Library, London. For a discussion of the reasons antisuffragists could support the idea of giving women votes for "domestic" legislatures while opposing their enfranchisement for "imperial" legislatures see Harrison, Separate Spheres, pp. 74-76.

[35]NUWSS, Ex. com. mins., May 5 and June 5, 1913, and March 5, 1914, Fawcett Library, London; Marshall Papers, Catherine Marshall to Lord Strathclyde, November 26, 1913; Correspondence of the National Union of Women's Suffrage Societies, 1913, Circular from headquarters regarding the Scottish Home Rule Bill, May 29, 1913, Fawcett Library, London; National Union of Women's Suffrage Societies, Annual Report, 1913, p. 27.

these bills, the lobbying efforts gave the NUWSS the excuse to argue the suffrage cause before a number of politicians and did secure the concession that women should have a vote for National Parliaments.

Further efforts were made, too, with the Irish, who had sparked the federalist movement. Working in close cooperation with the Irish Women's Suffrage Federation, the NUWSS tried to secure the inclusion of women in the Irish Home Rule Amending Bill, and it lobbied, unsuccessfully, to obtain a promise from Sir Edward Carson (Cons., Dublin University), that if a referendum were taken in the Ulster counties, women would vote in the referendum; the Ulster Unionist Council did, however, include women's suffrage in the scheme it drew up for forming a Provisional Government in Ulster.[36] The outbreak of war put an end to the NUWSS dealings with the Irish Unionists. Again, as in the case of Scotland and Wales, the negotiations were mainly valuable from the point of view of keeping open the channels of communicatiton between the suffragists and the politicians, and giving some vitality to the otherwise moribund state of the suffrage cause in Parliament.

Perhaps the most interesting example of the NUWSS efforts to keep the suffrage cause alive at Westminster was the introduction in the House of Lords of a bill to enfranchise women. It was the first time the House of Lords had debated and divided on the issue. The NUWSS realized that the Lords would be unlikely to pass any measure for women's suffrage, but it felt the debate and division would be valuable as a demonstration of suffrage activity and, in particular, suffrage activity in the Conservative Party.[37] Working in conjunction with the Conservative and Unionist Women's Franchise Association (CUWFA), the NUWSS lobbied to form a suffrage group in the House of Lords, trying to keep these plans as quiet as possible in case Lord Curzon, who headed the National League for Opposing Woman Suffrage, should hear of these activities and organize opposition to the bill.[38] Lord Selborne, who

---

[36]NUWSS, Ex. com. mins., March 19 and April 2, 1914, Fawcett Library, London; Archives of the Manchester Public Library, M/50, Box 1, Proceedings of the Provincial Council of the NUWSS, November 1914; National Union of Women's Suffrage Societies, Annual Report, 1913, pp. 42-43.

[37]NUWSS, Ex. com. mins., April 2, 1914, Fawcett Library, London.

[38]Proceedings of the Councils of the National Union of Women's Suffrage Societies, Proceedings of the Annual Council, February 27 and 28, 1913, Fawcett Library, London; NUWSS, Ex. com. mins., May 1, 1913, and February 19, 1914, Fawcett Library, London; South Western Federation, Annual Report, 1914 (n.p., n.d.), pp. 6-7; Marshall Papers, the Countess of Selborne to Catherine Marshall, October 15, 1913.

was closely allied with the NUWSS and the CUWFA, agreed to introduce a women's suffrage bill which would give votes to women who were on the municipal register--in other words, a Conciliation Bill. Both the NUWSS and the CUWFA preferred an "equal" suffrage bill, which would enfranchise women on the same basis as men were enfranchised, but they were overruled. Lady Selborne complained to Catherine Marshall: "Lord Newton rather thinks we should have a better chance with Conciliation, which seems incredible if one did not know how extraordinarily stupid the Conservative Party are."[39] The bill received its first reading April 2, and its second reading May 5, and it was defeated by a vote of 104 (80 Cons., 23 Lib., 1 Cross-bench) to 60 (31 Cons., 23 Lib., 6 Bishops).[40] The suffragists had expected the bill to lose, but the vote came as something of a surprise and delight to them, for the bill received more votes than either the 1910 Budget or the Home Rule Bill.[41] In terms of publicity value, the division showed that there was a surprising amount of suffragist sentiment in the Lords, and that some of the most influential Conservative peers were in favor of women's suffrage.[42] The prestigious Liberal journal, The Nation declared that the vote indicated "a sharpening Tory appetite for a Suffrage Bill" and predicted that the Conservatives, if returned, would introduce a bill to enfranchise women.[43] This kind of talk, however exaggerated, could only help the suffrage movement.

The NUWSS still hoped to persuade the party leaderships and party agents that the claims of the women suffragists would be difficult to evade and to convince them that the women's suffrage movement did have electoral power. Specifically, it wanted to be assured that whichever party formed the next Government would secure the enactment of some measure for women's suffrage.

As in 1912, relations between the Labour Party and the NUWSS remained close. The EFF, still under the capable direction of Catherine Marshall, continued to be the fighting arm of the NUWSS; its purpose was to build up pressure on the left of the Liberal Government

---

[39]Marshall Papers, the Countess of Selborne to Catherine Marshall, October 18, 1913.

[40]NUWSS, Ex. com. mins., May 7, 1914, Fawcett Library, London.

[41]Archives, Manchester Public Library, M/50, Box 1, Proceedings of the Provincial Council of the NUWSS, November 1914.

[42]Lord Willoughby de Broke, for example, supported the bill and lamented the opposition of his former ally, Lord Ampthill, to the bill: "I am sorry that he is going to die in a different ditch from what I am." As quoted in C. C., May 15, 1914.

[43]The Nation, May 9, 1914.

for women's suffrage. As Marshall told a suffragist colleague, the EFF was designed to bring the Liberal Party to the bargaining table:

> They are beginning to get really uneasy about our E.F.F. policy, and their fears are magnifying the sums which they think we are amassing. The more uneasy they are, and the richer they think we are, the better, especially just at this moment when they are anxiously watching to see which way every straw blows, that they may shape their policy accordingly for the next election.[44]

The NUWSS wanted to frighten the Liberals with the power of the Labour vote in the constituencies, to reduce the Liberal majority, and to make the Labour Party more powerful in relation to the Liberals. It wanted to make sure that if the Liberals were returned at the next election, they would be dependent on a Labour Party which was strongly committed to the enfranchisement of women. The smaller the Liberal majority and the larger the number of Labour MP's, the more the suffragists would benefit, particularly if the enactment of Home Rule had removed half of the Nationalist Party from Westminster.[45]

During 1913-14 the EFF expanded the activities that it had begun in 1912. In an attempt to rid the Liberal Government of its antisuffragist component and "produce a Cabinet united on women's suffrage which would make a Government Bill possible," the EFF extended its work in the constituencies of the antisuffragist ministers, particularly Rossendale, East Bristol, Rotherham, North Monmouth, and Accrington.[46] In these constituencies EFF organizers worked to build up the woefully inadequate Labour organization by canvassing and registering voters, and the NUWSS, to complement the more political aspect of the EFF's activities, tried to rouse organized labor to support the suffrage cause.[47] All this was groundwork which might make

---

[44]Marshall Papers, Catherine Marshall to Mrs. Hope, copy, June 12, 1913.

[45]Catherine Marshall, "Women's Suffrage and the Next General Election," Englishwoman, 19 (August 1913): 125-26. The suffragists believed that the Home Rule Bill would be enacted into law before the next General Election. Under the terms of this bill, the number of Nationalist MP's in the House of Commons would be substantially reduced.

[46]C. C., September 26, 1913.

[47]Marshall Papers: Ada Chew to Margaret Robertson, May 28, 1913; M. Hilton to Catherine Marshall, June 21, 1913; Report of the Election Fighting Fund to the Half-Yearly Council of the N.U.W.S.S. [October 1913]; C. C., July 18, October 10, 17, and 31, 1913; Manchester and District Federation, Annual Report, 1913, pp. 11-14.

it possible for the Labour Party to put up strong women's suffrage candidates in these constituencies at the next election. As a result of the EFF activities, the Labour Party definitely decided to contest East Bristol, North Monmouth, and Rotherham in the next General Election.[48]

In addition to this work, the EFF systematically went ahead with preparations for the General Election in a number of other selected constituencies where the NUWSS felt that it was particularly desirable that it should support the Labour candidate "because he was a specially active friend of the cause of Women's Suffrage, or because the Liberal was anti or unreliable," or because it seemed that the work of the EFF "might be the decisive factor in securing the seat for Labour."[49] These selections were made in consultation with Arthur Peters, chief agent of the Labour Party, and included constituencies such as Ilkeston (Col. Seely) and Glasgow, Bridgeton (A. MacCallum Scott), which were represented by prominent Liberal antisuffragists, as well as constituencies such as Barnard Castle (Arthur Henderson), where the Labour MP was in danger of losing his seat.[50] In 1914 the EFF further extended the defensive aspect of its election preparations and compiled a list of twenty-five Labour MP's whom it intended to give substantial support to at the General Election.[51]

The EFF devoted its main attention to industrial centers in the North—Blackburn (Snowden), Clitheroe (A. Smith, Lab.), N.E. Manchester (J. R. Clynes, Lab.)—and to constituencies in the Northeast—Bishop Auckland (Sir H. Havelock Allan, Lib.), Chester-le-Street (J. W. Taylor, Lib.), Houghton-le-Spring (T. Wing, Lib.), Mid-Durham (John Wilson, Lib.), Gateshead (H. L. Elverston, Lib.), and South Shields (R.

---

[48]Marshall Papers, Report of the Election Fighting Fund to the Half-Yearly Council of the N.U.W.S.S. [October 1913]; National Union of Women's Suffrage Societies, Annual Report, 1913, p. 54.

[49]Proceedings of the Councils of the National Union of Women's Suffrage Societies, Proceedings of the Half-Yearly Council, November 1913, Fawcett Library, London.

[50]Marshall Papers: Catherine Marshall to Eleanor Acland, copy, April 25, 1913; Report of the Election Fighting Fund to the Half-Yearly Council of the N.U.W.S.S. [October 1913].

[51]Marshall Papers, "Absolutely Confidential" Memorandum on Labour MPs [1914].

Rea, Lib.).[52] Funds and organizers were sent to these constituencies, and the EFF helped the Labour Party with "registration, canvassing, and all the other spade work which is necessary as the preliminary to a successful election"; in one constituency, Mid-Durham, the EFF organizer, Miss Dring, even went into the Revision Court as a Labour agent.[53] In addition to these preparations for the General Election, the EFF established NUWSS branches in the constituencies in which it was working, propagandized for women's suffrage among the trade unions and the Trade and Labour councils, and enrolled FWS.[54] The strategy of the EFF was to make the local labor forces more critical and independent of the Liberals, and to strengthen labor's support for women's suffrage. The NUWSS was so pleased by the EFF's work in these selected constituencies that it was considering enlarging the scope of EFF activities. Offensively, the NUWSS had used the EFF to attack antisuffrage Liberals. It contemplated changing its focus from quality to quantity, and contesting Liberal seats on a much wider scale. It would base its criteria for selection on the size of the Liberal majority and the strength of the Labour vote, rather than on the suffrage views of the Liberal candidates.[55] Grey told Marshall that he took this threat seriously, and estimated that there were forty constituencies in which the Labour vote was large and the Liberal majority small.[56] There, the presence of the EFF could make a real difference.

In 1913-14 the EFF also supported Labour candidates at four by-elections (see Table 5). Although none of the Labour candidates was victorious, Labour's decision to contest these elections cost the Liberals two seats: South Lanark and Leith Burghs. At the other two

---

[52]Marshall Papers, Report of the Election Fighting Fund to the Half-Yearly Council of the N.U.W.S.S. [October 1913]; Manchester and District Federation, Annual Report, 1913, pp. 11-14; NUWSS, Ex. com. mins., May 1, 1913, Fawcett Library, London.

[53]Marshall Papers: Catherine Marshall to Eleanor Acland, copy, April 25, 1913; Report of the Election Fighting Fund to the Half-Yearly Council of the N.U.W.S.S. [October 1913].

[54]Marshall Papers, Report of the Election Fighting Fund to the Half-Yearly Council of the N.U.W.S.S. [October 1913]; National Union of Women's Suffrage Societies, Annual Report, 1913, pp. 53-55.

[55]Marshall Papers, Catherine Marshall to Francis Acland, copy, November 4, 1913. The EFF had collected all the relevant information. See Marshall Papers, NUWSS Federation Reports on antisuffrage Liberals, enclosed in a letter from Mary McKenzie to Catherine Marshall, April 20, [1913].

[56]NUWSS, Ex. com. mins., December 18, 1913, Fawcett Library, London.

Table 5

By-Elections at Which the Election Fighting Fund Was Used,
1913-1914

Houghton-le-Spring--March 1913[a]		January 1910 election results[b]	
T. Wing, Lib.	6,930	R. Cameron, Lib.	10,393
T. Richardson, Cons.	4,807	Major H. Streatfield, Cons.	4,382
Alderman W. House, Lab.	4,165		
Lib. majority	2,123	Lib. majority	6,011
S. Lanark--December 1913[c]		**December 1910 election results**	
Hon. W. Watson, Cons.	4,257	Sir W. Menzies, Lib.	5,160
G. Morton, Lib.	4,006	Dr. C. M. Douglas, Cons.	3,963
T. Gibb, Lab.	1,674	Lib. majority	1,197
Cons. majority	251		
N.W. Durham--January 1914[d]		**December 1910 election results**	
A. Williams, Lib.	7,241	L. A. Atherly-Jones, Lib.	8,998
J. O. Hardicker, Cons.	5,564	J. O. Hardicker, Cons.	4,827
G. H. Stuart, Lab.	5,026	Lib. majority	4,171
Lib. majority	1,677		
Leith Burghs--February 1914[e]		**December 1910 election results**	
G. W. Currie, Cons.	5,159	Rt. Hon. A. C. Munro-Ferguson, Lib.	7,069
Provost M. Smith, Lib.	5,143	F. A. MacQuisten, Cons.	5,284
J. N. Bell, Lab.	3,346	Lib. majority	1,785
Cons. majority	16		

[a] *Common Cause*, March 28, 1913; *Dod's Parliamentary Companion, 1910*, p. 180.

[b] At the December 1910 election, the Liberal candidate, Cameron, was unopposed.

[c] *Common Cause*, December 19, 1913; *Dod's Parliamentary Companion, 1912*, p. 198.

[d] *Common Cause*, February 6, 1914; *Dod's Parliamentary Companion, 1912*, p. 189.

[e] *Common Cause*, March 16, 1914; *Dod's Parliamentary Companion, 1912*, p. 200.

by-elections, Houghton-le-Spring and N.W. Durham, the Liberal majorities were substantially reduced.[57] The Labour poll at all four by-elections was, at the least, respectable, particularly in view of the fact that in three of these constituencies, Labour had never before run a candidate.[58] The EFF took a major role in all four campaigns. Not only did it persuade Labour to put up candidates, but it also sent workers and funds to the constituencies, and, working closely with the local supporters of Labour, helped to set up party organizations and also NUWSS societies.[59] These organizational nuclei would help Labour contest these seats at the next General Election.

The NUWSS felt that these by-elections were valuable from the point of view of discomfiting the Liberals and encouraging Labour to be more independent of the Liberal Party, and also in building up support for women's suffrage in the constituencies. It took great pleasure in announcing that in the eight by-elections in which the EFF had participated, the Liberals had, on the average, lost 1,800 votes, while Labour had gained 1,100.[60] The Nation, voicing a Liberal view on the matter, commented that the Labour vote could "make all the difference between a small Liberal majority in Parliament (or an actual defeat of the party at a General Election) and a large sufficient one."[61] And P. W. Wilson warned his fellow Liberals of the dangerous situation they were creating by pushing the advocates of women's suffrage into the arms of Labour:

> In the constituencies, which determine all things, Liberalism and Conservatism are to-day threatened by Labour, and the central fact of the times which are ahead of us is the rapidly extending association of the workers with the political aims of women. . . . The restlessness of women, if it stood alone, might have been negigible, but when, as now, it is associated with the seething undercurrents of industrial discontent, when its satisfaction is the condition precedent to fundamental

---

[57]The N.W. Durham by-election was a real test of the NUWSS loyalty to the Labour Party because the Liberal candidate, Aneurin Williams, was a close friend of the NUWSS. See Papers of Millicent Garrett Fawcett, Correspondence concerning the N.W. Durham by-election, passim, Fawcett Library, London.

[58]C. C., March 20, 1914. Leith Burghs was the only constituency in which the Labour Party had previously sponsored a candidate.

[59]Ibid., February 28, March 28, November 18, December 12, and December 19, 1913; February 6, February 20, and March 6, 1914; The Election Fighting Fund: What It Has Achieved, NUWSS pamphlet (n.p., n.d.).

[60]The Election Fighting Fund; see also Chapter 5, Table 3.

[61]The Nation, May 20, 1914.

Liberal reforms, it can only be answered with evasion, at the
risk of a Liberal debacle. . . . the suffragists . . . are in
every direction reinforcing and influencing the balancing vote
on which depends the fate of Governments.[62]

In general the NUWSS was gratified by the results of its work
with the Labour Party. The election preparations and the propaganda
activities of the EFF had continued to strengthen the link between
Labour and the women's suffrage movement. There were however, still
the occasional rough spots, mostly caused by MacDonald's continuing
lack of enthusiasm for the suffrage cause and his complaints about the
women's stranglehold on the party.[63] The NUWSS was inclined to feel
that his attitude influenced the whole party and encouraged Labour to
be compliant with the Liberals. The NUWSS tended to be impatient with
Labour for being, as one member put it, "extraordinarily anxious to be
passive about everything" and not always standing up to the Liberals in
the manner in which the NUWSS desired.[64] The NUWSS was very unhappy
with Labour's support for the Plural Voting Bill, for example, which it
felt would secure "to the Government all that they really cared about
in the Franchise Bill of last session."[65]

At times, the Labour Party had specific complaints about the
NUWSS. The EFF's failure to support the Labour candidate at the
Keighley by-election made the party question the sincerity of the NUWSS
commitment to the Labour Party.[66] And there were some Labour MP's,

---

[62]P. W. Wilson, "Women's Suffrage and Party Politics," Englishwoman, 22 (April 1914): 2-11.

[63]See p. 150 above; also David Morgan, Suffragists and
Liberals, pp. 128-29. The NUWSS did not believe MacDonald would accept
the EFF's help at the General Election. See Marshall Papers,
"Absolutely Confidential" Memorandum on Labour MPs [1914].

[64]Marshall Papers, Kathleen Courtney to Catherine Marshall,
November 23, 1913; G. Evans to Catherine Marshall, October 4, 1913.

[65]On March 13, 1913, the Cabinet decided to proceed with the
Plural Voting Bill, which was designed to do away with the plural
voting system which was thought to be beneficial to the Conservatives.
The bill was passed twice by the House of Commons but had not passed
into law when World War I began. The Labour Party supported the bill
because it felt its passage would improve Labour's electoral fortunes.
See National Union of Women's Suffrage Societies, Annual Report, 1913,
p. 24.

[66]NUWSS, Ex. com. mins., November 20 and December 4, 1913,
Fawcett Library, London. The EFF's reasons for not supporting the
candidate were that it did not receive adequate notice to prepare for
the election and felt it would be impossible to put up an effective

including G. N. Barnes (Glasgow, Blackfriars), who continued to view the NUWSS as a group of "rich women" whose interests had nothing to do with the Labour Party.[67] On the whole, however, the Labour Party much appreciated the assistance that the EFF had given to the party in the constituencies.[68] Henderson, Peters, and Snowden cooperated closely with the NUWSS and worked to prevent misunderstandings between the party and the suffragists. On several occasions the Labour Party gave visible demonstrations of its support for women's suffrage: the Annual Conferences of the Labour Party and the ILP continued to pledge their support for women's suffrage; the TUC sent a deputation to the Prime Minister to demand women's suffrage; and the PLP, to remind the House of Commons of the women's demand, introduced an Adult Suffrage Bill.[69] The work of the EFF had done much to strengthen the Labour Party's commitment to women's suffrage. On the eve of the War, Arthur Henderson assured Marshall that the National Labour Party would, in all probability, make women's suffrage a test question at the next General Election, in the same way it had done with Taff-Vale in 1906; this would give a prominence to women's suffrage which it had never before enjoyed at an election and would oblige the Liberal party managers to put up suffrage candidates in any constituency in which the Labour vote was important.[70]

---

fight, and furthermore, that the Labour organization in the consitutency was extremely weak. Marshall Papers, G. Evans to Catherine Marshall, October 30, 1913.

[67]Marshall Papers, "Absolutely Confidential," Memorandum on Labour MPs [1914].

[68]C. C., March 28, 1913; Christian Commonwealth, March 26, 1913. On February 14, 1914, the NUWSS sponsored a demonstration in the Albert Hall which was attended by a number of Labour MP's. Henderson spoke and complimented the NUWSS on its work. C. C., February 20, 1914.

[69]C. C., February 16 and March 28, 1913; Electoral Reform and Women's Suffrage, 1914-1917, NUWSS pamphlet (n.d., n.p.); Archives, Manchester Public Library, M/50, Box 1, Proceedings of the Half-Yearly Council of the NUWSS, November 1914. In 1914, the Labour Party also tried to raise the demand for women's sufrage in an amendment to the address in reply to the King's Speech; Asquith, however, moved the closure, and the opportunity was lost.

[70]NUWSS, Ex. com. mins., June 18, 1914, Fawcett Library, London. The Taff-Vale decision of 1901 held that a trade union could be sued for the actions of its officers and members. The Labour Party wanted to reverse this decision.

At the same time that the NUWSS was, through the EFF, applying pressure for women's suffrage on the left of the Liberal coalition, it was also trying to convince the Liberals that the Conservatives were considering sponsoring a women's suffrage measure, should they be returned at the next election. If the Liberals wanted to prevent a recurrence of 1867, and another "dishing of the Whigs," it would be prudent for them to make some commitment to women's suffrage before the Conservatives grasped the initiative and climbed on the suffrage bandwagon. Francis Acland told Marshall that, given the present electoral qualifications, the Liberals believed that an "equal terms Bill—one that enfranchised women on the same terms as men"—would keep the Liberals out of office for a generation; the NUWSS wanted to play on this fear.[71] Aside from scaring the Liberals into taking action on women's suffrage, the NUWSS negotiations with the Conservatives were carried on with an eye to the General Election: the NUWSS wanted to secure a pledge from the Conservatives that they would introduce a women's suffrage bill if they were chosen to form a Government.

During 1913-14, the NUWSS, working hand in glove with the CUWFA, lobbied for women's suffrage in the Conservative Party and tried to promote the idea that women's suffrage would benefit the electoral fortunes of the Tories.[72] A number of the party's leaders, including both Balfour and Bonar Law, were nominally in favor of women's suffrage and it was not unreasonable to think that some concessions on women's suffrage could be wrung from the Conservatives on the grounds of electoral advantage. Lord Robert Cecil had told Marshall that he was convinced "the next Unionist Government will have to do something [about women's suffrage] if it comes in in the course of the next few months."[73] The NUWSS met with Bonar Law, organized deputations to MP's, and asked its members to help "make the Conservative Party realise the time has come when the Government cannot be neutral on

---

[71]Marshall Papers: Francis Acland to Catherine Marshall, November 9, 1913; Catherine Marshall to the Countess of Selborne, copy, November 13, 1913. Lady Selborne shared the belief that an "equal terms bill" would benefit the Conservatives. Marshall Papers, the Countess of Selborne to Catherine Marshall, October 18, 1913.

[72]Both Liberals and Conservatives agreed that a moderate bill, along the lines of the Conciliation Bill, would help the Tories at the polls. They assumed that this sort of legislation would enfranchise upper and middle class women who would vote Conservative. Though there does not seem to have been any foundation for this conviction, the conviction persisted. Wilson, "Women's Suffrage and Party Politics," pp. 6-7; Pugh, pp. 26-27.

[73]Marshall Papers, Lord Robert Cecil to Catherine Marshall, November 19, 1913.

women's suffrage."[74] Most important, it spent a great deal of time consulting with its close friends in the Conservative Party--notably Cecil, Lytton, and Selborne--to see if the Tories and the NUWSS could come to some agreement over women's suffrage before the General Election. These politicians, in turn, discussed the issue with Bonar Law, as well as with prominent antisuffragists, such as Curzon. Their aim was to impress upon the party that it must formulate some plan to deal with the suffrage question, in order to avoid drifting "into the same kind of position on the question as have the present ministry--to their lasting discredit."[75] Selborne emphasized to Cecil that they must be firm in pleading their cause:

> The essential thing is to have a plan and to let our colleagues know before a General Election what our plan is. . . . Some of them do not believe in the strength of our convictions, others like Curzon think that if only the decision is put off until the last moment we shall not be able to resist the pressure to join either without conditions or with only vague assurances.

Curzon must be made to realize:

> that unless he is prepared to agree to something Lansdowne and Bonar Law will have to choose between him and you and me. I do not think it would break his heart to lose us as colleagues, but I do not think that he would regard the position with equanimity. In fact I regard it as of great importance that he should understand that we will not under any circumstances be placed in the position in which the members of the present Government are placed.[76]

Three separate plans were discussed by the NUWSS and the Conservatives. One of these was the "Massingham plan," favored by Lord and Lady Selborne, by which the Government would introduce a women's suffrage bill, most probably on the Conciliation basis; if the bill passed, it would then be up to each constituency to decide by local

---

[74]NUWSS, Ex. com. mins., September 18, 1913; Correspondence of the London Society for Women's Suffrage, Circular from Philippa Strachey [1914]; Fawcett Library, London.

[75]Law Papers, 32/4/2, Lord Robert Cecil to Andrew Bonar Law, June 4, 1914.

[76]Selborne Papers, Ms. 79 f. 189, the Earl of Selborne to Lord Robert Cecil, copy, May 30, 1914.

referendum whether women should vote.[77] The "Lytton plan" called for an "initiatory referendum" on women's suffrage; the electors would be asked if they desired legislation on women's suffrage, and if so, the Government would introduce a suffrage bill.[78] A third plan, the "Cecil plan," called for a national referendum on women's suffrage, which would be held after a Government bill for women's suffrage had passed the House of Commons. The Cecil plan was similar to the Massingham plan, except that it would be up to the nation, rather than the individual constituencies, to decide whether women should be enfranchised.[79]

All these plans fell far short of what the NUWSS hoped for—that is, a straightforward Government bill on women's suffrage—but friends of the NUWSS in the Conservative Party had made it clear that, given the antisuffragist contingent in the party, no bill of that sort would be forthcoming from the Tories. Therefore, after some discussion with Cecil, Selborne, and Lytton, the NUWSS decided that Cecil's proposal would be the most palatable of the plans so far proposed.[80] But it was very distasteful. Marshall, speaking for her colleagues, told Cecil that they feared no referendum on women's suffrage would be successful:

> If only the apathetic and indifferent could be eliminated from the referendum I should not fear it. The active undoubtedly outnumber the active anti-suffragists. . . . You might get a majority in favor of repealing some grossly unjust or

---

[77]Law Papers, 24/4/91, the Countess of Selborne to Andrew Bonar Law, November 29, 1913; Selborne Papers, Ms. 79 f. 185, the Earl of Selborne to Lord Robert Cecil, copy, May 20, 1914; C. C., March 7, 1913; NUWSS, Ex. com. mins., March 6, 1913, Fawcett Library, London. Henry W. Massingham, the Liberal journalist, had formulated this plan, probably in an effort to help the Liberal Government deal with the conundrum of women's suffrage.

[78]NUWSS, Ex. com. mins., May 17 and May 21, 1914, Fawcett Library, London.

[79]Cecil Papers, Ms. 51075, Memorandum on Women's Suffrage by Robert Cecil, December 20 [1913]; Selborne Papers, Ms. 79 f. 179, Copy of Memorandum on Women's Suffrage by Robert Cecil, December 24, 1913; NUWSS, Ex. com. mins., December 4, 1913.

[80]NUWSS, Ex. com. mins., May 17 and May 21, 1914. Pugh, p. 25, says that the NUWSS flatly rejected the referendum proposal. This is not the case. In 1912, the NUWSS had objected to the referendum proposal because it had something better to bank on: the Conciliation Bill. By 1914, with no immediate prospects for women's suffrage, the NUWSS was much more willing to consider a referendum proposal, although it was not enthusiastic about it. See Chapter 4, pp. 128-130.

repressive measure, the evil of which has been proved by experience but I don't believe you would ever get a majority for <u>enacting</u> something new or untried.[81]

By August 1914, the NUWSS and the Conservative Party had not come to any agreement on women's suffrage: Bonar Law, though according to Cecil, "speaking more strongly than I have ever heard on the justice of the women's claim," had not struck any bargain with the suffragists.[82] Moreover, the bargain he was most likely to accede to, a referendum, was not appealing to the women. The main value of all this work had been to provoke considerable thought and discussion within the Conservative Party over the suffrage question. In June 1914, Marshall reported that the Conservatives were starting to grow anxious that the Liberals were preparing to take up the suffrage question; they feared the Liberals would introduce a bill along the lines of the Dickinson Bill, which would benefit the electoral fortunes of the Liberals. Cecil reported that a growing number of Conservatives were eager to see the women's suffrage question settled once and for all,[83] and the House of Lords vote on Selborne's bill seemed also to suggest that the Conservatives were becoming more responsive to the suffrage cause. Cromer reported that the prospect of a moderate women's suffrage measure had "hypnotized the Unionist Agents," and Steel-Matiland, chairman of the Party Organization, had approached the NUWSS about various proposals for the enactment of women's suffrage.[84] Even Arnold Ward (Cons., Herts., West), a leading antisuffragist, was agitated that the Conservative Party was going to adopt the Conciliation Bill.[85] Marshall could not resist dangling the prospect

---

[81]Marshall Papers, Catherine Marshall to Lord Robert Cecil, copy, November 24, 1913.

[82]Selborne Papers, Ms. 79 f. 189, Lord Robert Cecil to the Earl of Selborne, June 1, 1914. Militancy also damaged the fortunes of women's suffrage within the Conservative Party. Lord Robert Cecil testified to this when he wrote to Fawcett: "I am sorry your interview with Bonar Law was so unsatisfactory. . . . But I fear it is true that as long as militancy goes on nothing can be done with the Conservatives. . . . I was shocked at the kind of wild beast feeling displayed in the House during our little Cat and Mouse Debate on Wednesday." FLAC, vol. I, K, Lord Robert Cecil to Millicent Garrett Fawcett, July 25, 1913, Fawcett Library, London.

[83]NUWSS, Ex. com. mins., June 18, 1914, Fawcett Library, London.

[84]As quoted in Pugh, p. 26; NUWSS, Ex. com. mins., June 18, 1914, Fawcett Library, London; Archives, Manchester Public Library, M/50, Box 1, Proceedings of the Half-Yearly Council of the NUWSS, November 1914.

[85]Pugh, p. 26.

of a Conservative bill for women's suffrage before Lloyd George: "A propos of our bet, and your scepticism when I said that the Conservatives were beginning to concern themselves seriously with women's suffrage, you may be interested to hear, in confidence, that on Thursday I met at tea Mr. Balfour, Lord Robert Cecil, Lord Lytton, and Mr. Steel-Maitland and they all talked of nothing but women's suffrage for an hour and a half."[86]

By August 1914, the NUWSS had come around to the idea that the return of a Conservative Government might be better for the women than the return of the present Liberal Government with a greater majority. In order to embarrass the Conservatives, the Liberals might, in opposition, take up the cudgel of women's suffrage. Moreover, if a referendum on a Conservative measure for women's suffrage was held and the bill defeated, it could be construed not as a defeat for women's suffrage, but as a defeat for a Conservative women's suffrage bill.[87]

The NUWSS dealings with both the Labour and Conservative parties were carried on with an eye to the Liberal Party. The NUWSS wanted to alarm the Liberals with the prospect of harnessing the suffrage cause to the labor movement, and it also wanted to alarm them with the prospect of a Conservative Government enacting a women's suffrage measure framed in a manner that would destroy the electoral fortunes of the Liberals. The idea was that this pressure, conducted on two fronts, would "make the Government see that delay is likely to be more embarrassing than settlement."[88] According to Marshall, the Liberals were beginning to respond to the pressure: "the result of the fear of an 'equal terms' Bill on the one hand and pressure for an Adult Suffrage Bill on the other hand is to make the Liberals more inclined to think that the safest course would after all be to pass a Bill on Dickinson lines."[89]

For all its disillusionment with the Liberal Government, the NUWSS had not given up the conviction that the Liberals could, through an appeal to party self-interest, be brought to agree to bring in a women's suffrage measure if a Liberal Government were returned at the

---

[86]Lloyd George Papers, C11/1/68, Catherine Marshall to David Lloyd George, July 11, 1914. The Daily News took this threat seriously. See the Daily News, June 15, 1914.

[87]See NUWSS, Ex. com. mins., February 5, March 5, and June 18, 1914, Fawcett Library, London.

[88]Marshall Papers, Catherine Marshall's notes on an interview with Arthur Ponsonby, June 20, 1913.

[89]Marshall Papers, Catherine Marshall to the Countess of Selborne, copy, November 13, 1913.

next General Election. Throughout 1913-14 the NUWSS worked not only indirectly, through the Liberal and Conservative parties, but directly, through Liberal orgnizations and party politicians, to make the Liberal Party change its mind on the suffrage question. Although the NUWSS was much more hardheaded about the Liberals, and had taken its gloves off in dealing with the party, traces of the assumption that the Liberal Party was the natural champion of the suffrage movement still lingered. As Catherine Marshall wrote rather sadly to Sir John Simon (Lib., Essex, Walthamstow):

> The failure of a Liberal Government to recognize the biggest movement for political liberty of its day is very bitter to those of us who are liberals. I was burning with zeal for the great principles of Liberalism and as soon as I left school I started working for the Liberal Party almost as hard as I am working for women's suffrage now. It has been the greatest disillusionment of my life to find how little those principles count with the majority of Liberal men.[90]

The NUWSS devoted a great deal of attention to building up support within the Liberal Party for women's suffrage and to creating lobbies which would agitate for women's suffrage within the Liberal Party organization. Francis Acland, Willoughby Dickinson, and Sir John Simon were the closest allies of the NUWSS in this work: they supplied the NUWSS with information about the party's attitude on the women's suffrage question, discussed tactics with the NUWSS, and acted as emissaries between the NUWSS and prominent politicians such as Grey.[91] Simon was chairman of the Liberal Suffrage Committee in the House and active in the Society of Liberals, with headquarters in Manchester, which was pressing the suffragists' claims on the Government.[92] Acland and Dickinson, abetted by the NUWSS, were instrumental in forming the Men's Liberal Suffrage Society, which was designed to ensure that the next Liberal Government would bring in a measure for women's suffrage.[93] Acland's wife, Eleanor, who was active in the Women's Liberal Federation (WLF), was also a valuable contact for the NUWSS.

---

[90]Marshall Papers, Catherine Marshall to Sir John Simon, copy, August 10, 1913.

[91]Marshall Papers: Notes on an interview with Francis Acland, April 14, 1913; Notes on a planned interview with Sir Edward Grey, October 22, 1913; Francis Acland to Catherine Marshall, November 9, 1913; Francis Acland to Catherine Marshall, October 29, 1913.

[92]Much to the delight of the NUWSS, Simon was appointed Attorney-General with a seat in the Cabinet, October 19, 1913.

[93]Marshall Papers, Francis Acland to Catherine Marshall, November 9, 1913; NUWSS, Ex. com. mins., April 2, 1914, Fawcett Library, London; J. Malcolm Mitchell, "Women's Suffrage and the New Liberalism," Englishwoman, 22 (June 1914): 241-48.

At her instigation a Liberal Women's Suffrage Union was formed within the WLF to strengthen support for women's suffrage within the party and make sure that suffragist candidates were selected at the General Election.[94] Members of the NUWSS, including Margery Corbett-Ashby, were active in the new union, which also acted as a haven for suffragists who resigned from the NUWSS in opposition to the EFF. According to Acland, the Liberal Women's Suffrage Union had done much good in strengthening women's suffrage within the WLF.[95] At the annual council in 1914, the WLF decided that when an antisuffragist was standing, the WLF would not take any official steps to support him; it also urged the Government to make women's suffrage part of its program at the General Election.[96]

Aside from these indirect lobbying activities, the NUWSS also approached its friends in the Cabinet and tried to secure their help in pushing the Liberal Government to agree to introduce a women's suffrage bill after the next General Election. Grey and Lloyd George were the main targets. The NUWSS had an idea, shared by some Liberals, that if Home Rule were enacted before Parliament was dissolved, Asquith might step down as Prime Minister and Grey would replace him.[97] In this case, their having secured a commitment from Grey to give women's suffrage top priority would be extremely valuable. And even if Grey did not succeed Asquith, his public advocacy of women's suffrage would be important in terms of creating pressure within the party for women's suffrage and influencing the actions of the other suffragist ministers.[98] Francis Acland had told the NUWSS that Grey felt that,

---

[94]NUWSS, Ex. com. mins., May 5 and June 6, 1913, Fawcett Library, London; Eleanor Acland, "Prospects of a Government Suffrage Measure," Englishwoman, 19 (July 1913): 7-8.

[95]C. C., July 18, 1913; Marshall Papers, Eleanor Acland to Catherine Marshall, November 20, 1913; see also Chapter 5, pp. 154-55. There are no figures available on the number of members who resigned from the NUWSS as a protest against the EFF. On the basis of the archival evidence, it would seem that this number was not large. The Liberals do not seem to have tried to exploit the divisions within the NUWSS over the EFF.

[96]C. C., June 19, 1914; NUWSS, Ex. com. mins., June 18, 1914, Fawcett Library, London.

[97]Mitchell, "Women's Suffrage and the New Liberalism," p. 248. NUWSS, Ex. com. mins., July 3, 1913, Fawcett Library, London; Marshall Papers, Kathleen Courtney to Catherine Marshall, November 23, 1913.

[98]The most important suffragist ministers were Simon and Lloyd George. The NUWSS believed that if one Cabinet minister came out strongly for women's suffrage, others would follow. Marshall Papers, Eleanor Acland to Catherine Marshall, November 20, 1913.

depending on the circumstances of the next election, he could be very helpful to the suffrage cause: "Grey is quite certain that if we had to have a General Election on Ulster, i.e., to finish Home Rule, he could do nothing, but if we'd got the two big bills (Home Rule and Welsh Disestablishment) out of the way, he could do a good deal. I feel the same."[99]

Grey was very evasive with the NUWSS, however, and would make no guarantees about what action he would take on the suffrage question. At an interview with Marshall, he admitted that he could not indefinitely continue as a member of a Government which would not take up women's suffrage, but said he would not make any pledges to the NUWSS until after Home Rule was enacted.[100] His only offer of advice was the now hackneyed exhortation "to go on educating the country."[101]

The NUWSS dealings with Lloyd George were no more productive than those with Grey. The NUWSS was convinced that Lloyd George, for all his double dealings over the Conciliation Bill, was a suffragist at heart and that he could become the Liberal Lochinvar of the suffrage cause. The problem was to paint the women's suffrage movement in bold enough colors to attract the fancy of the Chancellor of the Exchequer and then to highlight Lloyd George's role in this movement in even brighter tones. This was just what the NUWSS set out to do, and using Catherine Marshall as its mouthpiece, it began its courtship of Lloyd George. An appeal to Lloyd George's ego, combined with a little flirtatious chiding, might convince Lloyd George, as Marshall archly told him, to come out of his "tent and lead the Women's Suffrage Cause to Victory."[102]

The courtship went on through most of 1913 and 1914, as Marshall painstakingly worked at convincing Lloyd George that the suffrage cause was related to the other causes he had championed, and that it could serve as a springboard to further his political career:

. . . it is a movement which holds big possibilities for the future, I think, if the right leader is forthcoming when the

---

[99]Marshall Papers, Francis Acland to Catherine Marshall, November 9, 1913.

[100]NUWSS, Ex. com. mins., December 18, 1913, Fawcett Library, London.

[101]An Account of the Northern Men's Federation for Women's Suffrage Deputation to Sir Edward Grey, October 22, 1913, NUWSS pamphlet (n.p., n.d.).

[102]Lloyd George Papers, C9/4/85, Catherine Marshall to David Lloyd George, July 26, 1913. I am indebted to Professor Bentley Gilbert for calling my attention to the Marshall letters contained in Lloyd George's papers.

time is ripe for action. It must be someone big enough to
see, and to make others see, the phenomenon of militancy in
its true proportion and not allow it to throw everyone's
judgment off its balance as it does at present, obscuring the
great fundamental principles which are at stake in our
struggle against the old enemies which have always barred the
way of progress—the spirit of monopoly and privilege (this
time not of class but of sex), the opposition of those who
possess power to those who demand liberty.

I thought at the time of your Bath speech that you were
going to be the leader whom the Suffrage movement needed—that
having successfully championed the cause of the poor, the old,
and the sick, you would turn your attention next to the cause
of the unrepresented sex, and help us to win our political
liberty.[103]

She scolded him and his suffragist colleagues for using militancy as an
excuse to ignore the suffrage cause and urged him to supply the
political leadership which the women's suffrage movement so badly
needed:[104]

What disappointed us so much was that you could not offer us
any assurance of a better chance for women's suffrage even
when Home Rule and Welsh Disestablishment are out of the way
than we have had hither to. . . . it is disappointing when
those who have the power to make your work bear fruit in an
Act of Parliament say, in effect: "Yes, you are good little
girls, we quite approve of the way in which you are working
and the object you are working for, and our advice to you is
to go on pegging away. Don't get tired and don't get cross.
Some day, when we have settled all our own business, we will
bring in a Bill to give you what you want—only of course we
cannot do anything so long as some of you are naughty and
throw stones." When we know that it is just that attitude
which makes naughty ones throw stones, we feel you are asking
us to work in a vicious circle.

---

[103]Ibid. On November 24, 1911, Lloyd George addressed the
National Liberation Federation meeting at Bath and announced his
support for women's suffrage.

[104]On August 8, 1913, a deputation from the NUWSS met with a
number of ministers, including Lloyd George, Birrell, Simon, Acland,
Thomas Macnamara (Sec. to the Admiralty), Thomas McKinnon Wood (Sec.
for Scotland), and J. Ellis Griffith (Under Sec. to the Home Office),
to discuss women's suffrage. The NUWSS was extremely disappointed with
the interview. See Lloyd George Papers, C9/5/10, Typescript account of
the NUWSS deputation to the suffragist ministers, August 8, 1913;
Papers of Millicent Garrett Fawcett, Circular letter from Millicent
Garrett Fawcett to "Gentlemen," August 11, 1913, Fawcett Library,
London.

I often wish you were an unenfranchised woman instead of being Chancellor of the Exchequer. With what fire you would lead the Women's Movement and insist the legislation was more important than the right of those whom it concerned to have a say in it.[105]

Marshall urged Lloyd George to "start a really effective demand for Adult Suffrage (which there never has been yet) at the same time as your Land Campaign. It would be a grand programme on which to go to the country."[106]

Yet these blandishments, coupled with threats that the Conservatives were about to take up the suffrage cause and descriptions of the EFF's successful work with Labour, did not produce the desired impact on Lloyd George: Lloyd George continued to be "most amiable but oh but indefinite."[107] There are indications in Lloyd George's papers that the Chancellor of the Exchequer was testing the wind in the Liberal Party before taking any action on the suffrage question, but he gave no hint of these plans to the NUWSS.[108] He informed the NUWSS that until Welsh Disestablishment, Home Rule, and the Land Campaign were out of the way, he could not make any promises to the suffragists. He would not make any pronouncements on what a future Liberal Government would do for the women, nor would he give the NUWSS any idea what role he, as a proponent of women's suffrage, might play in this government. His only advice to the NUWSS was to go on educating the public to erase the blot that militancy had placed on the suffrage cause.[109] Most discouraging of all, he hinted that as long

---

[105]Lloyd George Papers, C9/5/13, Catherine Marshall to David Lloyd George, August 11, 1913.

[106]Lloyd George Papers, C9/5/20, Catherine Marshall to David Lloyd George, August 29, 1913.

[107]Lloyd George Papers, C11/1/68, Catherine Marshall to David Lloyd George, July 11, 1914; Marshall Papers, Francis Acland to Catherine Marshall, November 21, 1913.

[108]The Lloyd George Papers contain memoranda which give complete information on how Liberal MP's voted on the women's suffrage bills and analyze the attitude toward women's suffrage of those Liberal candidates who had been selected to stand at the General Election. See the Lloyd George Papers, C17/5/26, Memorandum on Liberal MPs marked "private and confidential," December 1913; C17/13/27, Memorandum on Liberal Candidates marked "private and confidential," January 1914.

[109]National Union of Women's Suffrage Societies, Annual Report, 1913, pp. 33-34; Lloyd George Papers, C9/5/10, Typescript account of the NUWSS deputation to the suffragist ministers, August 8, 1913.

as militancy persisted, he would never champion the women's suffrage cause.[110]

In its efforts to come to an understanding with the Liberal Government before the next General Election, the NUWSS even went so far as to see Asquith to plead the cause of women's suffrage one more time. Asquith agreed to see the suffragists, because, as he told Fawcett, her request "has a special claim on my consideration and stands upon another footing from similar demands proceeding from other quarters where a different method and spirit is predominant."[111] On August 8, 1913, the Prime Minister held a discussion on women's suffrage with a deputation from the NUWSS. Although he was much more polite and sympathetic to the representatives than he had been in the past, it was clear that he had not changed his attitude. He rebuffed Fawcett's suggestion that he follow Wellington's and Peel's example and preside over the enactment of a measure to which he was opposed; he also ignored her appeal that he, like Lord Goschen, should temporarily stand aside from active participation in party politics and allow the Liberal Party to take action on the suffrage question.[112] Asquith admitted the suffragists' position "was one of great hardship," and acknowledged that their work with the working class had greatly impressed him. He did not, however, show any signs of abandoning his opposition to the enfranchisement of women.[113] Ten months later, in an interview with representatives from Sylvia Pankhurst's East London Federation, Asquith made it very clear that his position on women's suffrage had not fundamentally changed: he still opposed the enfranchisement of women.[114]

---

[110]NUWSS, Ex. com. mins., June 18, 1914, Fawcett Library, London. Marshall's comment that militancy "always tended to put him in a bad mood" is an understatement. There is no question that Lloyd George took the militants' activities very much to heart. The militants disliked him thoroughly, and he returned their dislike in kind. Indeed, their behavior did much to estrange him from the whole movement, and this was a great loss to the suffrage cause. Lloyd George may have been the most important casualty of the militant campaign.

[111]Papers of Millicent Garrett Fawcett, H. H. Asquith to Millicent Garrett Fawcett, July 31, 1913, Fawcett Library, London.

[112]The Duke of Wellington and Sir Robert Peel allowed the Catholic Emancipation Bill to pass in 1829, though they did not approve of this measure. In 1880, Lord Goschen temporarily withdrew from party politics because he disapproved of the enfranchisement of agricultural laborers.

[113]Asquith Papers, vol. 89 f. 47, Account of the NUWSS deputation to H. H. Asquith, August 8, 1913.

[114]Asquith Papers, vol. 39 f. 126, Account of the East London Federation of Suffragists' deputation to H. H. Asquith, June 20, 1914.

On the eve of World War I, the NUWSS had not received a
commitment from either the Liberals or the Conservatives that, if
chosen to form a government, they would introduce legislation for
women's suffrage. The Labour Party was firmly committed to the women's
cause, but there was no possibility that the Labour Party would govern.
The activities of the NUWSS had stirred the Liberals to fear that the
Conservatives might introduce an equal terms bill, and the
Conservatives to worry that the Liberals might enfranchise women on the
Dickinson basis,[115] but neither party was concerned enough about these
possibilities to take pre-emptive action on the suffrage question.
Both the parties stood at the edge of the chasm, but unlike Disraeli
they were afraid to take the "leap into the dark": the risks involved
in introducing a measure for women's suffrage seemed to outweigh the
dangers of inaction. The conundrum of women's suffrage had denied the
Liberals the comprehensive franchise reform which they so badly needed,
but Asquith, intransigent, preferred to forgo these reforms rather than
surrender.[116] A Conservative measure for women's suffrage would
compensate for the loss of the plural voter, but Bonar Law was
unwilling to risk the wrath of Curzon and other antisuffragists in the
party by sponsoring a women's suffrage bill. Liberals and
Conservatives were afraid of the electoral repercussions of women's
suffrage, and of the divisive effect that women's suffrage would have
within the parties. To them, women's suffrage was a Pandora's Box that
was best left unopened; fortunately, militancy, public apathy, and
more pressing political business--Ulster, Welsh Disestablishment, Land
Reform--all provided convenient excuses for postponing the opening.

As the NUWSS assessed the situation at the beginning of August
1914, the best thing it could hope for at the General Election seemed

---

George Dangerfield and Sylvia Pankhurst have argued that at this
interview, Asquith indicated that he had seen the light on women's
suffrage. This is not the case. In June 1914, he simply stated that
if women's suffrage was enacted, it must be done in a "thoroughgoing
and democratic way." This was very similar to the statement he had
made in opposing the Conciliation Bill in 1910. On both these
occasions, Asquith was discussing the terms on which women should be
enfranchised if they were to gain the vote; he was not showing any
support for the suffrage cause. See George Dangerfield, The Strange
Death of Liberal England, pp. 336-38, and E. Sylvia Pankhurst, The
Suffragette Movement, pp. 575-77.

[115]Archives, Manchester Public Library, M/50, Box 1,
Proceedings of the Half-Yearly Council of the NUWSS, November 1914.

[116]For a discussion of electoral reform in the 1906-14 period
see Pugh, pp. 3-46. The Liberal Government particularly wanted to
abolish the system of plural votes. It would have succeeded in doing
this had not war broken out in August 1914, preventing the passage of
the Plural Voting Bill. This stroke of fate came as a boon to the
Conservatives.

to be the return of a Liberal Government with a small majority, backed up by a strong Labour Party demanding the enfranchisement of women. The worst thing would be the return of a Liberal Government with a large majority, and with Asquith as Prime Minister. The return of a Conservative Government fell somewhere in between. The NUWSS did not like the Conservatives' idea of a referendum, but it shrewdly thought the Liberals out of office might come around to espousing the women's cause.

Speculations about the General Election abruptly came to an end on August 4, 1914, when England declared war on Germany. After two days of meetings, the NUWSS executive decided to suspend all political activity. The NUWSS organization was to be kept intact, but it was to be used not to agitate for women's suffrage, but "to help those who will be the sufferers from the economic and industrial dislocation caused by the war."[117] Fawcett, speaking for her colleagues, exhorted the members of the NUWSS to forget their grievances against the Government and support the war effort: "Now is the time for resolute effort and self-sacrifice on the part of every one of us to help our country. Let us show ourselves worthy of citizenship whether our claim to it be recognized or not."[118]

The women's suffrage movement had come to a sudden and unexpected end—but in terms of legislative progress, the women's suffrage movement had long since lost momentum. The NUWSS had succeeded in establishing strong roots for the suffrage cause in the labor movement and in bringing the suffragists' demands to the working class. Its educational and propaganda activities had helped to quell the hostility caused by the militants and to prove that the women's suffrage movement was not all sensationalism. The NUWSS had expanded the organizational basis of the suffrage movement, and by July 1914 it included over five hundred societies.[119] Over 100,000 suffragists were allied with the NUWSS—either as subscribing members or as Friends of Women's Suffrage—and the organization was raising over £45,000 a year.[120] The NUWSS had succeeded in establishing good relations with

---

[117]Correspondence of the National Union of Women's Suffrage Societies, 1914, Circular from the NUWSS executive committee, August 6, 1914, Fawcett Library, London.

[118]London Society for Women's Suffrage, Annual Report, 1914 (n.p., n.d.), p. 11.

[119]C. C., July 31, 1914.

[120]In February 1914, there were 98,998 suffragists allied to the NUWSS: 52,336 of these were subscribing members. It seems reasonable to suppose that this number exceeded 100,000 by August 1914, as the NUWSS was growing at the rate of 800 new members a month, not

many of the leading politicians and had helped to build up suffragist
sentiment within the Liberal, Labour, and Conservative parties. Yet,
although the NUWSS had done much to prepare the way for the enactment
of women's suffrage, it had not found the catalyst that would force
Government legislation on the women's suffrage question. World War I
proved to be the deus ex machina for the suffrage cause; paradoxically,
though it brought to an end the agitation for women's suffrage, it
released women's suffrage from its parliamentary limbo.

---

including FWS. No firm figures are availabale for 1914, as the NUWSS
did not issue a report. National Union of Women's Suffrage Societies,
Annual Report, 1913, pp. 17-18 and 65. Archives, Manchester Public
Library, M/50, Box 1, Proceedings of the Half-Yearly Council of the
NUWSS, November 1914.

CONCLUSION

In 1918 the Representation of the People Act became law, thereby enfranchising women over thirty who were either householders, wives of householders, occupiers of property worth £5 per year, or university graduates. The long campaign for votes for women had come to an end, and some 8,479,156 were soon to register as parliamentary electors.[1]

The Great War had created a climate which was, in a multitude of ways, much more conducive to the enactment of women's suffrage than that of the prewar period. In order to make it possible for members of the armed services abroad to vote, the Government was forced to revise the franchise laws, and thereby to resurrect the dormant issue of women's suffrage.[2] Snowden's prediction of 1913 proved prescient, and it was soon apparent that any Fourth Reform Act would include women. The war had abetted the women's cause not only by compelling the Government to take up the question of electoral reform, but also by creating a political environment which was favorable to women's suffrage. The establishment of a Coalition Government in 1915 put an end to a period of party strife in which the politicians had perceived every issue, including women's suffrage, as a potential pawn in the struggle for political supremacy; as the political rivalry at Westminster became less intense, and as cabinets drawing on all parties were formed in 1915 and 1916, compromise and cooperation became easier. The Coalition of May 1915 was also marked by the entry of a number of steadfast supporters of women's suffrage into the Government: Selborne, Cecil, and Henderson had been good friends to the suffragists in the prewar period and were to continue to be so during the War.[3] The women's suffrage forces within the Government were again strengthened in December 1916, when Lloyd George replaced Asquith as Prime Minister. Although the new Prime Minister was hardly the champion of the women's cause, he was certainly more sympathetic to the enactment of women's suffrage than his predecessor had been. Also, the

---

[1]H. C. Deb. 4s, vol. 117, July 9, 1919, c. 1947. In 1928 the voting age for women was lowered from thirty to twenty-one, and women were enfranchised on the same straightforward residence qualification as men.

[2]The existing law required male householders to have occupied a dwelling for at least one year prior to the July 15 preceding an election; this resulted in the disenfranchisement of most soldiers and sailors.

[3]The Earl of Selborne became president of the Board of Agriculture; Lord Robert Cecil became Minister of Blockade; and Arthur Henderson became president of the Board of Education.

cessation of militancy after war was declared undoubtedly gave Lloyd George and other politicians an incentive to adopt a more positive attitude to the enfranchisement of women.[4]

The War also helped marshall public opinion behind the cause of women's suffrage. As W. C. Anderson, chairman of the National Labour Party Executive remarked, the War shook conservatism out of people and made change, both political and social, seem less threatening.[5] The women's contribution to the war effort challenged the notion of women's physical and mental inferiority and made it more difficult to maintain that women were, both by constitution and temperament, unfit to vote. If women could work in munitions factories, it seemed both ungrateful and illogical to deny them a place in the polling booth.[6] But the vote was much more than simply a reward for war work; the point was that women's participation in the war effort helped to dispell the fears that surrounded women's entry into the public arena. A revolution within the private sphere—the family—did not accompany the upheaval within the public—the factories, transport services, and countless other areas in which women took the place of men. Thus, the lugubrious predictions of the opponents of women's suffrage were not fulfilled.

To admit, however, that the War created a climate that was favorable to the enactment of women's suffrage does not imply that the prewar labors of the NUWSS were not crucial to the enfranchisement of women. If women's suffrage had not already achieved some importance as a political issue, if the suffrage cause had not succeeded in establishing a strong organizational base in the country and in attracting public support, if the supporters of women's suffrage had not obtained considerable backing for their cause in Parliament and established valuable contacts with leading politicians, women's suffrage would not have been included in the Reform Bill of 1918. Because of the work of the NUWSS, these conditions had been met.

The NUWSS, through its work at Westminster and in the constituencies, was responsible for winning both public and

---

[4]On August 13, 1914, Emmeline Pankhurst suspended militancy for the duration of the War. Andrew Rosen, Rise Up, Women! p. 248.

[5]Marshall Papers, Report of a Meeting of Members of the NUWSS Executive Committee with W. C. Anderson, August 13, 1915. This meeting with Anderson was held to discuss relations between the NUWSS and the Labour Party. Martin Pugh, says that "after the outbreak of war the National Union came to believe that it was tied to a declining force in the Labour Party and withdrew from the alliance." This was not the case. See Pugh, Electoral Reform in War and Peace, 1906–1918, p. 28.

[6]For a discussion of women's work in the war see Arthur Marwick, The Deluge: British Society and the First World War (New York, 1965), pp. 87–94.

parliamentary support for women's suffrage. In the process of taking its demand to the British public, the NUWSS created a network of suffrage organizations throughout Britain, and for the first time in the history of the British women's suffrage movement, it made a concerted, national effort to attract the support of workers and to disabuse the populace of the notion that the women's suffrage issue was the exclusive property of the middle and upper classes. Through its lobbying activities in the House of Commons—in particular, its work for the Conciliation Bill and the women's suffrage amendments to the Franchise Bill—the NUWSS was responsible for welding together a group of staunch parliamentary supporters of women's suffrage. It cultivated the friendships of party leaders and established good relationships with a number of very influential politicians—Simon, Grey, Dickinson, Henderson, Selborne, Cecil, Lloyd George, and Bonar Law—and their goodwill ultimately proved valuable in winning the enfranchisement of women.[7] More important, however, than the concrete results of the NUWSS proselytizing in the country and in Parliament was the intangible contribution which the NUWSS made to the progress of the women's suffrage movement. At a time when the activities of the militants threatened to vitiate the women's suffrage cause and engender hostility to the very mention of women's suffrage, the work of the NUWSS succeeded in keeping women's suffrage alive as an issue. The WSPU's progression from demonstrations to arson spelled potential disaster for the suffrage movement. The NUWSS was able to counter the militants' influence and, despite the exploits of the WSPU, to win support, both public and parliamentary, for the cause. The fact that there was, in August 1914, still a movement for women's suffrage, is perhaps the greatest accolade that can be given to the NUWSS.

The metamorphosis of the NUWSS, though not spectacular like the burgeoning of the WSPU, was very impressive. Between 1897 and 1914 the NUWSS underwent a remarkable evolution. From a small organization of seventeen societies, the NUWSS in seventeen years mushroomed into a well-organized and well-financed national union of some five hundred branches, no longer expounding the claims for women's suffrage based on liberal individualist ideology but arguing for the enfranchisement of women on the basis of expediency. It also had a practical working force, the Election Fighting Fund, aimed at convincing the Liberal Government that it would be politically expedient to grant votes to women.

The severing of its ties to the Liberal Party was the political counterpart of the NUWSS decision to jettison its liberal argument for

---

[7]Sir John Simon, Sir Edward Grey, and W. H. Dickinson were members of the Speaker's Conference which was in charge of drafting a new measure of electoral reform. The conference met from October 1916, to January 1917. The NUWSS was apprised of the conference's thoughts on women's suffrage. See Papers of Millicent Garrett Fawcett, Memorandum on a conference held with Sir John Simon, W. H. Dickinson, and Henry Nevinson, December 15, 1916, Fawcett Library, London.

votes for women. Though its roots still bound it in some ways to the Liberal Party, the NUWSS in 1914 had broken its ties with the Liberals and, firmly allied to the Labour Party, was committed to a policy designed to reduce the number of Liberals at Westminster. Though it had for many years been satisfied to accept whatever crumbs the politicians were willing to give to the women—a resolution for women's suffrage or a private member's bill--the NUWSS had come to demand nothing less than a Government Bill for women's suffrage. And when the Liberals resisted the demand, the suffragists had proved powerful enough to prevent the franchise reform which the Government so desired. Inadvertently and ironically, the Liberal Government's obduracy over the women's suffrage issue contributed to the demise of the Liberal Party. The Liberal Party's failure to enact a Fourth Reform Bill on its own terms before the War was one of the reasons for its decline.

Despite the many changes which the NUWSS underwent between 1897 and 1914, the organization still retained an aura of Victorian middle class respectability. This static quality was as essential to the organization's success in winning support for the women's cause as were the innovations of the NUWSS in terms of its argument and its political policy. In an age in which the credentials of class and kinship were of paramount importance, and conformity to a certain code of behavior was the sine qua non of social and political acceptance, the presence of women such as Millicent Garrett Fawcett, Lady Frances Balfour, and Catherine Marshall in the councils of the NUWSS was reassuring to both politicians and public. These women, and others like them who, in a less grand fashion, led the branch societies throughout Britain, were tangible proof that politics and intellectual pursuits did not unbalance or unsex women; their championship of the women's suffrage movement made the cause itself less threatening and offered one more piece of evidence that the boundaries of the public sphere could be redefined without altering the structure of the private sphere. It may have been the WSPU that first attracted the attention of the country by flouting the staid convention of Victorian womanhood, but it was the suffragists of the NUWSS who created sympathy for the cause of women's suffrage by outwardly conforming to the very image which the Pankhursts and their colleagues rejected. In this respect the militants were a valuable foil for the suffragists and made the adherents of the NUWSS appear deceptively reasonable and moderate.

The enfranchisement of women in 1918 was a somewhat tardy epilogue to the prewar tale of the NUWSS as an organization fighting for votes for women. The NUWSS nurtured the suffrage cause and injected vitality into the suffrage movement--by giving it an organizational base, by cultivating political friendships, by pursuing a variety of propagandistic activities, by sheer hard work. It created an image of decency and fairness which all men and women could respond to. Had it not been for its activitites in the prewar years, the Representation of the People Act of 1918 might well not have included votes for women.

228

APPENDIX

APPENDIX A

NATIONAL UNION OF WOMEN'S SUFFRAGE SOCIETIES:

NUMBER OF SOCIETIES — 1907-1913

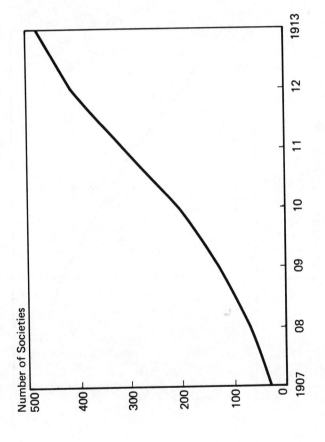

Number of Societies

Source: NUWSS Annual Reports, 1907-1913

APPENDIX B

NATIONAL UNION OF WOMEN'S SUFFRAGE SOCIETIES:

MEMBERSHIP — 1907-1913

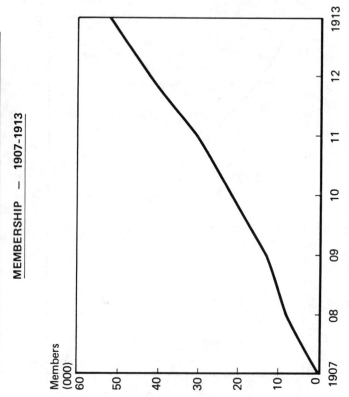

Source: NUWSS Annual Reports, 1907-1913

APPENDIX C

NATIONAL UNION OF WOMEN'S SUFFRAGE SOCIETIES:

ANNUAL RECEIPTS* — 1907-1913

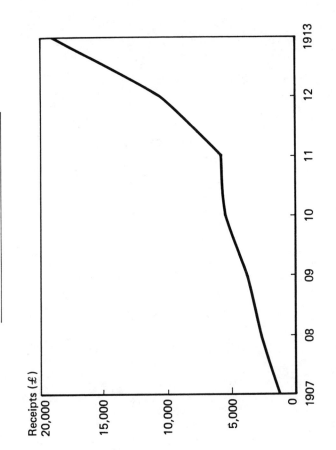

* - Annual receipts do not include receipts of the literature department and the Election Fighting Fund. These figures are only for headquarters and do not include receipts of branch societies

Source: NUWSS Annual Reports, 1907-1913

BIBLIOGRAPHY

(At the time the research for this study was done, the Fawcett
Library was located at 27 Wilfred Street, London. The entire contents
of the Library have since been moved to the City of London Polytechnic.
Thus, some of the sources cited in this dissertation may have been
recatalogued or reclassified.

The Papers of Andrew Bonar Law and Earl Lloyd George of Dwyfor
have been moved from the Beaverbrook Library to the House of Lords
Record Office.)

PRIMARY SOURCES

I. Manuscripts and Archives

A. Private Papers

Maud Arncliffe-Sennett Collection (British Museum, London).
Arthur, 1st Earl of Balfour Papers (British Museum, London).
Teresa Billington-Greig Papers (Fawcett Library, London).
Andrew Bonar Law Papers (Beaverbrook Library, London).
Sir Henry Campbell-Bannerman Papers (British Museum, London).
Robert, Viscount Cecil of Chelwood Papers (British Museum, London).
Emily Davies Papers (Fawcett Library, London).
Emily Davies Papers (Girton College, Cambridge).
Dame Millicent Garrett Fawcett Papers (Fawcett Library, London).
Dame Millicent Garrett Fawcett Papers (Manchester Public Library,
    Manchester).
Herbert, Viscount Gladstone Papers (British Museum, London).
Edward, Viscount Grey of Falloden Papers (Public Record Office,
    London).
George Lansbury Papers (British Library of Political and Economic
    Science, London).
Earl Lloyd George of Dwyfor Papers (Beaverbrook Library, London).
Reginald McKenna Papers (Churchill College, Cambridge).
Catherine Marshall Papers (Cumbria County Record Office, Carlisle,
    Cumberland).
Laura Puffer Morgan Papers (Schlesinger Library, Cambridge, Mass.).
Henry Woodd Nevinson Journals (Bodleian Library, Oxford).
Earl of Oxford and Asquith Papers (Bodleian Library, Oxford).
William Waldegrave Palmer, 2nd Earl of Selborne Papers (Bodleian
    Library, Oxford).
C. P. Scott Papers (British Museum, London).
Jane, Lady Strachey Papers (Fawcett Library, London).

B. Archival Collections

Central National Society for Women's Suffrage Archive (Fawcett Library, London).
Central Society for Women's Suffrage Archive (Fawcett Library, London).
Fawcett Library Autograph Collection (Fawcett Library, London).
Hitchin, Stevenage, and District Society for Women's Suffrage Archive (Fawcett Library, London).
Labour Party Archive (Transport House, London).
London Society for Women's Suffrage Archive (Fawcett Library, London).
National Union of Women's Suffrage Societies Archive (Fawcett Library, London).
Oldham Women's Suffrage Society Archive (Fawcett Library, London).
State Archives (Public Record Office, London):
    1. Cabinet Papers: CAB 37, 41.
    2. Home Office Papers, Series 45.
Suffragette Fellowship Papers (London Museum, London).
Women's Suffrage Collection Archive (Manchester Public Library, Manchester).

II. Printed Materials of Women's Suffrage Organizations

(All items are located in the Fawcett Library, London, unless otherwise noted.)

A. Collections of Materials

Cavendish Bentinck Collection.
Helen Blackburn Collection (Girton College, Cambridge).

B. Individual Reports, Leaflets
and Pamphlets

Actresses' Franchise League. Annual Report, 1913.
Artists' Suffrage League. Annual Reports, 1909-1911.
Bristol and West of England Society for Women's Suffrage. Annual Report, 1899-1900.
Central and East of England Society for Women's Suffrage. Annual Reports, 1898-1900.
Central and Western Society for Women's Suffrage. Annual Reports, 1898-1900.
Central Committee of the National Society for Women's Suffrage. Annual Reports, 1889-1897.
Central National Society for Women's Suffrage. Annual Reports, 1889-1897.
Central Society for Women's Suffrage. Annual Reports, 1901-1906.
Clapham Women's Social and Political Union. Annual Report, 1913.

Conservative and Unionist Women's Franchise Association. Miscellaneous leaflets (British Museum, London).

East Midland Federation. Annual Reports, 1911-1913.

Edinburgh National Society for Women's Suffrage. Annual Reports, 1903, 1907, 1913-1914.

Forward Suffrage Union of the Women's Liberal Federation. Annual Report, 1911 (Cumbria County Record Office, Carlisle, Cumberland).

Hitchin, Stevenage and District Society. Annual Reports, 1912-1914.

Jewish League for Woman Suffrage. Annual Report, 1913-1914.

Kentish Federation. Annual Report, 1913.

Lancashire and Cheshire Women's Suffrage Society, Lancashire and Cheshire Women Textile Workers' Committee, Manchester and Salford Women's Trade and Labour Council. Joint Report of Women's Suffrage Work, 1905-1906.

Leeds Woman's Suffrage Association. Report on the Conference of the International Woman's Suffrage Alliance held at Copenhagen, August 1906.

Leicester and Leicestershire Women's Suffrage Society. Annual Report, 1912.

London National Society for Women's Suffrage. Annual Report, 1869.

London Society for Women's Suffrage. Annual Reports, 1907-1915.

Manchester and District Federation. Annual Reports, 1911-1917 (Manchester Public Library, Manchester).

Manchester National Society for Women's Suffrage. Annual Reports, 1868-1896 (Manchester Public Library, Manchester).

Manchester Society for Women's Suffrage. Annual Reports, 1912-1914 (Manchester Public Library, Manchester).

Men's League for Women's Suffrage. Annual Report, 1912.

Men's Political Union for Women's Enfranchisement. Annual Report, [1910-1911].

National Society for Women's Suffrage. Annual Reports, 1872-1888.

National Union of Women's Suffrage Societies. Annual Reports, 1898, 1900, 1905-1913, 1915-1918.

National Union of Women's Suffrage Societies. Miscellaneous pamphlets and leaflets.

National Union of Women's Suffrage Societies. Scrap Book of Notices and Meetings, 1909-1913.

New Constitutional Society for Women's Suffrage. Annual Reports, 1910-1912.

North and East Ridings Federation. Annual Report, 1911-1912.

North Hertfordshire Society. Annual Report, 1909-1910.

North of England Society for Women's Suffrage. Annual Reports, 1898-1911 (Manchester Public Library, Manchester).

North-Eastern Federation of Women's Suffrage Societies. Annual Report, 1912.

North-Eastern Society for Women's Suffrage. Annual Report, 1909.

North-Western Federation. Annual Report, 1910-1911.

Petersfield Woman's Suffrage Society. Annual Report, 1912.

South Western Federation. Annual Report, 1914.

Surrey, Sussex, and Hants Federation. Annual Reports, 1911-1913.

West Lancashire, West Cheshire, and North Wales Federation. *Annual Reports*, 1912–1913.
West Midland Federation. *Annual Reports*, 1911–1913.
West Riding Federation. *Annual Reports*, 1912–1913.
Women's Emancipation Union. *Annual Reports*, 1892, 1894, 1896, 1899.
Women's Freedom League. *Annual Reports*, 1907–1908, 1910–1911.
Women's Freedom League. Miscellaneous pamphlets and leaflets.
Women's Social and Political Union. *Annual Reports*, 1907–1914.
Women's Social and Political Union. Miscellaneous pamphlets and leaflets.

III. Official Papers

Great Britain, Parliament. *Journals of the House of Lords* (1900–1914).
Great Britain, Parliament. *Hansard's Parliamentary Debates*, 4th and 5th series (1892–1919).

IV. Directories, Reference Works, and Year Books

Burke's Peerage and Baronetage. London, 1911.
Calendar for 1898 with Women's Suffrage Directory. Ed. Helen Blackburn. Bristol, 1897.
The Dictionary of Labour Biography. Eds. Joyce M. Bellamy and John Saville. London, 1972–1974.
The Dictionary of National Biography. London, 1901, 1908, 1912, 1937, 1949.
Dod's Parliamentary Companion. London, 1881–1914.
Girton College Register, 1869–1946. Eds. R. T. Butler and H. I. McMorran. Cambridge, 1948.
Lady Margaret Hall Register, 1897–1952. Ed. Christine Anson. n.p., 1955.
Somerville College Register, 1879–1959. Oxford, 1961.
The Suffrage Annual and Women's Who's Who. Ed. A. J. R. London, 1913.

V. Contemporary Newspapers and Periodicals

(Rather than list the individual articles already cited in the footnotes, I have listed only the periodicals in which they appeared.)

A. Dailies

Daily Chronicle. London, 1897–1914.
Daily Citizen. Manchester, 1912–1914.
Daily Express. London, 1900–1914.
Daily Mail. London, 1897–1914.
Daily Telegraph. London, 1897–1914.
Manchester Guardian. Manchester, 1897–1914.

Pall Mall Gazette. London, 1897–1914.
Standard. London, 1897–1914.
The Times. London, 1897–1914.

B. Weeklies and Monthlies

Christian Commonwealth. London, 1906–1914.
Common Cause. Manchester and London, 1909–1915.
Conservative and Unionist Women's Franchise Review.   London, 1909–1915.
Contemporary Review. London, 1866–1914.
Edinburgh Review. Edinburgh, 1860–1914.
Englishwoman. London, 1909–1915.
Englishwoman's Journal. London, 1858–1864.
Englishwoman's Review. London, 1866–1910.
Fortnightly Review. London, 1865–1914.
I. L. P. News. London, 1897–1903.
Labour Leader. London, 1900–1904.
The Nation. London, 1907–1914.
National Review. London, 1883–1914.
Nineteenth Century. London, 1877–1914.
Quarterly Review. London, 1870–1914.
Queen. London, 1900–1914.
Review of Reviews. London, 1900–1914.
Suffragette. London, 1912–1914.
Victoria Magazine. London, 1863–1880.
Vote. London, 1909–1914.
Votes for Women. London, 1907–1914.
Westminster Review. London, 1860–1914.
White Ribbon. London, 1896–1914.
Woman's Signal. London, 1895–1898.
Women's Franchise. London, 1907–1909.
Women's National Liberal Association Quarterly Leaflet. London,
    1895–1910.
Women's Suffrage. London, May–September, 1907.
Women's Suffrage Journal. London, 1870–1890.
Women's Suffrage Record. London, 1903–1906.

VI. Contemporary Books, Memoirs, Letters, etc.

The Amberley Papers. 2 vols. Eds. Bertrand and Patricia Russell.
    London: Hogarth Press, 1937.
Anderson, Louisa Garrett. Elizabeth Garrett Anderson, 1886–1917.
    London: Faber and Faber, 1939.
Balfour, Lady Frances. Ne Obliviscaris; Dinna Forget. 2 vols.
    London: Hodder and Stoughton, [1930].
Billington-Greig, Teresa. The Militant Suffrage Movement. London:
    Frank Palmer, 1912.

Black, Clementina. A New Way of Housekeeping. London: W. Collins Sons, 1918.

_____. Married Women's Work: Being the Report of an Enquiry Undertaken by the Women's Industrial Council. London: G. Bell and Sons, 1915.

Blackburn, Helen. A Handbook for Women Engaged in Social and Political Work. London: Edward Stanford, 1895.

_____. Record of Women's Suffrage. London: Williams & Norgate, 1902.

Brockway, A. Fenner. Inside the Left: Thirty Years of Platform, Press, Prison, and Parliament. London: George Allen & Unwin, 1942.

Butler, Josephine E. Personal Reminiscences of a Great Crusade. London: Horace Marshall & Son, 1911.

The Case for Women's Suffrage. Ed. Brougham Villiers. London: T. Fisher Unwin, 1907.

Cecil of Chelwood, Viscount. All the Way. London: Hodder & Stoughton, 1949.

Chamberlain, Austen. Politics from Inside. New Haven: Yale University Press, 1937.

Courtney, Kate. Extracts from a Diary During the War. London: Privately printed, 1927.

Davies, Emily. Thoughts on Some Questions Relating to Women, 1860-1908. Cambridge: Bowes and Bowes, 1910.

Drake, Barbara. Women in Trade Unions. London: G. Allen & Unwin, 1920.

Dugdale, Blanche E. C. Arthur James Balfour, First Earl of Balfour. 2 vols. New York: G. P. Putnam's Sons, 1937.

_____. Family Homespun. London: John Murray, 1940.

Fawcett, Henry, and Millicent Garrett Fawcett. Essays and Lectures on Social and Political Subjects. London: Macmillan & Co., 1872.

Fawcett, Millicent Garrett. Political Economy for Beginners. London: Macmillan & Co., 1870.

_____. Some Eminent Women of Our Times: Short Biographical Sketches. London: Macmillan, 1889.

_____. What I Remember. London: T. Fisher Unwin, 1924.

_____. Women's Suffrage: A Short History of a Great Movement. London: T. C. & E. C. Jack, 1912.

_____. The Women's Victory and After: Personal Reminiscences, 1911-1918. London: Sidgwick & Jackson, 1920.

Fawcett, Millicent Garrett, and E. M. Turner. Josephine Butler: Her Work and Principles and Their Meaning for the Twentieth Century. London: Association for Moral & Social Hygiene, 1927.

Ford, Isabella Ormston. Industrial Women and How to Help Them. London: Humanitarian League, [1900].

Ford, Isabella Ormston. Women and Socialism. London: Independent Labour Party, 1904.

Haldane, Richard B. An Autobiography. London: Hodder & Stoughton, 1929.

Hamilton, Mary Agnes. Arthur Henderson. London: William Heinemann, 1938.

Hammond, J. L. C. P. Scott of the Manchester Guardian. New York: Harcourt Brace & Co., 1934.

Housman, Laurence. The Unexpected Years. New York: Bobbs Merrill, 1936.

Journals of Lady Knightley of Fawsley. Ed. Julia Cartwright. London: John Murray, 1915.

Kenney, Annie. Memoirs of a Militant. London: Edward Arnold, 1924.

Lansbury, George. My Life. London: Constable, 1928.

Letters of Constance Lytton. Ed. Lady Betty Balfour. London: William Heinemann, 1925.

Linton, Elizabeth Lynn. Modern Women and What Is Said of Them. New York: J. S. Redfield, 1870.

Lowther, James W. A Speaker's Commentaries. 2 vols. London: Edward Arnold, 1925.

McKenna, Stephen. Reginald McKenna, 1863-1943. London: Eyre & Spottiswoode, 1948.

McLaren, Eva. The History of the Women's Suffrage Movement in the Women's Liberal Federation. n.p.: Women's Liberal Federation, 1903.

McLaren, Lady. The Women's Charter of Rights and Liberties. 4th ed. London: Grant Richards, [1909].

MacDonald, J. Ramsay. Margaret Ethel MacDonald. 3rd ed. London: Hodder & Stoughton, [1913].

Markham, Violet. Return Passage. London: Oxford University Press, 1953.

Martindale, Hilda. From One Generation to Another, 1839-1944. London: George Allen & Unwin, 1944.

Mason, Bertha. The Story of the Women's Suffrage Movement. London: Sherratt & Hughes, 1912.

Metcalfe, A. E. Woman's Effort. Oxford: Basil Blackwell, 1917.

Mill, John Stuart. The Subjection of Women. Intro. by Wendell Robert Carr. Cambridge, Mass.: MIT Press, 1970.

Mill, John Stuart, and Harriet Taylor Mill. Essays on Sex Equality. Ed. and with an intro. by Alice S. Rossi. Chicago: University of Chicago Press, 1970.

Mitchell, Hannah. The Hard Way Up. London: Faber, 1968.

Montefiore, Dora. From a Victorian to a Modern. London: E. Archer, 1927.

Nevinson, Henry Woodd. More Changes, More Chances. London: Nisbet & Co., 1925.

Nevinson, Margaret Wynne. Fragments of Life. London: George Allen & Unwin, [1922].

_____. Life's Fitful Fever: A Volume of Memories. London: A. C. Black, 1926.

Oxford and Asquith, Countess of. The Autobiography of Margot Asquith. 2 vols. London: Thornton Butterworth, 1922.

_____. More Memories. London: Cassell, 1933.

Oxford and Asquith, Earl of. Fifty Years of Parliament. 2 vols. London: Cassell, 1926.

_____. Memories and Reflections, 1852-1927. 2 vols. Boston: Little, Brown & Co., 1928.

Pankhurst, Christabel. Unshackled: The Story of How We Won the Vote. London: Hutchinson, 1959.

Pankhurst, E. Sylvia. The Life of Emmeline Pankhurst. London: T. Werner Laurie, 1935.

_____. The Suffragette. New York: Sturgis Walton, 1911.

_____. The Suffragette Movement: An Intimate Account of Persons and Ideals. London: Longmans, Green & Co., 1913.

Pankhurst, Emmeline. My Own Story. London: Eveleigh Nash, 1914.

Pethick-Lawrence, Emmeline. My Part in a Changing World. London: Victor Gollancz, 1938.

Pethick-Lawrence, F. W. Fate Has Been Kind. London: Hutchinson & Co., 1943.

Prison Letters of Constance Markievicz: Also Poems and Articles Relating to Easter Week by Eva Gore-Booth and a Biographical Sketch by Esther Roper. London: Longmans Green & Co., 1934.

Richardson, Mary R. Laugh a Defiance. London: George Weidenfeld & Nicolson, 1953.

Sharp, Evelyn. Unfinished Adventures: Selected Reminiscences from an Englishwoman's Life. London: John Lane, 1933.

Simon, Rt. Hon. Viscount. Retrospect. London: Hutchinson & Co., 1952.

Smyth, Ethel. Female Pipings in Eden. London: P. Davies, 1933.

Snowden, Ethel. The Feminist Movement. London: Collins, 1913.

Snowden, Philip Viscount. An Autobiography. 2 vols. London: Ivor Nicholson & Watson, 1934.

Spender, J. A., and Cyril Asquith. Life of Herbert Henry Asquith, Lord Oxford and Asquith. 2 vols. London: Hutchinson & Co., 1932.

Stephen, Sir Leslie. Life of Henry Fawcett. 2nd ed. London: Smith, Elder, 1885.

Stevenson, Frances. Lloyd George: A Diary. Ed. A. J. P. Taylor. New York: Harper & Row, 1971.

Stocks, Mary D. Eleanor Rathbone. London: Victor Gollancz, 1949.

_____. My Commonplace Book. London: Peter Davies, 1970.

Strachey, Ray. The Cause: A Short History of the Women's Movement in Great Britain. London: G. Bell & Sons, 1928.

_____. Millicent Garrett Fawcett. London: John Murray, 1931.

Swanwick, Helena M. The Future of the Women's Movement. London: Bell & Sons, 1913.

_____. I Have Been Young. London: Victor Gollancz, 1935.

Trevelyan, Janet Penrose. The Life of Mrs. Humphrey Ward. London: Constable & Co., 1923.

The Woman Question in Europe. Ed. Theodore Stanton. New York: G. P. Putnam's Sons, 1884.

Women and the Labour Party. Ed. Marion Phillips. New York: B. W. Huebsch, 1920.

Wright, Sir Almroth. The Unexpurgated Case Against Women's Suffrage. London: Constable, 1913.

VII. Contemporary Novels, Plays, Poems

Barrie, Sir James M. "The Twelve-Pound Look." Contemporary One-Act Plays. Ed. B. Roland Lewis. New York: Charles Scribner's Sons, 1922.

Black, Clementina. The Agitator. New York: Harper & Bros., 1895.
_____. The Princess Desirée. London: Longmans & Co., 1896.
_____. A Sussex Idyl. London: Samuel Tinsley, 1877.

Fawcett, Millicent Garrett. Janet Doncaster. London: Smith, Elder & Co., 1875.

Ford, Isabella Ormston. Miss Blake of Monkshelton. London: John Murray, 1890.

Gissing, George. The Odd Women. New York: W. W. Norton & Co., 1971.

Gore-Booth, Eva. Poems of Eva Gore-Booth. Intro. Esther Roper. London: Longmans Green, 1929.

Grand, Sarah. The Heavenly Twins. 3 vols. London: W. Heinemann, 1893.

Shaw, George Bernard. Mrs. Warren's Profession. London: Constable & Co., 1927.

Wells, H. G. Ann Veronica. New York: Boni & Liveright, 1909.

SELECTED SECONDRY SOURCES

I. Books

Askwith, Betty. The Lytteltons. London: Chatto & Windus, 1975.
_____. Two Victorian Families. London: Chatto & Windus, 1971.

Banks, J. A. Prosperity and Parenthood: A Study of Family Planning Among the Victorian Middle Classes. London: Routledge, Kegan Paul, 1954.

Banks, J. A., and Olive Banks. Feminism and Family Planning in Victorian England. Liverpool: Liverpool University Press, 1964.

Best, Geoffrey. Mid-Victorian Britain, 1851-75. St. Albans: Panther Books, 1973.

Blake, Robert. The Conservative Party from Peel to Churchill. New York: St. Martin's Press, 1970.
_____. The Unknown Prime-Minister: The Life and Times of Andrew Bonar Law, 1858-1923. London: Eyre & Spottiswoode, 1955.

Blewett, Neal. The Peers, the Parties, and the People: The British General Elections of 1910. Toronto: University of Toronto Press, 1972.

Branca, Patricia. Silent Sisterhood: Middle-Class Women in the Victorian Home. London: Croom Helm, 1975.

Briggs, Asa. The Making of Modern England, 1783-1867: The Age of Improvement. New York: Harper & Row, 1965.

Brittain, Vera. Pethick-Lawrence: A Portrait. London: George Allen & Unwin, 1963.

Brook-Shepherd, Gordon. Uncle of Europe. London: Collins. 1975.

Butler, David, and Jennie Freeman. British Political Facts, 1900-1968. 3rd ed. London: Macmillan, 1969.

Churchill, Randolph S. Winston S. Churchill. vol. 2: 1901-1914. Boston: Houghton Mifflin Co., 1967.

_____. Winston S. Churchill. Companion vol. 2, Part 3. Boston: Houghton Mifflin Co., 1967.

Clarke, P. F. C. Lancashire and the New Liberalism. Cambridge: Cambridge University Press, 1971.

Cross, Colin. The Liberals in Power, 1905-1914. London: Barrie & Rockliff, 1963.

_____. Philip Snowden. London: Barrie & Rockliff, 1966.

Dangerfield, George. The Strange Death of Liberal England. New York: Capricorn Books, 1961.

Davidoff, Leonore. The Best Circles: Women and Society in Victorian England. Totowa, N. J.: Rowman & Littlefield, 1973.

Emy, H. V. Liberals, Radicals, and Social Politics, 1892-1914. Cambridge: Cambridge University Press, 1973.

Ensor, R. C. K. England 1870-1914. Oxford: Oxford University Press, 1936.

Evans, Richard J. The Feminists: Women's Emancipation Movements in Europe, America, and Australasia. London: Croom Helm, 1977.

Fulford, Roger. Votes for Women. London: Faber and Faber, 1957.

Grigg, John. The Yound Lloyd George. London: Eyre Methuen, 1973.

Grimshaw, Patricia. Women's Suffrage in New Zealand. Auckland: Auckland University Press, 1972.

Halèvy, Elie. A History of the English People. Epilogue: vol. 2. London: Ernest Benn, 1934.

Hamer, D. A. Liberal Politics in the Age of Gladstone and Rosebery: A Study in Leadership and Policy. Oxford: Clarendon Press, 1972.

Harrison, Brian. Drink and the Victorians: The Temperance Question in England, 1815-1872. Pittsburgh: University of Pittsburgh Press, 1871.

_____. Separate Spheres: The Opposition to Women's Suffrage in Britain. London: Croom Helm, 1978.

Holroyd, Michael. Lytton Strachey: A Biography. Middlesex: Penguin Books, 1971.

Houghton, Walter E. The Victorian Frame of Mind. New Haven: Yale University Press, 1957.

Hynes, Samuel. The Edwardian Turn of Mind. Princeton: Princeton University Press, 1968.

Jenkins, Roy. Asquith: Portrait of a Man and an Era. New York: Chilmark Press, 1964.

_____. Mr. Balfour's Poodle. London: Heinemann, 1954.

Jones, Thomas. Lloyd George. Oxford: Oxford University Press, 1951.

Kamm, Josephine. Rapiers and Battleaxes. London: George Allen & Unwin, 1966.

Koss, Stephen E. Lord Haldane: Scapegoat for Liberalism. New York: Columbia University Press, 1969.

Kraditor, Aileen S. The Ideas of the Woman Suffrage Movement, 1890-1920. New York: Columbia University Press, 1965.

Lutzker, Edythe. Edith Pechey-Phipson, M.D.: The Story of England's Foremost Pioneering Woman Doctor. New York: Exposition Press, 1973.

McCormick, Donald. The Mask of Merlin: A Critical Study of David Lloyd George. London: Macdonald, 1963.

Mackenzie, Midge. Shoulder to Shoulder. New York: Alfred A. Knopf, 1975.

Magnus, Philip. King Edward the Seventh. London: J. Murray, 1964.

Manton, Jo. Elizabeth Garrett Anderson. New York: Dutton, 1965.

Marquand, David. Ramsay MacDonald. London: Jonathan Cape, 1977.

Marwick, Arthur. The Deluge: British Society and the First World War. New York: W. W. Norton & Co., 1965.

Matthew, H. C. G. The Liberal Imperialists: The Ideas and Politics of a Post-Gladstonian Elite. Oxford: Oxford University Press, 1973.

Mitchell, David J. The Fighting Pankhursts: A Study in Tenacity. London: Jonathan Cape, 1967.

_____. Queen Christabel: A Biography of Christabel Pankhurst. London: Macdonald and Jane's, 1977.

Morgan David. Suffragists and Liberals: The Politics of Woman Suffrage in England. Totowa, N. J.: Rowman & Littlefield, 1975.

Newsome, Stella. The Women's Freedom League, 1907-1957. London: n.p., 1958.

O'Neill, William L. The Woman Movement: Feminism in the United States and England. London: Allen & Unwin, 1969.

Pelling, Henry. A Short History of the Labour Party. London: Macmillan, 1961.

Petrie, Glenn. A Singular Iniquity. New York: Viking Press, 1971.

Playne, Caroline E. The Pre-War Mind in Britain. London: G. Allen & Unwin, 1928.

Postgate, Raymond. The Life of George Lansbury. London: Longmans Green & Co., 1951.

Pugh, Martin. Electoral Reform in War and Peace, 1906-1918. London: Routledge & Kegan Paul, 1978.

Raeburn, Antonia. The Militant Suffragettes. London: New English Library, 1974.

Ramelson, Marion. The Petticoat Rebellion: A Century of Struggle for Women's Rights. London: Lawrence & Wishart, 1967.

Read, Donald. Edwardian England, 1901-15. London: Harrap, 1972.

Robb, Janet Henderson. The Primrose League, 1883-1906. New York: Columbia University Press, 1942.

Robbins, Keith. The Abolition of War: The Peace Movement in Britain During the First World War. Cardiff: University of Wales, 1976.

_____. Sir Edward Grey: A Biography of Lord Grey of Falloden. London: Cassell & Co., 1971.

Roberts, Charles. The Radical Countess: The History of the Life of Rosalind Countess of Carlisle. Carlisle: Steel Bros., 1962.

Rose, Kenneth. The Later Cecils. London: Weidenfeld & Nicolson, 1975.

_____. Superior Person: A Portrait of Curzon and His Circle in Late Victorian England. London: Weidenfeld & Nicolson, 1969.

Rosen, Andrew. Rise Up, Women! London: Routledge & Kegan Paul, 1974.

Rover, Constance. _Love, Morals and Feminism_. London: Routledge & Kegan Paul, 1970.

_____. _The Punch Book of Women's Rights_. New York: A. S. Barnes & Co., 1970.

_____. _Women's Suffrage and Party Politics in Great Britain, 1866-1914_. London: Routledge & Kegan Paul, 1967.

Rowbotham, Sheila. _Hidden from History_. New York: Vintage, 1976.

Rowland, Peter. _The Last Liberal Governments: The Promised Land, 1906-1910_. London: Barrie & Rockliff, 1968.

_____. _The Last Liberal Government: Unfinished Business, 1911-1914_. London: Barrie & Jenkins, 1971.

Sanders, Charles Richard. _The Strachey Family, 1588-1932_. Durham, N. C.: Duke University Press, 1953.

Scally, Robert J. _The Origins of the Lloyd George Coalition: The Politics of Social-Imperialsim, 1900-1918_. Princeton: Princeton University Press, 1975.

Soldon, Norbert C. _Women in British Trade Unions: 1874-1976_. Dublin: Gill & Macmillan, 1978.

Speaight, Robert. _Hilaire Belloc_. New York: Farrar, Straus, & Cudahy, 1957.

Van Voris, Jacqueline. _Constance de Markievicz_. Old Westbury, N. Y.: Feminist Press, 1972.

White, Cynthia L. _Women's Magazines, 1693-1968_. London: Joseph, 1970.

Zebel, Sydney H. _Balfour: A Political Biography_. Cambridge: Cambridge University Press, 1973.

II. Articles

Blewett, Neal. "The Franchise in the United Kingdom, 1885-1918." _Past and Present_, XI (1968), 95-124.

DuBois, Ellen. "The Radicalism of the Woman Suffrage Movement: Notes Toward the Reconstruction of Nineteenth-Century Feminism." _Feminist Studies_, III (1975), 63-71.

Hale, T. F. "F. W. Pethick-Lawrence and the Suffragettes." _Contemporary Review_, 225 (August 1974), 83-89.

Harrison, Brian. "State Intervention and Moral Reform in Nineteenth-Century England." In _Pressure from Without in Early Victorian England_. Ed. Patricia Hollis. London: Edward Arnold, 1974.

Hollis, Patricia. "Pressure from Without: An Introduction." In _Pressure from Without in Early Victorian England_. Ed. Patricia Hollis. London: Edward Arnold, 1974.

Horne, Grenda. "The Liberation of British and American Women's History." _Bulletin of the Society for the Study of Labour History_, XXVI (1973), 28-39.

Jacoby, Robin Miller. "Feminism and Class Consciousness in the British and American Women's Trade Union Leagues, 1890-1925". In _Liberating Women's History_. Ed. Berenice A. Carroll. Urbana: University of Illinois Press, 1976.

Kanner, S. Barbara. "The Women of England in a Century of Social Change, 1815-1914: A Select Bibliography." In Suffer and Be Still. Ed. Martha Vicinus. Bloomington: Indiana University Press, 1973.

Liddington, Jill. "Rediscovering Suffrage History." History Workshop, 4 (1978): 192-202.

Martin, David. "Land Reform." In Pressure from Without in Early Victorian England. Ed. Patricia Hollis. London: Edward Arnold, 1974.

Millett, Kate. "The Debate Over Women: Ruskin vs. Mill." In Suffer and Be Still. Ed. Martha Vicinus. Bloomington: Indiana University Press, 1973.

Morgan, K. O. "Asquith as Prime Minister, 1908-16." English Historical Review, LXXXV (1970), 502-31.

Neale, R. S. "Working Class Women and Women's Suffrage." In Class and Ideology in the Nineteenth Century. Ed. R. S. Neale. London: Routledge & Kegan Paul, 1972.

Pugh, Martin. "The Politicians and the Women's Vote, 1914-1918." History, LIX (1974), 358-74.

Robson, A. P. W. "The Founding of the National Society for Women's Suffrage, 1866-1867." Canadian Journal of History (1973), no. 1:1-22.

Weeks, Jeffrey. "The Women's Movement." Bulletin of the Society for the Study of Labour History, XXIX (1974), 55-59.

Weston, Corinne Comstock. "The Liberal Leadership and the Lords' Veto, 1907-1910." Historical Journal, XI (1968), 508-37.

Wilson, Alexander. "The Suffrage Movement." In Pressure from Without in Early Victorian England. Ed. Patricia Hollis. London: Edward Arnold, 1974.

III. Unpublished Theses, Dissertations, and Manuscripts

Claus, Ruth Freeman. "Militancy in the English and American Woman Suffrage Movements." Ph.D. diss., Yale University, 1975.

Currell, Melville E. "Women in Politics." Ph.D. diss., University of Birmingham, 1965.

Jones, Donald J. "The Asquith Cabinet and Woman's Suffrage, 1908-1914." M.A. thesis, Memorial University of Newfoundland, 1972.

Leventhal, Fred. "The Conciliation Committee." Unpub. ms.

Rosen, Andrew. "Emily Davies and the Women's Movement, 1862-1867." Unpub. ms.

Walkowitz, Judith R. "We Are Not Beasts of the Field: Prostitution and the Campaign Against the Contagious Diseases Acts, 1869-1886." Ph.D. diss., University of Rochester, 1974.

INDEX